T0301837

Representative Bureaucracy in Action

Representative Bureaucracy in Action

Country Profiles from the Americas, Europe, Africa and Asia

Edited by

Patrick von Maravić

Department of Political Science, University of Alberta, Canada and Department of Public Management and Governance, Zeppelin University, Germany

B. Guy Peters

Maurice Falk Professor of American Government, University of Pittsburgh, USA and Professor of Comparative Governance, Zeppelin University, Germany

Eckhard Schröter

Department of Public Management and Governance, Zeppelin University, Germany

Edward Elgar

Cheltenham, UK • Northampton, MA, USA

Published by
Edward Elgar Publishing Limited
The Lypiatts
15 Lansdown Road
Cheltenham
Glos GL50 2JA
UK

Edward Elgar Publishing, Inc.
William Pratt House
9 Dewey Court
Northampton
Massachusetts 01060
USA

A catalogue record for this book
is available from the British Library

Library of Congress Control Number: 2012949449

This book is available electronically in the ElgarOnline.com
Social and Political Science Subject Collection, E-ISBN 978 0 85793 599 1

ISBN 978 0 85793 598 4

Typeset by Servis Filmsetting Ltd, Stockport, Cheshire
Printed and bound by MPG Books Group, UK

Contents

PART III   AFRICA, OCEANIA, AND ASIA

Contributors

Rhys Andrews is Reader in Politics at the Centre for Local and Regional Government Research at Cardiff Business School, Wales.

Robert Cameron is Professor of Political Science at the University of Cape Town, South Africa.

Giliberto Capano is Professor of Political Science and Public Policy at the University of Bologna, Italy.

Nadia Carboni is Associate Professor in the Department of Political Science at the University of Bologna, Italy.

Gerrit S.A. Dijkstra is a researcher in the Department of Public Administration at Leiden University, the Netherlands.

Sonja M. Dudek works at the Berlin Anti-Discrimination Office, Germany. Her main tasks are to coordinate Berlin's activities against racism and to introduce diversity approaches within the administration.

Alain-G. Gagnon holds the Canada Research Chair in Quebec and Canadian Studies in the Department of Political Science at the Université du Québec à Montréal, Canada.

Bas van Gool is a lecturer in Governance Studies at Vrije Universiteit Amsterdam, the Netherlands.

Sandra Groeneveld is Associate Professor in the Department of Public Administration at Erasmus University Rotterdam, the Netherlands.

Daniel Kübler is Professor for Research in Democracy and Public Governance in the Department of Political Science and Centre for Democracy Studies at the University of Zurich, Switzerland.

Moshe Maor is the Wolfson Family Professor of Public Administration in the Department of Political Science at The Hebrew University of Jerusalem, Israel.

Patrick von Maravić is DAAD Visiting Associate Professor in the Department of Political Science at the University of Alberta, Canada, and at the Department of Public Management and Governance at Zeppelin University, Germany.

Frits M. van der Meer is Professor of Comparative Public Sector and Civil Service Reform in the Department of Public Administration at Leiden University, the Netherlands.

Katja Michalak is Reader in the Department of Public Management and Governance at Zeppelin University, Germany.

Chantal Milne is research assistant at the Centre for Conflict Resolution at the University of Cape Town, South Africa.

María del Carmen Pardo is Professor of Public Administration at El Colegio de Mexico, Mexico.

B. Guy Peters is Maurice Falk Professor of American Government at the University of Pittsburgh, USA, and Professor of Comparative Governance at Zeppelin University, Germany.

Eckhard Schröter is Professor of Comparative Public Administration in the Department of Public Management and Governance at Zeppelin University, Germany.

Rodney Smith is Associate Professor in the Department of Government and International Relations at the University of Sydney, Australia.

Luc Turgeon is Assistant Professor in the School of Political Studies at the University of Ottawa, Canada.

Lieselot Vandenbussche is a PhD student in the Department of Public Administration at Erasmus University Rotterdam, the Netherlands.

Steven van de Walle is Professor in the Department of Public Administration at Erasmus University Rotterdam, the Netherlands.

Frank de Zwart is Associate Professor in the Department of Public Administration at Leiden University, the Netherlands.

1. Representative bureaucracy: concept, driving forces, strategies

B. Guy Peters, Eckhard Schröter and Patrick von Maravić

For more than two decades the study of public administration has been occupied with the peculiarities, causes, and consequences of what has been termed New Public Management (NPM). Representative bureaucracy and diversity management also raises questions about the link between workforce and performance, but more importantly brings society back into the study of public administration. The study of representative bureaucracy is concerned with the multiplicity of relationships between the composition of the public workforces and the socio-demographic characteristics of the society it serves, the consequences of the workforce composition for society at large, specific societal groups, and internal organizational performance as well as the (formal and informal) institutionalization of group rights and privileges. It directs the attention to the relationship of the socio-demographic, -linguistic and -ethnic compositions of societies and the workforce of the public sector and raises questions about the extent to which public sector workforces mirror the composition of the societies they are supposed to serve and the consequences this has for the quality of delivering services, the management of large organizations, the legitimacy of the state as such as well as questions of sharing power between societal forces.

This book seeks to advance the comparative study of representative bureaucracy. It will do so by examining this phenomenon in a number of diverse countries. The concern with representativeness within the public sector is a general phenomenon but it is interpreted and implemented differently in different settings. The country studies in this book illustrate why and how the issue of 'representativeness' and 'diversity' matters in public sector employment, and what driving forces propel the debate forward. Not only traditional migration countries such as the United States, Canada or Australia cope with questions of the ethnic–cultural compositions of their societies but essentially European countries with

a growing diversified ethnic–cultural composition, often enough concomitantly to the existing linguistic–ethnic cleavages, as for example in
Switzerland or Belgium. How issues of representativeness play out insti-
tutionally varies tremendously between the countries, as does what representativeness actually means and to which groups it refers. Is it a question
of geographic representation as in the case of Southern Italy, an issue of
indigenous groups in Mexico, people of African or European descent in
South Africa or religious groups as in the Netherlands and formerly in
Switzerland?

What representativeness actually means appears to be highly contingent
on the prevailing societal conflicts and cleavages, the specific function of
the civil service within society, as well as its traditions and mechanisms of
recruitment. The capacity to produce representativeness within the public
sector may also depend upon developments in the labor market, developments of migrations as well as new hegemonic ideas and fashions about
group rights, identity, and the role of the civil service within society. Thus,
although government may attempt to produce more or less representative
personnel systems, their efforts may be shaped in part by the nature of the
surrounding society and market.

But how can we bring order to the variety of strategies and trajectories
towards 'representative bureaucracies' across country cases? This chapter
aims at highlighting a selection of descriptive as well as explanatory categories that will guide the reader in viewing the developments and the
institutional variety through an analytic lens, which has been informed by
insights from old and new institutionalism. The chapter continues with a
discussion of the normative foundations of the concept of representative
bureaucracy, highlighting the core 'beliefs' and shaping ideas behind this
concept. It will then proceed by briefly sketching the different understandings of public service employment, which can differ significantly and may
help to understand the variation between countries and within countries
over time. In addition, we ask what diversity in the public sector actually
means and suggest distinguishing between four different definitions. In the
third subsection, the question is how one could conceptualize institutional
change, a topic that is nothing new for students of public administration,
and to what extent such an analytical framework could be helpful in studying and comparing developments across countries, levels of government
or between organizations. The fourth subsection will then propose two
different analytical perspectives in addressing the ultimate 'why' question
in order to understand the driving forces between current developments
more systematically.

CONCEPTUAL BACKGROUND I: NORMATIVE FOUNDATIONS OF REPRESENTATIVE BUREAUCRACY

It is difficult to bring all, or at least the principal elements of an established line of theoretical and empirical research under one umbrella without doing injustice to individual works and their authors. It may just as well be necessary and helpful for our future discussion to shed some light on the shared normative foundations and belief systems of the 'representative bureaucracy community'. To be sure, membership of this research community tends to be in flux and is difficult to define neatly as the boundaries are fuzzy and tend to overlap with neighboring epistemic communities. Moreover, their common intellectual project is nourished by various theoretical sources and normative convictions. Having said this, we still suggest the mainstream of the 'representative government' literature can be seen as a line of thinking in organization studies and public administration that exposes a common set of core beliefs and values.

The term 'representative bureaucracy' is used by students of public administration when referring to the relationship between the demographic makeup of the public sector workforce (particularly with regard to race, ethnicity, cultural traits such as language and religion, and gender) and the society it is supposed to serve (Kingsley, 1944; Meier, 1975; Krislov, 1974; Dolan and Rosenbloom, 1981; van der Meer and Roborgh, 1996). In very general terms representative bureaucracy can be described as the 'body of thought and research examining the potential for government agencies to act as representative political institutions if their personnel are drawn from all sectors of society' (Dolan and Rosenbloom, 2003, p. xi). One central empirical question in this field of research is whether the bureaucracy looks like a given segment of the population in terms of its ethnic, racial, social, gender, or occupational characteristics. An associated question is whether the bureaucracy advocates interests of a specific segment of the population (Mosher, 1968).

The argument for researching the issue of representative bureaucracy often comes from a normative position assuming that the question of having or not having an ethnically representative public bureaucracy has implications for fair and effective policy-making and implementation, the aim of integrating minorities into society by giving them the chance to be part of government, or even to control a bureaucracy that is dominated by a (ethnic) majority group and which does not care for the problems of minorities (Subramaniam, 1967; Dolan and Rosenbloom, 2003; van Gool, 2008). It is not surprising that this has institutional consequences for administrative regimes such as the accessibility, recruitment, self-understanding, and management of the civil service, which go in hand with the *opening* of the civil service for personnel with a migration background. The issue of representation and staffing carries important implications for the delivery of public services and the sharing of power in a society. Additionally, it symbolizes equal opportunities and equity (Groeneveld and Van de Walle, 2010).

Conventionally, the theorems of representative bureaucracy are couched in terms of a search of control over administrative power. Sparked by the concern to keep public bureaucrats responsive to the public at large (Subramaniam, 1967) and further fuelled by the deeply ingrained belief that existing external constraints of bureaucratic power are inherently inadequate, the design of representative bureaucracy was meant to serve as an effective internal measure of controlling government officials' behavior. In contrast to the logic of external control mechanisms, protagonists of representative bureaucracy tend to see achieving attitudinal congruence between administrative officeholders and the general public as key to their approach. In addition to this well-established account of representative bureaucracy's conceptual foundation, however, a more fundamental value base can be identified on which most of the modern architecture of diversity strategies in the public and, for that matter, private sectors has been built. For this purpose, we take a number of hints and pointers from cultural theory as a navigating tool to chart the terrain and locate the representative bureaucracy research community.

Arguably, the prevailing notion of human nature employed by the advocates of representative bureaucracy serves as a good starting point of our cursory overview of their value and belief systems. Clearly, the anthropological picture of (wo)man that guides most of the normative debates and empirical studies on workforce diversity is that of a social animal or *zoon politikon*, defined by a strong sense of group identity and driven by a strong impetus for communication and interaction with other members of their community. It flows from this that a strong collectivist undercurrent can be discerned in the representative bureaucracy approach – not unlike the dominant strand of the participatory democracy literature. Advocates of representative public sector organizations hold organizational values diametrically opposed to the concept of impersonality as manifested in ideal-typical bureaucracies, i.e. organizations that are structurally and culturally geared to let real people and their feelings, identities and non-work-related qualifications vanish behind the veil of abstract rules and neatly delineated office structures (Kingsley, 2003; Dolan and Rosenbloom, 2003). In a similar vein, protagonists of market-driven social coordination (Self, 1993, 2000; Lindblom, 2002) – based on assumptions of rational action – tend to be just as far away from the core values of the 'representative school of thought'. It is not the uniformly defined model of man or woman with externally pre-set utility functions and cost–benefit calculations to guide their behavior that appeals to advocates of diversity strategies in public, or for that matter, private sector organizations. Rather, their belief system rests on the assumption that organization members are defined by their ethnic, linguistic, or religious backgrounds – to name just a few sources of identity – and that they rely on social interaction with other individuals to develop their own preference structures as well as for the purpose of self-actualization.

The high value accorded to groups and particularly to group rights is another defining feature of the 'diversity cluster' in the recent public administration and management literature (Groeneveld and Van de Walle, 2010). This collectivist undercurrent in the representative bureaucracy mainstream, however, is intimately coupled with a deeply rooted commitment to a pluralist representation of group interests and an inherently inclusive approach to group interest mediation (Taylor and Gutman, 1994). This peculiar cross of 'high-groupness' and the (quasi-multicultural) endorsement of plurality in group representation sets the pro-diversity approach apart from normative foundations of public management that only accept the methodological individualism as a legitimate yardstick to evaluate human behavior (as preached by adherents to the creeds of the 'new institutional economics' and the 'new public management'). By the same token, it alienates followers of the 'diversity band wagon' from the tenets of more 'grid'- and 'single group'-oriented supporters who, as for the former, primarily believe in the legitimacy of formal structures (if they do public management the hierarchist way to paraphrase Christopher Hood, 2000) or, as for the latter, consider the shared norms and values of a given single group as their first and foremost point of reference (as do outright 'egalitarians' to use Hood's terminology again).

It flows from this more inclusive group-oriented stance of members of the 'representativeness' camp that models of interest representation and political decision-making that operate under the 'winner-takes-it-all' rule do not resonate well with them. Consequently, a distinctly more consociational, consensus-oriented and power-sharing style seems to be in order. Necessarily, any elitist assumptions of strong leadership, quick, uniform, and efficient – in a nutshell: non-participatory – decision-making procedures, or 'experts-know-best' attitudes are sources of potential clashes with the worldviews of 'diversity' advocates. In this regard, the 'representativeness' community shows a greater proximity to exponents of 'egalitarianism', but a similarly large distance to the camps of 'hierarchists' and 'individualists'.

On the ground level of organization practice, this rather abstract

pattern of assumptions about the human nature and societal values trans-
lates best into principles of organization that empower employees, gives
them greater participation in administrative decision-making and subjects
them less to superiors and procedural controls. Empowerment is seen as
conducive to foster the connection between passive and active representation as employees enjoy greater discretion and flexibility in dealing with
clientele groups and the public at large. Clearly, advocates of representative bureaucracy would find it difficult to see organizations as a 'nexus
of contracts' as suggested by neo-institutional economics or to subscribe
to the Weberian notion of an 'iron cage'. Their preferred mode of social
control does not (primarily) rely on 'intelligently designed' incentive
structures or formal procedures. Rather, organizational cultures and sub-
cultures seem to play a decisive role in how organizations are governed.
Given this set of underlying values and normative expectations, advocates
of representative bureaucracy appear predisposed to expect diversity strategies to translate into a broad range of consequences positively associated
with organizational performance.

CONCEPTUAL BACKGROUND II: FUNCTIONS OF PUBLIC SECTOR EMPLOYMENT AND DIVERSITY

Employment in the public sector means different things to different
people, ergo representation has many faces. In order to develop a more
differentiated understanding of the relationship between diversity and
the public sector workforce we need to distinguish different meanings
of public sector employment. This is necessary in order to illustrate the
multi-faceted nature of this phenomenon. We will first broadly distinguish
four different meanings of public sector employment and then show that
also the discourse on representative bureaucracy touches upon different
dimensions of public sector employment.

Employment in the Public Sector *Means Different Things* to *Different People* . . .

Public administration refers first of all to a collection of people that are
meant to pursue collective goals. The dominant concern from an *organizational function* perspective is the management of human resources within
a set of rules and authority relationships and how people are linked to the
delivery of different public services (Bekke et al., 1996, p. 2). This perspective draws the attention to the way public servants are being recruited – by
merit or by patronage (Peters, 2001, chapter 4) –, the values they hold, their

socio-demographic composition, and dominant career patterns. But it also raises questions about the institutional setting in which employees perform their tasks, which can mean working in a structurally differentiated task environment that is being coordinated by means of hierarchy or can also mean to bundle activities, capacities and different abilities in teams. The *organizational function* of public sector employment links people to tasks and raises questions about their efficiency and effectiveness. However, public sector employment also has a *macroeconomic function*. The relationship between the public service and national labor markets stands here in the limelight of attention. Differing from country to country the public employment encompasses between 8 to 10 percent of the national labor force in countries such as Germany or Switzerland and can rise up to 25 percent in Sweden (Rose, 1984, 1985; see also Derlien and Peters, 2008). It is therefore very much an instrument of public sector employment and can have significant effects on the development of wages and the unemployment rate, but also employment standards, where the public sector takes the role of a 'model employer', for example when it comes to equal employment regulations. The third is crucial for any political system as it concerns the *political function* of the public service. The public sector regulates access to political decision-making, functions as a tool of interest representation of societal groups, and raises questions about patronage and clientelism. Last but not least, the public sector employment has a *socio-cultural function* as an important vehicle of social mobility, which is an important element of a free society (Mosher, 1968, pp. 17–21). Of course, social mobility relates to questions of the labor market but also to the socialization into democratic political systems. Whenever one talks about public sector employment it is necessary to be aware of the different connotations it carries, which are not totally independent from the disciplinary and professional background of the people referring to it. And as much as the public service has different faces, also diversity in the public sector workforces raises a number of different questions.

The reader of this book may bear these differences in mind when reading the different country reports as these investigations are highly contingent upon different traditions but also of the different roles the public service has in societies as well as current challenges.

Diversity in the Public Sector Workforce *Raises Questions* about . . .

Diversity in the public sector workforce raises a number of distinct questions, which are worth considering. When debating the notion of 'representative bureaucracy', four key dimensions seem to dominate the debate: the *functional*, the *power*, the *symbolic*, and the *administration-society* dimensions of the concept. Students of 'representative bureaucracy' in the United States have treated all of these issues in one or the other way since the mid-1970s. Without reviewing here the whole literature on representative bureaucracy, we will draw upon this rich body of research to illustrate these four functions of this discourse, which seem to form the core of this debate.

Functional Needs: To *What Extent* can *Representativeness* be *Linked* to *Performance Improvement*?

The *functional* dimension addresses the impact of the ethnic, cultural, etc. composition of society on the composition of the civil service itself and therefore the delivery of public services to the citizens. In the eyes of advocates of representative bureaucracy this is not only about guaranteeing equal rights and access to bureaucracy or skillfully drafting legislation but to gain societal 'support for policies' by drawing a 'wide segment of society into government to convey and merchandise a policy' (Krislov, 1974, pp. 4–5). In contrast to Weber, this position views the 'human potentialities' (Krislov, 1974, pp. 4–5) in their whole variety as a prerequisite for a well-performing administration. Good administrative performance in multi-ethnic environments depends to a great extent on the quality of judgment, information and social skills that bureaucrats bring into the administration. The 'immense social advantage', which Krislov (1974, p. 4) sees, lies in the active representation of societal needs. The problem can be illustrated by the example of policing of white police squads in multi-ethnic neighborhoods or the recruitment of teachers of foreign origin for specific neighborhoods. That this question is not a theoretical one is shown by the riots and violent protests by young immigrants in the suburbs of Paris in 2005, 2006, and 2007 (Meier and Hawes, 2008). One might therefore ask whether the ethnic composition of the police squad influences their ability to work towards a stable, secure, and calm neighborhood or that of teaching staff creates a better learning environment for students in high school (Keiser et al., 2002; Meier and Stewart, 1992).

Power Issues: To *What Extent* does *Representativeness Relate* to *Questions* of *Power* and *System*-wide *Legitimacy* of *Public Sector Organizations*?

The *power* dimension puts the problem of legitimacy on the agenda of the civil services in ethnically fragmented societies. The classical question of students of democratic theory – who rules and how can people be represented in democratic decision-making and power be shared? – comes back here with its specific focus on bureaucracies. With what kind of procedures and rules do bureaucracies in multicultural societies guarantee a 'good bureaucracy' and what does 'good bureaucracy' mean in the context of a multicultural society? Do equal opportunities for access to public office really exist? Are entry exams really impartial? The whole problem is about reconciling the 'basic principles of representative government with the powerful roles that unelected civil servants collectively play in the formulation and implementation of public policies' (Dolan and Rosenbloom, 2003, p. xi).

Symbolic Politics: To *What Degree* are *Moves Toward Representativeness* to be *Interpreted* as *Symbolic Actions*?

The *symbolic* function is viewed in the passive as well as active promotion of equal opportunity and equality. The civil service may even serve as an example and trigger change in broader society, such as private enterprises, or compensate for inequality and discrimination in other institutions (Krislov, 1974). Often the public service takes the role of a kind of 'model employer' when it comes to regulating employment, especially vis-à-vis the private sector. Also, it is argued that the employment patterns in the public sector should represent 'best practice', providing greater opportunities for minorities and women.

Administration and Society Relations: What can *Representativeness* in *Public Bureaucracies Contribute* to the Integration of *Ethnic Minorities*?

One of the most relevant links for political scientists to study is the role of public administration within society and how it develops relationships to either specific groups or society at large. In the debate on representative bureaucracy two different streams can be distinguished, which shall be described in some more detail in the remainder.

The clientele claim: improved external relations

The third dimension of the performance claim focuses on the relationship between an organization and its clientele or customers. Although the nature of external relations overlaps in part with the 'power' and 'function' categories, it also taps a different dimension as it acknowledges the value of having close and deeply rooted relations with more specifically defined target groups as a quality of public organizations in its own right. Moreover, it adds a distinct demand-side to the approach of representative bureaucracy: how do people at the receiving end of public service delivery value the fact that they interact with representative bureaucracies and, more specifically, with representatives of their own community? On top of that, this dimension recognizes also the profound political nature of external relations. Not only can representative bureaucracies contribute to governmental legitimacy, they can also opportunistically use their well-established ties with supportive citizens as a resource for political bargaining and bureaucratic politics.

As a closer look reveals, this dimension is, in turn, divided into two major categories: one stream of arguments is primarily driven by concerns about customer relations, whereas the other strand of thought is nourished by considerations about democratic accountability. As perceived in much of the private management literature, diversity allows for tailor-made products, new markets, better access to specific clientele, and a focus on customer demand (Thomas and Ely, 1996), whereas in the public (pre-NPM) literature the focus lies more on questions of responsiveness and accountability of government (cf. Subramaniam, 1967) and has to be read against the historical circumstances of the 1940s and 1960s (Groeneveld and Van de Walle, 2010, pp. 241, 245). The claim that citizens are better served in a representative bureaucracy is present in Kingsley's and Mosher's work as already mentioned in the 'output'-oriented section (cf. the 'pooling diverse streams of experience' as Kingsley (1944, p. 18) put it, or Mosher's idea of bringing together 'different perspectives, knowledge, values, and abilities' (1968, p. 16)) improves the quality of governance. In principle, advocates of representative bureaucracy share the idea that a bureaucracy that mirrors the composition of the society it serves is more responsive to public interests and will therefore, as Selden and Selden point out, 'better serve democratic principles' (Selden and Selden, 2001, p. 308).

It does not come as a surprise that this focus seems to shift in the backwater of 'new public management' reforms more to questions of customer satisfaction of public services. In keeping with the customer-oriented 'performance claim', Bradbury and Kellough (2008) found that African-American citizens respond particularly favorably to governmental behaviors that specifically target the interests of the African-American community and that African-American citizens and administrators hold markedly different attitudes from white administrators. In any event, catering to diverse communities seems to present an extra challenge to public service providers. So, Andrews et al. (2005, p. 501) observe lower levels of consumer satisfaction with public services in more ethnically diverse neighborhoods.

The 'diffuse system support' claim
Last but not least, it seems conceptually valuable to distinguish a 'diffuse system support' category, a term borrowed from Easton's classic work (1965; 1975, pp. 440–450), to denote a cluster of benefits that society

at large can derive from fostering public bureaucracies that mirror the demographic makeup of the communities they serve. When Easton talks about the 'diffuse support' of a system, he means the more general evaluation of what an object *is* and not what it *does* and refers to a 'reservoir of favorable attitudes of good will' (Easton, 1975, p. 444) that helps members of a society to accept decisions although they might be opposed to them or might even have negative consequences for them. This means that in the short run the level of support is independent of specific outputs or performance.

Though the smallest portion of work has been done on this dimension of the performance claim, it seems to be implicitly present in many studies mentioned before. So, Krislov's statement comes to mind that representative bureaucracy is also about gaining societal 'support for policies' by drawing a 'wide segment of society into government to convey and merchandise a policy' (Krislov, 1974, pp. 4–5). The 'diffuse system support' claim becomes especially visible when authors argue that a representative bureaucracy could be of advantage when it comes to implementing controversial policy programs, unpopular policy decisions, e.g. redistributive measures or budget cuts, and therefore help the organization in critical times, for example in times of economic recession or, more generally, in times of environmental uncertainty (Pitts et al., 2010, p. 882).

The central claim is that a representative bureaucracy would not only improve performance, as spelled out before, but enhance its legitimacy overall (Groeneveld and Van de Walle, 2010, p. 240), which in Easton's understanding of the concept of legitimacy would mean that passive representativeness could support a person's conviction 'that is right and proper [. . .]' and that it 'reflects the fact that in some vague or explicit way [a person] sees these objects as conforming to his own moral principles, his own sense of what is right and proper in the political sphere' (Easton, 1975, p. 451). On the other hand, it does not come as a surprise that 'separatist ethnic and linguistic groups' (Easton, 1975, p. 451) do not consider a political authority legitimate that turns them into second-class citizens and deprives them of their rights. In accord with this view, Mosher was convinced that a passively representative bureaucracy would carry some 'independent and symbolic values' (1968, p. 17) that are the prerequisite for a democratic society as it underlines such things as equal opportunities and an open civil service. And also Selden and Selden express the opinion that advocates of representative bureaucracy stress the importance of 'a symbolic commitment to equal access to power' (2001, p. 309) that goes in hand with passive representativeness. An open civil service to which everyone has access was in Mosher's eyes the fulfillment of Lincoln's dream of a government 'by the people' and this not only for symbolic reasons but Frederick Mosher was convinced that public employment is an important vehicle of social mobility, which is an important element of a free society (Mosher, 1968, pp. 17–21). Groeneveld and Van de Walle even use words such as 'harmonious society' (2010, p. 241) to which a representative bureaucracy could contribute, and the authors continue to maintain that representing 'those who count' is a means to balance and share the power among different groups and resembles the picture of a 'consensual and equalitarian ethos of the community' (Subramaniam, 1967, p. 1014). What also shines through these statements, however, is the possibility to use instruments of 'passive group representation' opportunistically as symbolic politics as already Frederick Mosher observed (Mosher, 1968, p. 17).

These four dimensions of the representative bureaucracy illustrate nicely the complexity of the theme from an empirical–analytical perspective but bring also into the open the high normative expectations that some students of representative bureaucracies attach to this topic.

THE RISE OF THE DIVERSITY DEBATE IN THE PUBLIC SECTOR IS DRIVEN BY A RANGE OF FACTORS . . .

The rise of the diversity debate is driven by a number of different factors, which may vary from country to country. At least four distinct developments seem to have an impact on why this issue has received such prominent attention during the past decade: socio-demographic development, new political ideas about group representation, cultural and attitudinal changes in societies, and socio-economic changes.

Socio-demographic *Development*

In European societies, there seems to be a clearly discernible trend towards greater cultural variety in what used to be more rigidly defined 'nation states'. The fast and widespread growth of geographical mobility in a common European market and a globalized economy resulted in more and more people migrating for work, but also on humanitarian grounds or to find political safe havens. The accelerated process of European integration has not only lowered the hurdles for a free movement of people, but stipulated also the right of EU-citizens to join the civil service of another member state (even though specific restrictions often remain). As a consequence, member states are facing a continuously growing diversity of their resident populations with political and social pressure building up to accommodate the specific interests and needs of the new, but sizable minority groups (Bauböck, 1996; Riggs, 2002, p. 35). This functional pressure can therefore not be separated from wider demographic developments.

New *Ideas* about *Political Representation*

Political and normative considerations find a common focal point when the argument in favor of representative bureaucracies follows the discourse of the 'politics of identity' or 'politics of recognition' debate (cf. Taylor and Gutman, 1994; Bauböck, 2004; Parekh, 2006; Kymlicka, 2010). In such a (philosophical) line of thought, the inclusion of cultural minorities is not contingent on functional necessities or politically opportunistic behavior but rather a manifestation of minority rights per se. From this flows a politically powerful symbolic meaning attached to pressures to open public sector organizations because working for 'government' can be interpreted as a strong signal of a successful integration of minority groups into statehood and society majority.

Cultural and *Attitudinal Changes*

When reflecting upon the causes that propel this debate one probably cannot turn a blind eye on the pessimistic, often enough openly negative or hostile view of citizens on the role of government in society. More than ever before government agencies and their employees are facing public criticism, intense media coverage by investigative and populist investigations, self-appointed government watch-dogs, e.g. Amnesty International or Transparency International, and the popular fashion of bureau-bashing as had been visible under the Thatcher and Reagan administrations in the 1980s and '90s. Popular television series, such as 'Yes, Minister', had been developed on the theoretical premises of public choice theory and then used as political instruments in order to uncover what advocates of this school of thought saw as the main problem to effective and responsive government. These (new) demands for greater accountability and responsibility of government activity must not be underestimated when it comes to a debate about who is actually represented by the public service workforce.

Socio-economic Changes

Important socio-economic changes are also affecting governments and their employment programs. As the financial resources supporting distributive welfare programs are drying up, 'recognition' becomes a new currency to foster 'social peace' and inclusion. Promoting more representative hiring is one means of creating that recognition of the claims of minority group members in society.

INSTITUTIONAL CHANGE: HOW CAN WE BRING ORDER TO VARIATION ACROSS COUNTRIES?

Institutional change is one visible consequence of the drive towards greater representativeness in the countries studied in this book. Representative bureaucracy takes, as the authors in this volume show, different institutional contours in different countries. But how can we actually systematically make sense of these transformations that concern not only changes to legal provisions but also training programs with a greater emphasis on the management of diversity as well as the introduction of new values within the bureaucracy? In the remainder, we shall propose an analytical grid that distinguishes between three different dimensions or 'pillars' of institutions. This institutional perspective may help the reader view the country studies through this distinct perspective of institutional change in order to grasp the high variety of developments.

Any institutional analysis has to tackle the question: what do we mean by 'institutional change', how can it be recognized, and is it a revolutionary or evolutionary process (Campbell, 2004, chapter 2)? To be sure, answers to these questions are highly contested and tend to differ significantly depending on the author's loyalty to the various schools of thought in institutional theory (Selznick, 1948, 1996; March and Olsen, 1989; DiMaggio and Powell, 1991; Hall and Taylor, 1996; Stinchcombe, 1997; Immergut, 1998; Katznelson and Weingast, 2005; Peters, 2011). Bearing in mind that we are skating on thin ice, we follow Scott in conceiving institutions as 'multifaceted, durable social structures, made up of symbolic elements, social activities, and material resources' (Scott, 2001, p. 49). According to this understanding, institutions have a formal as well as informal dimension. Important ingredients are rules, norms, and cultural beliefs but this understanding encompasses also material resources as well as behavior. Furthermore, they are resistant to change, transmitted across generations, maintained and reproduced, and institutions consist of different pillars – regulative, normative, cultural–cognitive (Scott, 1994, chapter 3): The *regulatory* pillar concerns those processes and structures that are designed to constrain and regularize behavior, which is rule-setting, monitoring, and sanctioning. They are considered to be the most conscious aspects of institutions. The *regulatory* pillar is affected when quotas, positive measures, or other requirements aim to increase immigrant employment. Stating intercultural skills as a job requirement can be a sign that an organization actively promotes diversity;[1] installing a diversity manager with an annual budget, staff, and formal authority places the institutional adaptations beyond the creation of an image. The *normative* pillar emphasizes the prescriptive dimension of social life, which relates to norms and values. Terms such as 'diversity' and 'multicultural' are often in the organization's mission statement or management explicitly defines diversity as an organizational goal. Norms and values define what is desirable and what not, define goals, e.g. tolerance towards difference or making profit, and prescribe legitimate or appropriate means to pursue specific goals. On the one hand, normative systems constrain behavior, but on the other hand do they empower to act in a specific way. As action is social insofar as actors attach meaning to behavior, the *cultural–cognitive* pillar looks at factors that shape the meaning being attributed to objects and action. Symbols, gestures, words, or signs are therefore considered to be central elements of institutions. They are the basis of the unconscious, culturally formed, and taken-for-granted assumptions about reality. The *cultural–cognitive* pillar is for example affected by having employees participate in intercultural communication seminars, a management that promotes diversity in its own ranks, and the maintenance of concepts or ideologies of multiculturalism. This can then form the ideological super-structure for an organization that affects the way terms are used. To a certain extent this politicizes the topic and starts to drift away from purely functional criteria. These pillars are not mutually exclusive but can be considered to be three relevant elements on a continuum moving from 'the conscious to the unconscious, from the legally enforced to the taken for granted' (Hoffman, 2001, p. 36). Together they form an integrated conception of what institutions are and allow a differentiated analysis of institutions as well as institutional change.

INSTITUTIONAL STRATEGIES: HOW CAN WE EXPLAIN THE OPENING OF PUBLIC SERVICES?

All authors in this book cope with the 'why' question. Why do bureau-cracies actually embark on diversity strategies – consciously or not – in order to make the public service more accessible for ethnic minorities, migrants, women, disabled persons or other groups. Though there seem to be significant differences between the countries we shall propose in the remainder a relatively simple distinction between a passive and an active mode of 'opening-up' the public sector. These two distinct analytical per-spectives shall guide the readers' eyes towards two dominant explanatory mechanisms. That is, one way to understand representation is purely passive, meaning that merely having personnel that look like the society is sufficient. The more active version is that these employees will in fact promote the interests of their ethnic, or gender, group once in office.

Against this background, we argue that there are two dominant rationalities for 'opening-up' public services and making them more accessible for minority groups. One way of reasoning about diversity is driven by functional requirements and operational needs of public sector organizations; another way of arguing for cultural representativeness revolves around the external pressure of organized interested groups. To be sure, in reality these rationalities often mix and overlap but analytically these are two distinctive categories.

A first and foremost *functionality*-driven strategy suggests that trends towards more ethnic diversity – or the lack of them – simply reflect the match or mismatch between staffing needs of an organization and the quantity and quality of available labor at any given time. In turn, we can distinguish between reactive and proactive variants of this functional explanation. As for the former, it seems to be worth drawing on insights developed by 'old institutionalists' such as Selznick or Stinchcombe in the 1940s, '50s, and '60s – which have almost been forgotten in the meantime – that any organization has 'basic needs', which are essentially related to the self-maintenance of it, such as 'integrity' or 'continuity' (Selznick, 1948, p. 29). A functional reason for recruiting personnel would solely look at the internal operational *needs* of the organization, which can of course also be intercultural competencies or the command of several languages. These needs are rationally determined by their function in the administrative production process and influenced by factors such as the labor market. Accordingly, a tendency towards an ethnically and culturally diverse workforce can even be seen as an accidental side effect of certain labor market necessities. From this vantage point, local government employers show no regard for the ethnic, linguistic or cultural background of applicants, but purely seek to fill staff positions according to their established operational job requirements. A *passive or reactive* stance on diversity issues like this might in fact, although not intended, lead to a sizeable influx of foreign-born employees, particularly at the lower end of the pay-scales (where employment is least attractive for the established middle classes – that serve as the archetypical talent pool for public sector employment) and specific top-paid expert positions (where demand can often not be met by supply from the local labor market).

In contrast, a more *proactive* strategy towards ethnic or linguistic diversity in public organizations values the contribution that new entrants make to the performance of the organization specifically based on their cultural background. While the underlying rationale is still entirely based on the functional and operational needs of the organization, a proactive stance on diversity recognizes the value of having a multi-cultural staff 'on board' in order to improve their organizational performance.

Another perspective opens up, if we consider motives and reasons for change that are based on *normative or political* considerations. As a matter of fact, more recent experience has shown a certain politicization of the whole issue and therefore also a stronger role of external actors pressing towards an opening-up of the civil service. Typically, factors grouped into this category are not necessarily inherent to the functioning of the organization, but externally driven, for example by coalitions of representatives of minority groups, political parties, non-governmental organizations (NGOs), or so-called 'integration commissioners'. They have a primarily political dimension as they infuse non-managerial norms, values, and interests into the decision-making process. Political and normative considerations find their common focal point when the argument in favor of representative bureaucracies follows the discourse of the 'politics of identity' or 'politics of recognition' debate (Taylor and Gutman, 1994). In this (philosophical) line of thought, the inclusion of cultural minorities is not contingent on functional necessities or politically opportunistic behavior. Rather, the concept of representative bureaucracies is a manifestation of minority rights that exist per se. It flows from this that there is also a politically powerful symbolic meaning attached to those pressures to open-up public sector organizations as working for 'government' can be interpreted as a particularly strong signal of a more successful integration of minority groups into statehood and the majority society. As with many political and administrative power-sharing arrangements, for example in cases of ethno-federalist systems or consociational democracies, the inclusion of cultural minorities is believed to increase system trust and overall legitimacy of politico-administrative institutions. From a different angle, of course, the interest of minority groups to be represented in official positions can also be in seen in the light of rent-seeking (Krueger, 1974) or as a struggle for collective goods provided by government and being able to influence, change, or get them (Wimmer, 1997). Admittedly, there might also be a considerable degree of potential overlap between political considerations and what we earlier coined as organizational–functional requirements. In particular, it could be argued that the quest to enhance system trust and overall legitimacy through measures towards representative bureaucracies falls into the category of functionally defined rationales, as they are also concerned with improved administrative performance. And yet, we find that the distinction between overall 'system performance' – as with the normative–political rationale – and functional requirements at the level of individual organizations is heuristically meaning- and useful especially when it comes to comparing developments in the countries studies in this book.

CONCLUDING THOUGHTS

As issues of ethnicity, gender, and equality have become more central to political life, representative bureaucracy also has become more significant to the study of the public bureaucracy. Although the issue is important, it is also the subject of substantive conceptual and political conflict. The conceptual conflicts are based on different understandings of the meaning of the term, and in particular whether passive representation is sufficient to claim that representation has been achieved.

The political questions center on the obligations of the State to recruit individuals in order to create greater equality of opportunity. This pattern of recruitment may also produce greater difficulties in managing the public sector, with a more socially diverse workforce. This may also force some reconceptualization of the relationships between state and society, emphasizing the need to link the two. This linkage also raises questions about the capacities of the public sector to manage diversity, especially in the context of the performance emphasis of the NPM.

This volume, and its companion volume, *The Politics of Representative Bureaucracy*, addresses the core questions of the research agenda in representative bureaucracy. It builds on the well-established research community within public administration, and attempts to raise a number of new questions for research. In particular, the comparative emphasis in this volume also emphasizes the multiple interpretations of this concept, and the importance of understanding context when attempting to understand representative bureaucracy. This concept appears simple, but its political, normative and managerial implications are significant and merit the careful consideration that it is given by the scholars writing in this volume.

NOTE

1. In the case of public administration this might also be due to laws. Berlin, for example, passed a Law on Integration and Participation in 2010, which makes training in intercultural skills mandatory for certain positions and promotion.

PART I

The Americas

2. Representative bureaucracy in the United States

B. Guy Peters

The increasing diversity of most contemporary societies, especially in the developed democratic systems, poses challenges to many of the ways in which governance has been practiced in the past. Many of the assumptions about how to manage in the public sector and what policies to pursue must be reconsidered in light of the increased social complexity and the need to deliver services to the more diverse population (Smith, 2004). Further, not only are societies more complex but also numerous minority social groups (or majority groups in the case of women) have become mobilized politically in order to press demands for greater equality and integration into the dominant society.

The public bureaucracy has been one obvious target for the mobilization of minority social groups, whether they have been resident in the country for decades or centuries, or whether they are relatively recent arrivals. The bureaucracy is important both as a potential source of employment for members of minority groups and also because it delivers public services, including a number that may be especially relevant for the minority groups. In contrast, members of the dominant community may attempt to preserve many public sector jobs for themselves, using a variety of legal and often extra-legal mechanisms to maintain their positions. Further, that dominant community may not be particularly concerned with the equality of the services being delivered to minorities, so that these questions of representative bureaucracy involve to some extent the exercise of political power.

The literature on representative bureaucracy began rather simply, looking at the extent to which the public bureaucracy, and especially the senior levels of the public bureaucracy, resembled the population as a whole. The initial concern in the literature was with the class origins of the members of the civil service (see Kingsley, 1944). At the time of the development of the concept class was perhaps the principal division in society, and many European societies were relatively homogeneous in religious and especially in ethnic terms.[1] The class conception of representative bureaucracy was especially important as Welfare State programs became central to European governance and that in turn involved more service delivery to working class clients.

In contemporary terms representative bureaucracy is discussed more in terms of ethnicity and gender than class. These dimensions have become more prominent in discussions of social inequalities, even though ethnicity, at least, often correlates highly with class. This change reflects the political activation of the gender cleavage, as well as the increasing heterogeneity of many European societies resulting from immigration. Politically these social cleavages have become more activated through the prevalence of identity politics, making understanding representative bureaucracy all the more important (Jenkins and Sofos, 2006).

In the academic discussions of representative bureaucracy there has been a marked shift away from the simple statistical representativeness of these structures to consider more the real consequences of the representativeness, or lack thereof, on the behavior of public servants. Beginning in the 1970s, scholars began to ask more probing questions about representativeness. Does the social background of the public bureaucracy matter for other than symbolic reasons, as important as that symbolism may be? Do minority group members use their positions in the bureaucracy to favor members of their own group, or are they more passive participants in the system? And do governments consciously use recruitment to the bureaucracy to attempt to influence social patterns and the behavior of other employers in the economy?

In one of the more comprehensive studies of the subject Sally Selden (1997) studied representative bureaucracy within one agency in the United States and differentiated between active and passive forms of representation. She found that simply having more members of a minority group was not necessarily related to agency behaviors that would treat minorities equally, or perhaps even preferentially. The individual minority group members within the agency had to adopt more active conceptions of their role as representative of their groups if there were to be more equal outcomes. Further, even within the same organization individuals would not necessarily adopt the same role conceptions. In her case it was especially important that many of the officers at the lower levels of the organizations, actually making the decisions about home loans, were more likely to have an active conception of the role.

Thus, as we investigate representative bureaucracy it may be necessary, but not sufficient, to detail the levels of employment provided to minority group members and women. The question is also the extent to which those numbers can and do translate their attributes and allegiances into actions. With that perception the usual emphasis on representativeness at the top of the bureaucratic pyramids may be somewhat misplaced. Given that the street-level bureaucrats (Meyers and Vorsanger, 2004) are the ones in contact with the public, and are generally then the ones who make decisions about who gets what, or who gets arrested, or suspended from school, then the representativeness of these individuals may be substantially more important than that of the upper levels of the bureaucracy.

The level of discretion available to public employees, or perceived to be available to them, appears to be related to the active exercise of discretion by public employees (Sowa and Selden, 2003). Administrators who perceive that they have discretion appear willing to exercise it, and when combined with minority status they are likely to provide differential benefits for minority clients. This perception can also be related to attempts in contemporary public management to "empower" lower level employees, and to enhance discretion. If that movement is successful then the attempts to build representative bureaucracies that deliver service are also likely to be successful.

REPRESENTATIVE BUREAUCRACY IN THE UNITED STATES

Like all political systems employment in the public bureaucracy of the United States has been dominated by males from the dominant ethnic group (Van Riper, 1958). This dominance has been, and to a great extent remains, especially true in the upper levels of the bureaucracy. The large majority of members of the Senior Executive Service in Washington, and analogous positions at the state and local levels of government, are white males. This pattern persists even after decades of attempts through affirmative action and equal opportunity programs to create greater equality within public employment. Further, as the social complexity of the United States becomes all the more pronounced the need to create more representative employment in the public sector becomes all the more important (see below).

Race has been the dominant social issue in representativeness in the United States. Although class differences certainly exist and to some extent are becoming more important, contemporary conceptions of the issue of equality have been expressed primarily in terms of black and white. That said, historically the Jacksonian version of public bureaucracy for the United States was founded on the logic of equality for the mass public (see White, 1954). That conception has never fully died, especially at the state and local levels and the populist tradition in American politics still extols the capacities and rights of the "little man".[2] That in turn can be translated into a conception that the public service should be representative of class and have a significant number of those "little people" included.

The conception of equality in employment has become more complex as the Hispanic population has grown and become more politically active, and as the Asian population also grows significantly.[3] In part, these questions become very important for local employment and for local service delivery in areas of high levels of minority population, as well as being more general national issues (see Table 2.1). Further, as in all countries, gender equality continues to be an important issue for employment in the United States. Merely having had a number of women (including one African-American woman) in high profile political positions, e.g. Secretary of State, does not alleviate concerns about employment throughout the administrative systems at all levels of government.

The question of representative bureaucracy and the concept of "minority" has also become more problematic in the United States as white Anglos cease to be the majority population group. This shift has already happened in some states and many localities but is clear in national demographic trends as well. While the white community will continue for some time to maintain its status as the dominant economic and social group, that position may also be threatened, again especially locally. Thus, representative bureaucracy ceases to have the rather unambiguous meaning that it once did. Representativeness remains important but the issues of dominance appear to be transforming.

The clarity of issues of representative bureaucracy may also be waning in terms of gender. This change is perhaps not immediately visible in employment patterns but it is also visible in educational terms. Higher education – and perhaps especially graduate and professional education – is the pathway to employment in the upper echelons of the public service. Perhaps more so in Europe than in the United States, given the adoption of mass higher education much earlier, the principal barrier to achieving a higher civil service job has been success in the educational system. This was especially important as a barrier for working class aspirants, but also true for creating equality on the basis of gender.[4]

In the United States, and in a number of other industrialized democracies, males have become a vanishing species in higher education and even in professional education. In 2009, over 60 percent of enrolment in four-year colleges and universities was female, and the proportion of women in graduate and professional education was even higher. Among African-Americans the disparity is even more marked. In 2010 some 64 percent of African-Americans in higher education were female. The pool of qualified employees for many public service positions, especially those toward the top of the hierarchy, therefore is becoming increasingly female and employment should begin to demonstrate that increasingly as the cumulative effect of higher rates of female education persist.

The educational statistics for minority group members in the United States cannot be expected to have the same positive effects as for women. The rate of attendance in higher education for African-Americans has stabilized or dropped very slightly over the past several years. On the other hand, the already high rate of participation in higher education for Asians has persisted, while that of Hispanics has tended to increase slightly. Thus, given that educational attainment is central to the opportunities to achieve high-level positions in the public bureaucracy, then the capacity to improve representativeness for African-Americans in particular appears diminishing. The continuing financial crisis in many states also means that tuition fees for public institutions will be increasing, thus posing a higher barrier to less affluent minority students.

Finally, I should note that although race and gender are probably the more important dimensions of variation, class retains some importance. Class issues remain relevant in a number of social programs and in labor market programs, with some evidence about the differential treatment of applicants for programs based on the social backgrounds of the public servants administering the programs. The increasing income inequality in the United States is likely to contribute to the relevance of class considerations in representative bureaucracy.

The rapidly increasing economic inequality in the United States will apparently pose some even greater class barriers for access to public sector employment. The impacts of the economic slowdown have been concentrated disproportionately on members of minority groups, with fewer minority group members entering universities. That pattern will then soon translate into fewer individuals being eligible for higher level jobs in the public sector. Further, the adoption of anti-immigrant laws in states such as Alabama and Arizona has reduced the opportunities for even legal immigrants (especially Hispanics).

THE EVIDENCE

The evidence concerning representative bureaucracy in the United States provides a rather predictable picture of the patterns of employment in the public sector. The evidence is relatively rich for the federal level of government, but is somewhat less available for the other levels of government, so that much of this discussion will be of the federal level. That is somewhat unfortunate given that many social and labor market programs are delivered by lower levels of government. Thus, it is at this level that the face-to-face contacts between citizens and the bureaucracy occur, and hence where the representativeness of the bureaucracy may be most relevant. That said, we do know that in most administrative systems the lower levels of the bureaucracy tend to be more representative than do the upper echelons, so we would expect the "street levels" of sub-national governments in the United States to be relatively representative.

The evidence that is available without conducting one's own attitudinal surveys can only address the passive dimension of representativeness. There is substantial evidence on employment of women and minorities at various grades in the federal government, and this is available across a substantial period of time. The evidence on state and local government is more limited, but still provides some picture of how well some categories of employment do represent the public. In particular, there is evidence on two of the most important state and local services that are in direct contact with citizens – elementary and secondary teachers, and the police.

EMPLOYMENT BY RACE: FEDERAL GOVERNMENT

As noted, employment by race and other minorities has tended to be perhaps the dominant consideration in representativeness in the United States. The data in Table 2.1 provide some evidence on the development of federal employment by race over a 20-year time period, along with

Table 2.1   Federal government employment by race, 1990–2010 (in percentage)

	1990	1995	2000	2005	2010
African-American	13.6	14.8	15.8	16.0	16.5
Hispanic	4.4	5.1	7.2	7.5	7.5
Asian, Native American	4.5	5.2	7.2	7.4	7.7
Total Population by Race					
African-American	12.3	12.1	11.8	11.7	11.6
Hispanic	10.7	11.2	12.2	14.1	16.4
Asian, Native American, etc.	3.9	4.4	4.8	5.3	5.6

Notes: These numbers are somewhat problematic because of self-identification of respondents in multiple categories, e.g. African-American and Hispanic.

Source: Bureau of the Census (various years), Office of Personnel Management (various years)

comparisons to the distribution of the total population in the same demographic categories. The obvious point here is that federal employment as a whole is not unrepresentative of the population, except that to some extent it has higher levels of minority employment than there is in the population as a whole. For example, the entire population of the United States in 2010 was 11.6 percent African-American, while federal employment is 16.5 percent African-American (see Table 2.1). When postal employment is added the figure increases to 18.1 percent.

When federal employment is broken down by level within the administrative system, the representativeness is not as apparent. For example, approximately one-quarter of all employees in the eight lower grades in the civil service are African-American, while only 6 percent of the executive grade employees are African-American. Likewise, approximately 10 percent of the lower grades in the civil service are Hispanic while less than 4 percent of the senior positions are Hispanic. The figures for Asian Americans are approximately the same as are those for Hispanic employees.

In some ways the above information is both good and bad news. On the one hand it is clear that minority group members are not doing well in competition for higher levels positions in the federal bureaucracy, despite some progress over time. On the other hand, the opportunities for the active conception of representative bureaucracy being exercised at the street-level do appear positive, and the chances of a client of a public program who is a minority group member encountering a service deliverer who is also from a minority group is reasonably high.[5]

In addition to these general questions about the level of employment of minority group members in government, there is also a question about whether minority employees are employed differentially in particular types of organizations (see Durr and Logan, 1997). Indeed, many minority managers are employed managing programs to enhance diversity, and many others are in social service programs. Thus, although the overall diversity is increased there may still be ghettos within the public sector.

EMPLOYMENT BY GENDER: FEDERAL GOVERNMENT

Unlike many administrative systems the US federal bureaucracy is not over half female. This is in large part because unlike many other systems there are relatively few members of traditional female occupations – nurses, school teachers, etc. – employed in the federal government. These positions are more prevalent at the state and local level. In addition, secretarial and clerical positions have been declining in response to the increased use of information technology. The proportion of females in the federal government has been stable or declining slightly during the past decades.

Women are better represented in the upper echelons of the federal government than are African-Americans or Hispanics. In the most recent data available women comprise just over 11 percent of employment in senior positions in the federal civil service. There are also relatively large percentages of women in middle-management positions so that with mobility within the service there may be an increasing number of females in senior positions.

EMPLOYMENT CHANGES OVER TIME

The evidence over time is that there has been a slight increase in the proportion of African-Americans and Hispanics in the upper echelon positions of the federal civil service. This increase is, as noted, painfully slow, but it still does represent some change in public employment. The proportion of African-Americans in senior positions has increased from under 5 percent to over 6 percent from 1990 to 2008. The proportion of Hispanics has increased somewhat more proportionately, going from 1.5 percent to 4 percent. The Hispanic population has also been increasing more rapidly than the African-American population so that in absolute terms there has been a sizeable increase in the number of Hispanics in senior positions.

Employment by gender has been changing somewhat more rapidly. Female employment in the upper levels of the federal civil service has increased from 6 percent in 1990 to 11 percent in 2007. Thus, it increased approximately five times as rapidly as did employment for African-Americans in these positions. As already noted, some of this effect may be a function of the gradually increasing levels of participation of women in higher education, and especially graduate and professional education. This can be seen in part because most of the gain in female employment was in the latter portions of the time period.

EMPLOYMENT IN STATE AND LOCAL GOVERNMENTS

As noted, most data sources on state and local government employment are not as detailed as those for the federal government, in large part because of the difficulties in assembling data from 50 states and over 100 000 local governments, many with their own personnel systems that do not correspond to one another. This level, however, is where the bulk of public employment in the United States is found. Federal civilian employment is just over 2 million, while over 22 million people work for state and local governments.

The available data on employment at the sub-national levels in the United States focuses on full-time employees. This focus is in some ways unfortunate for understanding representativeness in bureaucracies, given the number of part-time employees in schools, hospitals and social agencies at these levels. Further, many of these part-time employees are women and minority group members so much of the available information tends to understate the levels of employment by those groups.

For full-time employees over half of employment (2007) at the state and local levels (excluding school systems) is male and is approximately 65 percent white. The proportion of non-white employees is somewhat greater than in the population as a whole, with African-Americans being the largest minority group by far. The professional and administrative levels are very heavily white and male, with administrative support and professional and para-professional employees being predominantly female and with a higher proportion of minority employees than in the population as a whole.

If we examine two especially important groups of state and local government employees – schoolteachers and the police – the evidence is somewhat mixed.[6] Well over half of schoolteachers are female, and the number of African-American and Hispanic teachers has been increasing rapidly and has become roughly proportionate to the population. This is one instance in which there are arguments for hiring more males to attempt to achieve balance and to provide boys with male role models. The police remain largely male and white, although again there are changes in both categories of representativeness.

ISSUES IN REPRESENTATION

Having in mind some of the basic evidence and ideas in representative bureaucracy, there are several additional issues that should be considered in the American context, or indeed more generally. As is true for most political and social phenomena representative bureaucracy is not static, but rather is constantly evolving.

THE MODEL EMPLOYER

Historically government, and especially the federal government, has played a role as "model employer" (Merit System Protection Board, 2006). Even when this has been an aspiration for government, it has not always been a reality. Especially at the upper levels of the public bureaucracy the federal government has not been able to create employment that was truly representative of the population. That said, the public sector has been to some extent a model providing reasonably well-paying, stable, white-collar jobs to African-Americans, and then later Hispanics. For example, even in the South, the US Post Office would hire many more African-Americans for what were considered good jobs than would the private sector. Later this pattern of hiring was extended to a range of other positions in the federal government so that at least in the lower echelons the federal government had a much higher level of minority employment than did the economy as a whole.

The other traditional source of public employment, and some upward mobility, for minority group members was the military. These jobs available here were again generally not at the top of the income scale but especially for minority group members from the South they represented employment and also perhaps more importantly training for what might be better positions after serving in the forces. These opportunities are not, of course, as desirable in wartime but they have been jobs that have offered some opportunities when there might not otherwise be many available.

The sense of the public sector becoming a model employer has been institutionalized in various pieces of employment legislation for government. Most of these have a general effect across the economy, but have been enforced perhaps more stringently in the public sector, especially at the federal level. The Office of Personnel Management at the federal level, and analogous organizations at other levels of government, have created their own processes for encouraging minority hiring and ensuring greater representativeness. Again, however, the majority of the impact of these provisions may have been at the lower levels of the bureaucracies rather than at the upper levels of the system.

In addition to the apparent effects on outcomes of public programs for minority groups, there is some evidence that representation has more general positive effects. Meier et al. (1999) demonstrate that in school systems with more representative bureaucracies (the teacher corps) were more successful with all students, not just their minority students. This positive effect was found even controlling for the usual socio-economic characteristics that might influence the findings. In addition to the differences in substantive policy delivery, the representative nature of public bureaucracy may also present a more positive image of government and hence help legitimate the public sector.

NEW DIMENSIONS OF REPRESENTATION

As already noted, the traditional dimensions of social representation that have been important for the public bureaucracy in the United States have been race, ethnic origins, and gender. Implicitly, there has been a concern with class representativeness, given the extent of overlap of ethnic origins and class. These dimensions of difference remain highly relevant in the public bureaucracy but others also are becoming politically relevant and forcing more consideration of the role of the public sector as an employer. Perhaps the most important of the emerging, or emerged, dimensions of difference is disability.

The Americans with Disabilities Act (1990) placed into law the principle that people with disabilities should not be discriminated against in any area of public life including employment. The basic logic has been that potential employees should be assessed on their abilities, rather than disabilities, and if the individual can perform the requisite tasks he or she should be hired. Further, employers were required to make modifications of the workplace to make it possible for people with disabilities to perform the jobs. Similarly, educational institutions were required to accommodate the disabilities of their students, including learning disabilities.

In some ways this version of representative bureaucracy is simply a replay of the earlier stories of race and gender, although there are perhaps two significant differences. The first is that unlike other bases of representation disability may impose substantial costs on employers for modifying facilities and equipment. Many employers may therefore seek to avoid employing disabled workers on financial grounds rather from overt discrimination.[7] The other question is that of efficiency and effectiveness. While there is little doubt that many disabled employees can perform their jobs as well as anyone there are also more borderline questions where individual rights, employer responsibilities to the employee, and government responsibilities to citizens may come into conflict.

Finally, a question in which I have an increasing interest is the question of ageism in employment. As American society, and indeed all industrialized societies, becomes older rather rapidly the age representativeness of the civil service may become an issue. While formal retirement ages are largely things of the past, the opportunity for individuals who want to work after normal retirement ages is there. One of the attractions of civil service employment historically was its rather generous retirement program. Although this program has become less generous, there are still incentives for people to leave government when they reach a specified period of service.[8]

POLITICS AND POLITICAL CONTROL

Finally, there are issues about the relative powers of political officials and their own bureaucracies in shaping policy outcomes (see Meier and O'Toole, 2006). There is some evidence that public administrators are more self-directing than often assumed and that political controls can be relatively ineffective in shaping their behavior. The good news in this finding is that from the evidence presented above, the attitudes of public employees the services may be oriented toward providing services on the basis of equality or perhaps toward offering compensatory levels of service to more deprived citizens. Thus, left to themselves the public servants may provide better services to clients than might be required by law.

Although much of the concern with representative bureaucracy has an implicit or even explicit concern with providing enhanced services to minority groups and/or the poor, there is also a democratic issue about the extent to which civil servants should deviate from legal requirements or the instructions from their superiors. There is an inherent question of both responsible bureaucracy as well as representative (and responsive) bureaucracy (see Bovens, 1998). These are all important values in a democratic society, and some balance must always be struck to create a humane and a responsible administrative system.

The emergence of stronger pressures for fiscal controls in the American states, and to a lesser extent at the federal level, has placed these street-level bureaucrats under greater pressure to make decisions that defend the public purse more than even in the past. The anti-immigrant policies are particularly difficult for the service providers, requiring verifications for eligibility before providing the services, including allowing students to enroll in the public schools. Given these constraints, even those public servants who may want to respond more to the needs of minority clients face real difficulties.

CONCLUSION

The story for representativeness of the public bureaucracy in the United States is rather mixed. On the one hand, although the public service as a whole is broadly representative of the ethnic and gender distribution in the United States, the upper echelons of the bureaucracy remain much less representative. There have been some significant improvements in the level of representativeness of these upper levels, but there is some distance to go, especially for African-Americans and Hispanics. Women have made major gains at the upper levels of the federal bureaucracy, but even for them the system is not as representative as many European countries.

On the other hand, the system is more representative toward the bottom of the administrative system. These are the public servants who actually have regular contacts with the population and who make decisions about individual claims for benefits, or who teach children on a daily basis. Thus, the image of government that the public receives is that the public sector is more like themselves than would be true at the top of government. Further, from what we know about active versus passive representativeness, these lower level employees may make decisions that are also more representative than would the employees at the upper levels of the system. Thus, enhancing the relative autonomy of lower echelon organizations may also influence the services delivered to citizens.

NOTES

1. As Putnam (2000) points out, the assumption that class of origin affects behavior once in office in the bureaucracy is "plausible but not proven". Many officials appear to adopt the middle-class perspective of their occupation regardless of their origins. Other bases of representative democracy are less mutable.
2. Interestingly, while governor of the State of Georgia, the arch-segregationist Lester Maddox appointed African-Americans to the state prison authority, arguing that since a large proportion of the prisoners were black, it made sense for them to be represented on the board governing the prisons. This decision constituted a rough and ready conception of representative bureaucracy.
3. These issues have been somewhat less relevant for Asian Americans as many immigrants are professionals in engineering, medicine and similar professions. Still, for some Asian communities (the Vietnamese in particular), the American dream has been less available.
4. The United States avoided some of the worst of these barriers by having a relatively high level of African-Americans in higher education, albeit often in inferior segregated institutions. Similarly, a number of women's colleges – some of them quite prestigious – produced somewhat higher levels of higher education among women than in many other societies. For example, institutions such as Vassar, Wellesley, Smith and the like were founded in the middle of the nineteenth century and produced a cadre of educated women.
5. If the data were broken down by area the likelihood might be even higher. From limited data the proportion employment of minority group members in urban areas with large minority populations is a great deal higher than the national average.
6. These groups are particularly important because teachers have such pervasive impacts on the population and obviously because the police have such power at their disposal and have been subject to a number of claims of racism and sexism.

7. Similarly, in some cases individuals may be able to eliminate or ameliorate the disability themselves.
8. The above being said, the civil service to some extent has the opposite problem of attracting enough qualified young people to fill positions. The economic downturn, and the loss of luster of some private sector employers, is helping that problem, but hiring the "best and brightest" in government is still a problem in the United States.

3. Representative bureaucracy in Canada

Luc Turgeon and Alain-G. Gagnon

INTRODUCTION

Most studies of representative bureaucracy have tended to look at policies and programs adopted in the administrative structure of nation-states such as the United States or France as yardsticks. This chapter is slightly different in that it explores the politics of representative bureaucracy within a multinational and multilingual state, Canada. In addition to ensuring the representation of minority groups (women, gays and lesbians, and people with disabilities) and ethnic minorities (groups resulting from immigration), multinational states also have to ensure the representation of a third community, namely national minorities.

In a multinational country such as Canada, ensuring that the public service is representative of the linguistic and ethno-cultural diversity of the population is not only a question of social justice and fairness: It is also a question of political stability and trust. Indeed, the public service is often a central locus of conflicts that sometimes characterize multinational states.

First, citizens' relations with the central state often require contact with "street-level" bureaucrats (Lipsky, 1980). A weak representation of members of national minorities in the public service and the difficulty of these minorities to be served in their own language can not only lead to serious challenges to a state's legitimacy, but also to its efficient working. Second, the exclusion or underrepresentation of members of national minorities in administrative positions within the central state can be a major source of conflict and resentment since such positions are often considered desirable due to the high salaries or benefits they guarantee, bringing forward issues of social justice and fairness. Moreover, as Milton Esman (1999) notes, public servants can favor members of a specific national group with respect to the implementation of government programs, and thereby increase the discontent of those who do not enjoy such benefits, which in turn contributes to a rise in issues of trust and political stability. We point to three factors that encourage the development of a more representative bureaucracy: a normative factor (social justice and fairness), a political factor (trust and political stability), and a functional dimension (the ability of citizens to communicate with the bureaucracy).

However, if those factors undoubtedly explain the emergence of pressures to improve the representativeness of the bureaucratic apparatus, they are not sufficient to understand the types of change that are adopted. In this chapter we argue that it is also important to pay attention to a state's definition of the political community, as this definition provides legitimacy to certain actors and will favor the adoption of certain measures over others. A public service tradition also matters, as measures adopted must be compatible with organizational traditions and culture. In short, we show in this chapter that Canada's federal civil service was significantly transformed in the post-1960 period to reflect Canada's redefinition of itself as a bilingual and multicultural country without compromising the merit principle.

In the first section of this chapter, we present data on the cultural and linguistic diversity of the Canadian mosaic. In the second section, we offer a brief overview of the politico-administrative, as well as the ideological, setting that continues to mark the politics of representative bureaucracy. In the third and fourth sections, we survey the measures that have been put in place to ensure a proper representation of French-speaking Canadians and Aboriginals, as well as members of ethno-cultural groups, generally referred to in Canada as visible minorities. We also explore in the latter two sections the main public debates pertaining to the representation of these groups within the federal public service.[1]

SETTING THE STAGE: AN OVERVIEW OF THE CANADIAN MOSAIC

Canada is one of the world's most culturally diverse countries. As such, Canadians often refer to their country as constituting a cultural mosaic. This is reflected by the presence of a large linguistic minority, an ethnically diverse population, and indigenous peoples.

English and French are the two official languages of Canada. In 2006, the proportion of Canadians whose mother tongue was French was 22.1 percent and 21.4 percent of the population mostly spoke French at home, a significant decline since the post-war period (Statistics Canada, 2007, p. 15).[2] French-speakers are concentrated in the province of Quebec. In 2006, of Canadians who had French as their mother tongue, 85.8 percent lived in that province (Statistics Canada, 2007, p. 34). Although Canada is officially a bilingual country, the rate of bilingualism is much higher

Table 3.1   *Immigrant population as a percentage of total population, Canada, 1981–2006*

Year	1981	1986	1991	1996	2001	2006
Percent	16	15.6	16.1	17.4	18.4	19.8

Source: Statistics Canada, "Chart 2. Immigrant population as a percentage of total population, Canada" in Canada at a Glance 2009, available at: http://www45.statcan. gc.ca/2009/cgco_2009_001-eng.htm, accessed June 7, 2011.

amongst Canadians whose mother tongue is French. Only 9.4 percent of Canadians who have English as their mother tongue are considered bilingual (French–English) compared with 42.4 percent of Canadians who have French as their mother tongue (Statistics Canada, 2007, p. 26).[3] As will be shown below, such a difference in rates of bilingualism has had an important impact on the politics of bureaucratic representation in the country.

The decline in the number of French-speakers in Canada over the last four decades is the result both of a fall in their birth rate as well as the significant growth in the immigrant population that have acquired English as the language of social mobility outside of Quebec (see Table 3.1). In 2006, 20 percent of the population was foreign-born and the percentage of Canadians aged 15 and over who were foreign born, or had at least one foreign-born parent, was 39 percent.

Most of the Canadian foreign-born population belongs to a visible minority. In Canada, visible minorities are defined, according to the Employment Equity Act (1995, section 3), as "persons, other than Aboriginal peoples, who are non-Caucasian in race or non-white in colour." In 2006, the visible minorities population accounted for 16.2 percent of Canada's total population (Statistics Canada, 2008a, p. 12) (Table 3.2). It is significant to note that, as attitudes towards immigration were becoming more negative in other countries, the number of Canadians who stated that Canada should accept significantly fewer immigrants has declined over the last two decades (Simon and Sikich, 2007).

Canada's aboriginal population is composed of First Nations (North American Indians), Métis, and Inuit.[4] In 2006, the Aboriginal peoples accounted for 3.8 percent of the population (Statistics Canada, 2008b, p. 9). As a result of the appropriation of their land by the French and English settlers, First Nations lived on reserves that were often far from Canada's urban centers. However the percentage of those who live in urban areas has increased significantly over the last two decades.

Table 3.2   Visible minority population in Canada, 2006

	Total visible minority population	South Asian	Chinese	Black	Filipino	Latin American	Arab
Number	5 068 095	1 262 865	1 216 565	783 795	410 700	304 245	265 550
Percentage of total Canadian population	16.22	4.04	3.89	2.51	1.31	0.97	0.85

	Southeast Asian	West Asian	Korean	Japanese	Visible minority, not included elsewhere	Multiple visible minority
Number	239 935	156 695	141 890	81 300	71 420	133 120
Percentage of total population	0.77	0.50	0.45	0.26	0.23	0.43

Source: For the total Canadian population: Statistics Canada, "Ethnocultural Portrait of Canada Highlight Tables" in 2006 Census, available at: http://www12.statcan.ca/census-recensement/2006/dp-pd/hlt/97-562/sel_geo.cfm?Lang=F&Geo=PR&Table=2, accessed June 7, 2011. For visible minorities data, see: Statistics Canada, "Table 13.6 Visible minority population, by province and territory, 2006" in Ethnic Diversity and Immigration, available at: http://www41.statcan.gc.ca/2009/30000/tbl/cybac30000_2009_000_t06-eng.htm, site visited on accessed June 7, 2011.

Institutions and Ideology in Canada: A Liberal Multicultural State

Canada has often been viewed as the product of a compact between two founding nations: French and English. Indeed, this interpretation remains dominant in Quebec. The decline in the second half of the twentieth century of the British connection that had been central to the identity of English-speaking Canadians contributed to attempts to "reimagine" Canada. Largely under the leadership of Pierre Elliott Trudeau who was the Prime Minister for most of the period between 1968 and 1984, Canada was redefined as a multicultural country in which individuals speak one of two official languages. The lynchpins to such a redefinition were two programs: official bilingualism and multiculturalism.

Trudeau's Liberal government instituted official bilingualism in federal institutions in 1969 while opposing the efforts of successive Quebec provincial governments to make French the common public language of Quebec. As for Canada's policy of multiculturalism, it was adopted in 1971, entrenched in the Constitution in 1982, and revisited and strengthened in 1988.[5] The program was adopted in part to counteract the claim that Canada was a bi-cultural or bi-national country. The main objective of the program is not only to assist cultural groups to retain their identity but, as stated in the Canadian Multiculturalism Act (1988, section 3(1)(c)), to "promote the full and equitable participation of individuals and communities of all origins in the continuing evolution and shaping of all aspects of Canadian society and assist them in the elimination of any barrier to that participation."

The institutional and ideological renewal of Canada that started in the 1960s led, in more concrete terms, to the creation of a liberal multicultural state. Such a state can choose to accommodate local institutions with a view to providing an area of autonomy for national minorities, such as sub-national governments where a national minority constitutes the majority of the population on that given territory. However, the "benevolent neutrality" of the liberal multicultural state prevents it from acknowledging its multinational character within central institutions. It sees its task not as structuring relations among communities, according to Alain Dieckhoff (2000, p. 160, our translation), "but rather as providing a framework for egalitarian relations among all citizens." This liberal framework was entrenched in the Charter of Rights and Freedoms, adopted in 1982 without the consent of the province of Quebec.

As will be shown below, the adoption of official bilingualism and multiculturalism played an important role in attempts from the 1960s on to make Canada's federal public service more representative of the cultural and linguistic make-up of its population. At the same time, those policies, premised as they were on the protection of individual rights, meant that measures such as quotas, which are usually adopted to ensure the representation of certain communities, would be perceived as illegitimate and as such rejected.

THE REPRESENTATION OF FRENCH CANADIANS IN THE FEDERAL PUBLIC SERVICE

Prior to the 1960s, the issue of the representation of French Canadians in the federal public service did not lead to significant debates. In 1867, when the Canadian federation was established, a number of government departments, including education and justice, "maintained [an] integrated bilingual establishment, others were linguistically split right down the middle, starting at the top with the political head and going down to the subdivision of the various branches" (Wilson and Mullins, 1978, p. 517).

However, the professionalization of the Canadian bureaucracy, following the adoption of the Civil Service Commission (1908) and the passage of the Civil Service Act (1918), which is often viewed as marking the introduction of the merit principle, led to a significant decline in the representation of French Canadians in the bureaucracy, as the political influence that had ensured their representation was removed from the selection process. As a result, the proportion of French-speakers working in the federal public service dropped from 21.6 percent in 1918 to 12.5 percent in 1944–45. In the senior public service, the proportion was even more alarming. While in 1918, 14 percent of federal senior officials were francophones, their number gradually declined to 0 percent in 1946 (Wilson and Mullins, 1978, p. 520). This absence of representation reflected the belief, widespread amongst anglophones at the time, according to the late James Mallory (1971), that to require competence in a specific language in the federal public service would constitute a challenge to the merit system.

The lack of representation of francophones in the public service is said to have been one of the factors that contributed to the rise in support for Quebec independence in the 1960s. According to the Royal Commission on Bilingualism and Biculturalism (1969, p. 95), "[t]he possibility of national disintegration has forced a re-examination of the linguistic policies of the Public Service. The debate is no longer about efficiency, merit, patronage, and representation, but rather between thoroughgoing reform and schism. Change is imminent and no institution requires reform more urgently than does the federal administration." As such, it is clear that concerns with stability played a key role. However, it was also part of the efforts of Pierre Elliott Trudeau to make bilingualism a defining characteristic of a new Canada.

The Act formally acknowledged the equal status in Canada of French and English, and led to the creation of the position of Commissioner of Official Languages (2005), whose task is to ensure implementation of the principles on which the Act is based. The Commissioner produces an annual report on the state of bilingualism in the country, which is similar to a "name and shame" review of the federal government's linguistic practices, and asks political authorities to make appropriate changes to attenuate problems in the implementation of the Act. The Official Languages Act stated that members of both linguistic groups should have equitable opportunities for employment in federal institutions and that federal employees should be able to work in the official language of their choice in designated areas.

However, the Official Languages Act of 1969 was rather vague and did not present concrete measures to ensure a greater representation of French-Canadians in the public service (Dion, 1973, p. 257). The system that is currently in place was gradually implemented over the next 20 years.

First, in 1973, the Parliament of Canada passed a resolution on Official Languages in the Public Service (see Hudon, 2009). To increase the representation of French-Canadians without undermining the merit principle, bilingualism became an additional criterion of merit. Specific regions were designated bilingual, in which both English and French were to be the languages of work for civil servants, including the National Capital Region (Ottawa-Gatineau), and in which some key positions were declared to require the knowledge of both official languages. Considering, as illustrated previously, that more French-speaking Canadians are bilingual, such measures contributed to augment their presence in the public service and brought a fairer representation of both language groups in federal institutions.

Second, in 1977, the Treasury Board issued a series of temporary guidelines to ease the implementation of such measures. Included were provisions that stated that unilingual employees could be appointed to bilingual positions if they agreed to take language training, the reorganization of basic language training at public expense, and the adoption of a bilingualism bonus as an incentive for employees to augment their linguistic capability. While those measures were supposed to be implemented for a period of 6 years, they largely remain in place to this day.

Third, in 1981, new regulations were adopted by the Treasury Board stating that all senior management positions in a bilingual region would henceforth be designated bilingual. However, the Treasury Board has kept implementing measures that exempt certain public servants from the bilingualism requirements; measures that continue to be strongly denounced by the Commissioner of Official Languages. For example, to this day, deputy ministers do not have to be bilingual.

Finally, the federal government adopted the Official Languages Act (1988), a revision of the original Act, to incorporate the principle of equality of languages that was a cornerstone of the Charter of Rights and Freedoms, which was entrenched in the Constitutional Act of 1982. Indeed, section 20 (1) of the Charter states that "[a]ny member of the public in Canada has the right to communicate with, and to receive available services from, any head or central office of an institution of the Parliament or government of Canada in English or in French (. . .)." The 1988 Act contains sections dealing with the provisions for service to the public (part IV), language of work (part V) and the participation of French- and English-speaking Canadians in the federal public service (part VI). Moreover, part X provides the option to seek legal remedy before the Federal Court if certain rights guaranteed in the Act are violated. The Act (section 39(3)) stipulates that nothing in the Act "shall be construed as abrogating or derogating from the principle of selection of personnel according to merit."

The Treasury Board has also issued guidelines related to the measures that can and cannot be adopted to ensure that federal institutions, as stated in the 1988 Official Languages Act (section 39(1)(b)), "reflect the presence of both official languages communities of Canada." While measures such as ensuring that the linguistic composition of selection boards reflects the pool of applicants are allowed, setting quotas is strictly forbidden.

The measures adopted by the federal government since the 1970s have led to a reversal of the historical underrepresentation of French-speaking Canadians in the federal public service. Key to this transformation has been the creation of bilingual positions. In 2009, 40.4 percent of all positions in the core public administration were designated bilingual, a significant increase from 1978, when 25 percent of positions were designated bilingual (Treasury Board of Canada Secretariat, 2010a, p. 12).[6] A clear majority of those bilingual positions are occupied by Francophones. For example, in 2009–10, of the "bilingual imperative" appointments to the public service, 62.3 percent were Francophones and 37.7 percent were Anglophones (Public Service Commission of Canada, 2010, p. 34). As a result, French-speaking Canadians have become slightly over-represented in the public service. While the proportion of Canadians whose first official language is French represents 23.6 percent of the Canadian population,[7] the participation rate of Francophones in 2009 was 27.1 percent for all federal institutions, and 31.5 percent for the core public administration (Treasury Board of Canada Secretariat, 2010a, p. 4). Francophones are now better represented at the senior echelons, as 31.5 percent of executives of the core public administration are francophones (Treasury Board of Canada Secretariat, 2010a, p. 17).[8] However, those data hide the significant volatility in the representation of francophones at the higher echelons of the public service. For example, in 2000, only 15.6 percent of deputy ministers were francophones (Mattar, 2002, p. 8).

While significant improvements have been made with respect to the presence of French-speaking Canadians in the public service, important challenges remain. Despite the fact that, of those occupying bilingual positions and providing personal and central services, 92.5 percent met the language requirements of their position (compared to 69.7 percent in 1978) (Treasury Board of Canada Secretariat, 2010a, p. 14), studies have shown that French is underused in the workplace. A 2002 study found that while anglophones working in a bilingual setting spend 14 percent of their time using French, francophones working in a bilingual environment spent on average 43 percent of their time using English (reported in Commissioner of Official Languages, 2003, p. 94).

While there are limited public opinion data related to bilingualism requirements, a 2006 CROP/Radio-Canada survey found that 80 percent of Canadians believe that senior public servants should be bilingual (reported in Commissioner of Official Languages, 2007, p. 29). All major political parties support the system in place, although some politicians in English-speaking Canada and in the Conservative Party have denounced the Canadian policy of bilingualism.

While the introduction of measures to improve the representation of French-speaking Canadians and a bilingual public service have led to some backlash, overall the policy has largely become accepted. This can in part be explained by the fact that bilingualism has usually been viewed as an element of individual merit rather than as a form of quota developed to ensure the hiring of a given percentage of francophones in the bureaucracy.

REPRESENTATION OF VISIBLE MINORITIES AND ABORIGINALS

As mentioned earlier, Canada's policy of multiculturalism explicitly made as one of its goals the promotion of full participation of individuals of all origins in the evolution and shaping of all aspects of Canadian society. Such lofty sentiments did not lead to the adoption of specific measures to improve the representation in the public service of Canada of members of the different ethno-cultural communities during the decade following its adoption in 1971. Nevertheless, the policy of multiculturalism encouraged interest group activities around the representation of minority groups. One of these organizations, the Canadian Ethnocultural Council (CEC), which was in part financed by the federal government, pressured the government to ensure equity in the labor market by implementing a series of public policies (Abu-Laban and Gabriel, 2002). To respond to such demand, the Liberal government established in 1983 the Royal Commission on Equality and Employment presided by Judge Rosalie Abella.

Some of the recommendations contained in Judge Abella's final report were adopted in the Employment Equity Act in 1986. The goal of the Employment Equity Act is to correct disadvantages in employment experienced by women, Aboriginal peoples, persons with disabilities, and members of visible minorities. As such, while the adoption of Canada's multicultural policy contributed to the creation of a climate favorable to the adoption of the Employment Equity Act, normative concerns about fairness and social justice were also crucial.

The Act required employers to eliminate barriers to the workforce participation of four target groups (as mentioned above, women, Aboriginal persons, persons with disabilities, and members of visible minorities) and develop an equity plan to augment their representation. However, the Act only applied to federally regulated companies with 100 employees or more.[9] While the federal public service was not covered under the Employment Equity Act, in the same year as the Act was passed the federal public service adopted an employment equity program that required departments and agencies to "develop three-year employment equity plans that include special measures to correct imbalances in the workforce and contain quantitative and qualitative objectives, activities, schedules and monitoring mechanisms" (quoted in Bakan and Kobayashi, 2000, p. 15).

Repercussions of the Employment Equity Act seemed to have been limited (Lum, 1995), and as a result a revised Act was later adopted. The Employment Equity Act (1995) requires that employers (including the federal government) monitor the employment status of the four targeted groups. More specifically, the Act imposes a number of duties to an employer including the development of an employment equity plan that specifies measures to be taken for the elimination of employment barriers and, in a situation of underrepresentation, numerical goals for the hiring and promotion of people in the designated groups to augment their presence. With respect to the numerical goals, the Employment Equity Act (1995) specifies that they should not simply be based on the overall representation of a group in the general Canadian population, but on the following five factors:

1. The degree of underrepresentation of persons in each designated group in each occupational group within the employer's workforce;
2. The availability of qualified persons in each designated groups within the employer's workforce and in the Canadian workforce;
3. The anticipated growth or reduction of the employer's workforce during the period in respect of which the numerical goals apply;
4. The anticipated turnover of employees within the employer's workforce during the period in respect of which the numerical goal apply; and
5. Any other factors that may be prescribed.

Much like the Official Language Act, the Employment Equity Act states that the obligation to implement employment equity does not require employers in the public sector "to hire or promote persons without basing the hiring or promotion on merit (. . .)." The Act also stipulates that the Human Rights Commission, which is responsible for the enforcement of obligations imposed on employers, may not give a directive to impose a quota on an employer (Section 33).

By the turn of the decade, it was clear that the federal government had not reached its own employment equity objectives with regard to visible minorities. This contrasted with the situation of women, Aboriginals and people with disability.[10] For these three groups, their representation in the public services was above their workforce availability (WFA), the indicator used to measure the representation of designated groups in Canada under employment equity.[11] As a result, the Embracing Change Initiative, which identifies specific hiring objectives in order to increase the representation of visible minorities in the federal public service, was launched. This initiative, adopted in earnest in 2000, set a number of benchmarks for the hiring of visible minorities, including a one in five target for the hiring of visible minorities by 2003, and a one in five target for executive hiring by 2005 (Standing Senate Committee on Human Rights, 2007, p. 10).

Those benchmarks were not attained at first, although in the past few years the federal government has finally achieved its one in five benchmark for the federal public service. In 2009–10, 21.2 percent of individuals appointed to the public service from advertised external processes were members of visible minorities (Public Service Commission of Canada, 2010, p. 54). However, overall, visible minorities continue to be underrepresented. In 2008–09, they represented 9.8 percent of the core public administration, below their 2006 WFA of 12.4 percent (Treasury Board of Canada Secretariat, 2010b, p. 24). Their representation in the Executive category (6.9 percent) was also below their Executive Category WFA of 7.6 percent.

Politicians and interest groups pay close attention every year to the Annual Report of the Treasury Board on Employment Equity. The federal public service supports the National Council of Visible Minorities (established in 1999), whose mandate is to identify issues that affect its constituents, lobby on their behalf, and advise federal public service management on issues related to the development and implementation of employment equity programs and policies. Moreover, this issue has been the subject of task forces and numerous reports over the last decade, demonstrating the pressure on the public service to improve the representation of visible minorities. Some members of the Conservative Party of Canada have at times, much like for official bilingualism, denounced the "quotas" they argue are the product of the Act, although once in power they have made no attempt at reforming it.

CONCLUSION

In this chapter, we have studied representative bureaucracy in Canada, showing that concerns over stability and fairness were central in putting the issue of bureaucratic representation of linguistic and ethnic minorities at the forefront of the country's policy agenda. Moreover, we have shown that Canada's liberal multicultural model has had a defining impact on the type of measures that were adopted.

Canada has aimed to ensure a degree of representation of national minorities while officially rejecting any form of quota. However, the Canadian liberal multicultural model, in so far as it is based on respect for cultural differences, has to take cultural diversity into consideration in order to ensure both participation of minorities and equal opportunities. To the extent that these objectives can be met, trust is gained and, concomitantly, political stability is secured. The federal government has done so starting in the early 1970s, with regards to the representation of French-speaking Canadians, by making the mastery of French a merit criterion at the time of hiring. As for the representation of visible minorities, while no quotas have been put in place, the annual exercise of name and shame associated with the publication of the Treasury Board Annual Report has led to intense pressure to increase their representation.

To a certain extent, Canada has been able to reconcile principles of fairness, representation and political stability, though it has taken over 100 years before Canada's federal government began to worry about the problem of French-speakers' underrepresentation in the public service, and only seriously started to redress the underrepresentation of visible minorities over the last 15 years. For visible minorities, the task of ensuring fairer representation in the public service remains an ongoing challenge, while much still remains to be accomplished to ensure that the organizational culture of the public service reflects Canada's linguistic duality.

ACKNOWLEDGMENTS

We wish to acknowledge the financial support of the Institute of Public Administration of Canada and the Secrétariat au Affaires Intergouvernementales Canadiennes of the Government of Québec, and the assistance of Xavier Dionne, Jenna Martinuzzi, and Christopher Leite.

NOTES

1. Because of limited space, we do not discuss measures that have been adopted in the ten Canadian provinces and three territories to ensure a more representative public service.
2. In 1951, French was the mother tongue of 29 percent of the population (Leacy et al., 1983, Series A1-247).
3. Bilingualism is defined here as the capacity to hold a conversation in both official languages.
4. First Nations refers to members of indigenous population that are not Inuit or Métis. Inuits refers to the Aboriginal population living in Arctic Canada. Métis refers to Aboriginals of mixed First Nation and European ancestry who self-identify as Métis.
5. As such, Canada's policy of multiculturalism was adopted almost 20 years before debates about multiculturalism that raged in the 1990s and 2000s, and in which Canadian academics such as Charles Taylor and Will Kymlicka played a prominent role.
6. Core public administration refers to federal public servants employed by the Treasury Board that are not employed by crown corporations, federal tribunals, arm-length agencies such as the Canada Revenue Agency, the Royal Canadian Mounted Police or the Canadian Forces.
7. This data is slightly different than the proportion that has French as their mother tongue, since it is limited to which one of the two official languages an individual usually spoke.
8. Executives are those positions located, according to the Treasury Board's definition, "no more than three hierarchical levels below the Deputy or Associated Deputy level and that have significant executive managerial or executive policy roles and responsibilities or other significant influence on the direction of a department or agency."
9. Federally regulated companies, as opposed to provincially regulated companies, are essentially those in banking, transportation, and communication sectors.
10. However, Aboriginals are underrepresented at the executive level and in a number of departments.
11. Workforce availability refers to the "distribution of people in the Employment Equity designated groups as a percentage of the total Canadian workforce. For federal public service purposes, WFA is based on Canadian citizens in those occupations in the public services and is derived from Census statistics."

4. Representative bureaucracy in Mexico

María del Carmen Pardo

INTRODUCTION

By 2005 Mexico's indigenous population amounted to 10 103 571 persons, including almost 62 ethno-linguistic groups representing 9.8 percent of the country's total population. While this figure has decreased relative to the rest of the Mexican population, in absolute numbers it had increased significantly during the last decades – while in 1970 indigenous people aged 5 years or more equaled 3.1 million, by 2005 this figure had almost doubled to more than 6 million (CDI, 2006). That same year, the profound economic, social, and political disparities between the indigenous community and the rest of the country – dating back to the Colonial past – were still evident. In recent times, for example, the Human Development Index (HDI)[1] started to be measured in Mexican municipalities[2] having indigenous populations. The municipality with the lowest HDI in the country – the largely indigenous village of Batopilas, in the State of Chihuahua – had an indicator of 0.3010, even worse than that of the country with the lowest HDI in the world – Nigeria, in West Africa (HDI of 0.3300; PNUD, 2010, p. 15). However, this was not an isolated case. In recent years, Mexican municipalities with a high share of indigenous population have exhibited the lowest human development levels, mainly in access to health services and education (PNUD, 2010, p. 33).

Since the Partido Revolucionario Institucional (PRI) lost its hegemony in 2000, after more than seven decades of having controlled nearly all power positions, Mexico's democratic process was expected to deepen and it was assumed that the indigenous population – a traditionally marginalized sector of the Mexican society – would have more opportunities to enhance its rights and access to public life, especially in political representation and democratic participation. However, as we will see, things have not gone exactly this way in the near past. Particularly, we should consider the status of representation of this social sector within the Mexican public administration, not only in terms of the equal implementation of public policies aimed at indigenous development, but also to the essential fact of indigenous direct participation – with members of their community – in the Mexican bureaucracy.

This chapter will focus on trying to answer the following: why is it that Mexico – in contrast with other countries with significant ethnical diversity – has not made clear and distinctive efforts aimed at strengthening a representative bureaucracy for Mexican indigenous minorities, for example, in the form of affirmative action policies? This question does not suggest that Mexico has not had highly relevant intellectual and political movements – and even governmental organizations, as will be seen – intended specifically at improving the identity, opportunities, and rights of indigenous peoples (Villoro, 2005). What is striking is that the type of representation of Mexican indigenous people has been radically different from those in the United States, India, or Brazil, among others.

Actually, the term "representative bureaucracy" as such has been rarely used in academic debates, by the mass media or, generally, in the Mexican public arena. Thus, the point here is that the Mexican public opinion has not revealed a clear concern that would have led to having indigenous civil servants in government, not as an expression of the official rhetoric but as an instrument of genuine representation. Indigenous representation in Mexico has stemmed mainly from the active representation of minorities, rather than from Hanna Pitkin's (1967) passive or descriptive representation of indigenous,[3] meaning that those who are represented recognize themselves, physically and culturally, in those who represent them. Why is this so? How does this impact Mexican public life?

During the twentieth century, representative bureaucracy in Mexico was associated, first of all, with the consolidation of State power and national unity, and, only as a resulting effect, with the expansion and strengthening of the "citizen" status among the governed, including indigenous people. In contrast, in other countries such as the United States, public institutions and democratic practices were deeply rooted in society. As a result, the "structural" weakness of the Mexican State has represented a series of challenging barriers to the expansion of rights and warranties associated with citizenship. In other words, in Mexico the model of representative bureaucracy as power has prevailed vis-à-vis the model of representative bureaucracy as equality of opportunities (Groeneveld and Van de Walle, 2010).

The representation of ethnic minorities came about as a result of a difficult process based on the fragmented and differentiated discourse and practice regarding "the indigenous" issue both in the Mexican public sphere generally and the national public administration particularly.

In turn, this situation resulted in the prevailing logic of representative bureaucracy as equality of opportunities has been fundamentally subordinated to that of representative bureaucracy as power, due to the fact that – as we will see later – citizenship would not be generally bestowed to indigenous people – in general on the basis of acknowledging their difference – but only to those able to gain the privilege of becoming citizens through their commitment to the goals of the new post-revolutionary national state, shaped around the ideal of a different ethnic category, namely, the "mestizo" (Dawson, 1998, p. 306).

More recently, the concept of citizenship, associated with the increasing strength of the so-called neo-liberal State, experienced a second shift, entailing a relative emptying in the "citizen" status of its explicit content of rights and warranties; that is, an attempt at taking out those rights and warranties their public foundation establishes, and associating them instead with the discourse on performance, "empowering" people, and sustainable development (Escalante, 2006).

A BRIEF REVIEW OF INDIGENOUS INEQUALITY IN MEXICO

For the Mexican indigenous population one could ask who those allegedly represented in representative bureaucracy are; that is, the individuals and villages of the Mexican indigenous community. As mentioned, this sector of the Mexican society represents almost a tenth of the total, though it still surely endures particularly adverse social and economic conditions. According to data from the 2000 and 2005 censuses, the major share of the indigenous community is concentrated in nearly 500 municipalities with a native population level of 70 percent or more, and these municipalities are located mainly in Mexico's central and southern states that have a traditionally high indigenous population rate, including Chiapas, Estado de México, Oaxaca, Puebla, Quintana Roo, and Yucatán (see Table 4.1 and Figure 4.1). However, we must stress that an increasing share (17.1) percent of the indigenous population has moved to the major Mexican cities, including Mexico City, Monterrey, Cancún, and Guadalajara, mainly as a result of the collapse of productive options in their home towns (CDI, 2006).

In- and out-migration in Mexico has become increasingly relevant not only in material terms, but also for the transformation of public and social orders within indigenous communities. Actually, states with a considerable share of native communities, such as Oaxaca, Veracruz, Yucatán, and Puebla, present the highest indigenous emigration rates, certainly as

Table 4.1 Indigenous and non-indigenous population in Mexico, 2000–05

Population	2000		2005	
Mexican United States	97 483 412		103 236 388	
Indigenous Mexico	10 253 627	10.5%	10 103 571	9.8%
Male	5 294 143	50.3%	4 959 484	49.1%
Female	5 101 051	49.7%	5 144 087	50.9%

Source: CDI (2006)

a result of the overall collapse of the so-called "welfare state" in the last decades (PNUD, 2010, p. 53).

Clearly, disparities in living conditions among the Mexican social groups also result from asymmetries in opportunities and access to public services resulting from being part or not of an indigenous community. Seemingly there is a direct proportional link between a large proportion of indigenous population in a municipality, and scarce opportunities for that municipality to attain a considerable level of development (PNUD, 2010, p. 33). This dynamic is not fortuitous: according to the National System of Indigenous Population Indicators in Mexico, the levels of literacy among the indigenous aged 15 years or more registered a slight increase in 2000–05 – rising from 72.6 to 74.3 percent – but still 46.5 percent of the population has no or limited elementary education. This disparity is even stronger between men and women inside the indigenous community (see Tables 4.2 and 4.3). The same contrasts appear in the health dimension. In 2000, while the infant mortality rate of indigenous infants was 344 per 10 000 births, the rate among non-indigenous population equaled 216 per 10 000 births. This gap between indigenous and non-indigenous children is unlikely to improve much in the immediate future (PNUD, 2010, p. 16). Similar gaps are found in the access to other public services at home, including running water, drainage, and cement floors, as well as access to goods that may be considered key to being fully engaged in society, such as television, computers, and internet (CDI, 2006).

From this brief review of the situation of Mexican indigenous people it is clear that, while there have been substantial efforts by the Mexican State to improve the living conditions of indigenous communities during the last decades, there are enduring asymmetries resulting from the fact of being part of the indigenous population, which are likely to assume new forms and perhaps increase with the withdrawal of the post-revolutionary "social state."

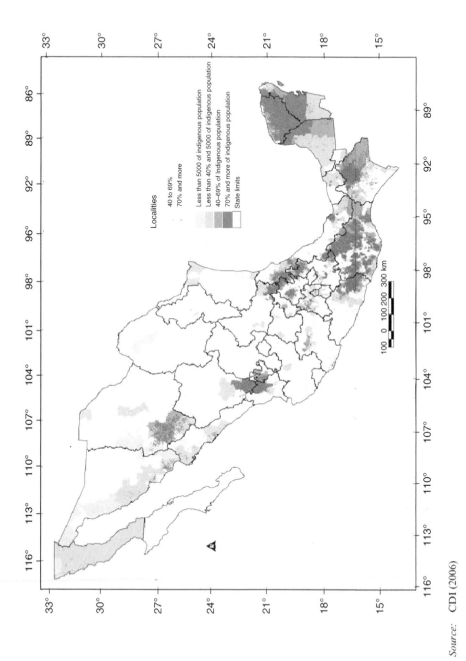

Localities

40 to 69%
70% and more

Less than 5000 of indigenous population
Less than 40% and 5000 of indigenous population
40–69% of Indigenous population
70% and more of indigenous population
State limits

100 0 100 200 300 km

Source: CDI (2006)

Figure 4.1   Localities with 40 percent and more of indigenous population, and type of municipalities, Mexico, 2000

52

Table 4.2   Indigenous and non-indigenous population aged 6–14 years attending school, Mexico, 2000–05

Population	2000		2005	
United States of Mexico	17 991 514	91.8%	18 201 308	94.7%
Indigenous Mexico	2 136 257	87.0%	2 049 611	91.5%
Male	1 091 207	88.2%	1 042 670	92.1%
Female	1 045 050	85.8%	1 006 941	91.0%

Source: CDI (2006)

Table 4.3   Illiterate indigenous population aged 15–64 years, Mexico, 2000–05

Population	2000		2005	
United States of Mexico	4 392 339	7.6%	3 968 172	6.3%
Indigenous Mexico	1 351 897	23.9%	1 220 511	21.6%
Male	458 762	16.8%	426 307	15.7%
Female	893 171	30.6%	794 204	27.1%

Source: CDI (2006)

REPRESENTATIVE BUREAUCRACY MODELS

During the second half of the twentieth century the main focus of Anglo-Saxon studies on the representative bureaucracy phenomenon was the split in democratic regimes between the power and public servant interests and the citizens, in particular those that were part of an ethnic minority (Wise, 2003). This resulted from an increasing relative power of the former – the bureaucrats – not only vis-à-vis the common citizen, but even with regard to other State powers and actors, along with the well-known rationalization logic of public administration. All these processes have been identified with the "excesses" of the Weberian bureaucratic model (Aberbach and Rockman, 1998).

While the drawbacks of some political systems were a result of the "excesses" of the bureaucratic model described by Max Weber, some others – as the Mexican case in the nineteenth and twentieth centuries – seem to have faced exactly the opposite: the State was simply too weak. Or, more precisely, the State was too weak to act as mediator of social interests and guarantor of basic individual rights. Paradoxically, however, the State was at the same time strong enough to extort especially vulnerable segments of society, such as the indigenous people (Escalante, 2009).

We have mentioned that the term representative bureaucracy has not been extensively used in the Mexican public sphere; however, this does not mean that the term is trivial for a discussion on Mexico's modern public life. A review of the intellectual history of this concept will show that at first it was usually associated with a process of stabilization of State power, through the inclusion of the major political groups in public administration and the cooptation or neutralization of rival groups (Groeneveld and Van de Walle, 2010, p. 241).

According to Groenveld and Van de Walle (2010, p. 241), unlike the model of representative bureaucracy as equality of opportunities, there are alternative views to representative bureaucracy, such as the model of representative bureaucracy as power whose concern for an active representation by the public sector of the interests of disadvantaged groups is secondary and may be even subordinated to the determination of centralizing and stabilizing state power. This second model – representative bureaucracy as power – seems more appropriate to understanding the ambiguous position of Mexican indigenous people vis-à-vis the status of citizens in recent times. As stated by Luis Medina Peña (2010, pp. 19–21), it was in the course of this recent period when the history of a splintered political space took form: on the one hand, the political arcadia, limited to a liberal elite in Mexico City and a few other State capitals, and on the other hand, a system of relationships and patronage pyramids which served the Mexican society to face the lack of a citizenry, as in the case of the indigenous population.

Half-Citizens: A Splintered Representation

In Mexico, the major obstacle to consolidating the State's hegemony was its having imposed its own logic of obedience over the logic of other political structures that demanded loyalty to themselves, in particular local communities – the political unit of most indigenous villages. In addition, since communities constitute a limited social system, their main concern was to eliminate risks for the immediate group. Therefore, the obedience logic generated a strong internal cohesion, distributive demands (irrespective of the social status), reciprocity among members, and above all, clientelistic relationships as a mechanism of basic social exchange (Escalante, 2009). The nascent liberal State, on the contrary, was based on eliminating local loyalties, the uniformity of authority throughout the Mexican territory and, ultimately, even the dissolution of indigenous communities, as evinced by the mid-nineteenth century aggressive elimination of ecclesiastic and communal lands.

The institutional frameworks required to cut the distance between these two political structures – the national political class and the villages – were complex and diverse, depending on the economic and social local conditions, but they always involved the figure of the political mediator, who was charged of the unequal distribution of rights and public services that in theory belonged to the entire citizen community (Escalante, 2009). This was, thus, the genesis of a logic that promoted development of personal relationships, the elaboration of obsequious and courtesy manners, the cultural assimilation of corruption, and the use of bureaucratic rules and procedures as mechanisms of exclusion, rather than as an instrument of ethnic and national integration (Lomnitz, 2000, p. 131).

While this practice was deeply rooted in nineteenth-century stormy political life, things did not change that much by the end of the period and throughout the next century (Fox, 1994). During the consolidation of state power – expressed in the 70-year hegemony of the official party – by the 'Partido Revolucionario Institucional' the

> Mexican political classes [had] a very clear goal: thriving with [public] resources through their mediation between State institutions and local clienteles. [. . .] The State expansion in the course of several decades was a process of continuous incorporation of the political medium class at the same time as new social movements emerged. (Lomnitz, 2000, p. 146)

As in the case of other incipient states enduring major political transformations (Groeneveld and Van de Walle, 2010), the Mexican bureaucracy did not agree to represent society as a whole but only a few groups with a progressive political descent, namely, the emergent middle classes.

The differentiated distribution of rights and representation, based on the "purchase" of privileges whether it was through cash payments or future corporative compromises, had a deep impact on the public perception of the legitimacy of the State, especially on the most vulnerable groups. However, due to the lack of both a supreme authority and the mediation of the State, which did not reasonably represent the interests of the whole, the result was a fragmentation of the notion of citizenship. The Republican notion of citizenship, therefore, did not emerge from a legal equality based on rights, but was rather an upshot of divisions among elites:

> In sum, the early Mexican constitutions contained two clashing thrusts: on the one hand, they eradicated caste and slavery in order to create a wide-based nationality encompassing each person born in Mexico and each resident in the country, who were catholic and willing to observe Mexican laws; on the other hand, they only gave access to public positions to independent male owners

capable of reading and writing. The status of citizen was not (and still is not) equal to that of "national" in the legal discourse, though they appeared mixed in the political discourse; their relationship was in fact hierarchical. (Lomnitz, 2000, p. 134)

In line with Claudio Lomnitz, (2000, p. 135) there are two aspects we should mention. First, while the status of citizen was relatively broad and modern, involving the will to enforce a single law for all nationals, it is clear that it retained a markedly conservative concern about the degree of representation that "the rabble," "the masses," or "the savages" – including, particularly, the national indigenous community – might attain within this embryonic democracy. Therefore, the prospect for them to become part of the State as a civil servant was completely out of the question.

The solution for this tension within the nascent Mexican democracy – our second major issue – was equally categorical and biased: the notables were charged with safeguarding the interests of those who were incapable of "fending for themselves," that is, minors, illiterates, and especially, indigenous people (Lomnitz, 2000, p. 136), all of them wrapped into the same category of degraded citizens. While it would have been easier to ignore them or get rid of them, because of their number they were a key factor to preserve the balance between groups with conflicting projects: the liberals and the conservatives (Escalante, 2009, p. 372).

Therefore, even as one could indeed talk of a Mexican citizenry, the citizens varied in degree and type. An official rhetoric emerged then, in which the population was divided into the "good people" and the "bad people" (Lomnitz, 2000, p. 139). The main conclusion that we can draw from this is that the fragmentation of the citizen status would become rooted in the ambivalent stance that the Mexican State would later take vis-à-vis the indigenous community, which, on the one hand, was seen as a heinous mass, genuinely dangerous to democratic life, in which case they were excluded or disciplined; while on the other hand, indigenous were perceived as a vulnerable and helpless mass, unable to get by without governmental actions aimed at their eventual emancipation and the resulting condition as true citizens (Dawson, 1998). In any case, the possibility of the indigenous population becoming a legitimate part of civil society was dependent on their modernization and broad commitment to the project of the post-revolutionary national State, and this would only be attained as a result of the action of the State, intermarriage, or education, but never through widening or deepening their dissimilarities (Lomnitz, 2000, p. 136).

The Mutations of the Mestizo Nation

We have asserted that the model of representative bureaucracy as power fits better the indigenous lack of representation during the last century in Mexico. This has been also a contributing factor for both the structural weakness of the State, and a population predominantly poor and isolated from the center of the political and social life, resulting in a fragmented system of access to the right of citizenship in Mexico (Fox, 1994). In this context, mediators played an extremely important role in strengthening the link between the early national political authority and the local caciques that had most indigenous communities under their dominion.

Even in the immediate post-revolutionary period the situation did not change much: the local caciques were replaced by the strong revolutionaries, but the representation of the communities remained indirect and clientelistic in nature (Medina Peña, 2010, p. 20). After the tumultuous period of the 1910 armed struggle, more explicit efforts at consolidating and promoting development of the indigenous communities became apparent, whose main expression was setting up government agencies for that specific purpose. However, the revival of the indigenous past under the mantle of the revolutionary nationalism proved to be a double-edged sword for the indigenous communities – and for their representation within bureaucracies created on their behalf. On the one hand, efforts were made at documenting and mapping the indigenous cultures in Mexico. It was even claimed that at the origins of these societies there was a primitive form of socialism endorsed by early post-revolutionary administrations, mainly that of President Lázaro Cárdenas (1936–40). Also, economic and social development policies were put into practice in Mexico's native communities, resulting in probably the most important agrarian reform ever.

On the other hand, the nationalist alliance entailed a commitment by the indigenous communities with the long-term project of the post-revolutionary national State, even at the expense of that which made them different. The creation of a sphere of citizens that were equal before the law was yet limited by both the corporatist relationship resulting from the distribution of lands to collective social unities – rather than to individuals – and the strengthening of the PRI's hegemony, organized by sectors – the military, worker, agricultural and urban-popular sectors (Lomnitz, 1996). In other words, the possibility of integrating the indigenous populations into the national community was largely determined by their losing their distinctive culture and identity.

This process regarding indigenous identity and culture was only seemingly paradoxical, for it responded to a wider logic for developing a new model of citizenship based on the figure of the mestizo that emerged during the previous century. The example of the African-American in the US political culture may help clarify this process, as has been suggested by the Mexican anthropologist Claudio Lomnitz (1996). Like the African-American community, the indigenous was viewed as the reverse of the citizen standard; while the ideal citizen was an individual with properties and schooling, who spoke the national language and, of course, was part of the racial orthodoxy of the nation, African-American and indigenous people allegedly lacked those attributes. But in contrast with African-Americans, after the first decades of the twentieth century, the Mexican natives were claimed to be the spirit of the post-revolutionary nationality – though just as a sort of raw material (Lomnitz, 1996). However, the indigenous concept that was thus revived did not correspond to true flesh and bone natives, but to a sublimated version. Indeed, to reach civil legal status the indigenous population would have to be transformed along the way by means of the State action, education, and racial mixing (Lomnitz, 1996).

The ambiguity of this definition of "the indigenous," and as a result, of "the mestizo" in the construction of the national subject is also rooted in the ambivalent stance of the State concerning the representation of the indigenous interests (Dawson, 1998, pp. 283, 292). As accurately stressed by Alexander S. Dawson:

> From its very inception, the DAAI [Departamento Autónomo de Asuntos Indígenas, one of the first governmental agencies intended for indigenous development, created in 1935] divided the Indian population of Mexico primarily in two groups: those that deserved the rights of the citizenship, and those that did not. That division was justified by differentiating between cultures that needed substantial tutelage from the State (such as the Yaquis and Mayos of the North, specific sierra cultures of Central Mexico, and southern groups, such as the Lacandones and Chamulas), and those that did not need specially tailored aid (highland culture with a long history of contact). (Dawson, 1998, p. 306).

As Dawson (1998, p. 283) points out, at the core of the nationalist imaginary was placed an indigenous "individual" who would not turn anymore to the obscure competition between national authorities and local caciques to secure political and material marginal resources, but had become instead the architect of his own development. What is worth stressing here is that any political and representative logic of national communities that might counter the post-revolutionary logic of consolidation of the State power was in outright contrast to what was perceived as legitimate by the ascending political groups.

By 1917, as the revolutionary conflict began to fade, the Direction of

Anthropology arrived on the scene, marking the inception of a large series of public organizations established explicitly by the post-revolutionary governments to promote the interests of the indigenous population, as a particularly disadvantaged segment of the Mexican society. A group of public officials and anthropologists undertook the task of promoting and documenting the indigenous cultures in the country, in keeping with the nationalist drive that sprouted during the first decades of the previous century; all of them driven by logic of the mestizo nationalism.

The Direction of Anthropology was followed by the Cultural Missions (1922), the House of the Indigenous Student (1926), the Socialist Education (1934), the above-mentioned Autonomous Department for Indigenous Affairs (1935), and the creation of the National Institute of Anthropology and History (INAH), as part of the continued efforts by the federal government to give visibility and relevance to indigenous communities in Mexico (Dawson, 1998, p. 281).

Just a decade after the creation of the INAH, the National Indigenist Institute (INI) was founded in 1948, charged with coordinating and planning the governmental policies on this subject for more than 50 years, until the establishment in 2003 of the National Commission for the Development of the Indigenous Peoples, which replaced the INI in the federal public administration as a decentralized autonomous agency. Thus, in the post-revolutionary period – and especially perhaps in the Lázaro Cárdenas administration (1936–40) – the indigenous communities were imagined by the public as subjects seeking out to get personally in charge of their own development, not any longer as a result of the government officials' propaganda, but through their own and deeply rooted "civilizing" conviction.

It is perhaps in this picture of the Indian where a key for understanding indigenous representation and bureaucracies in Mexico is found. Since:

> In their public representations of Indian communities and in their intra-governmental correspondence, ethnographers and bureaucrats increasingly couched their representations of Indians and request for [governmental] aid in terms that implied that they were merely passing on the demands of Indians themselves. Limiting and removing their own authorial voices, these Indigenistas often created an impression that the Indian was speaking directly to the Mexican executive, or the Mexican public. (Dawson, 1998, p. 304)

In this context, it is easy to understand why the issue of passive or descriptive representation – in contrast with the active representation in organizations such as the INAH or the INI – was never really brought up as a problem, in need of a solution, in the public arena. Since "official" anthropologists and bureaucrats conveyed the demands of the indigenous in a transparent and reliable way – and if this were not enough, also in an authoritative and scientific way – why "bother" to include them as government officials?

Representative Bureaucracy in Mexico Today

By the end of the twentieth century the issue of the indigenous representation went through deep transformations, though not completely dissociated from the processes discussed previously. It is important to point out those changes to have a clear view of the representative bureaucracy in Mexico. The first change is related to the weight that sustainable human development reached, which became visible in the UN Declaration on the Rights of Indigenous Peoples (2007), endorsed by Mexico. Also, it is important to note the impact of the reforms on the Mexican administrative system in the last decade; these reforms were to a great extent – though not entirely – shaped by New Public Management (NPM), drastically changing the profile of representative bureaucracy in Mexico. This is indicated by the role played by the agency currently in charge of the indigenous population within the federal administration: the National Commission for the Development of Indigenous Peoples (CDI).

Second, it is important to consider an actor that became increasingly relevant in the political arena after the opening of the political system – one that has been called in a rather imprecise way the 'civil society.' It is evident, thus, that these pieces of the puzzle constitute the most relevant group of the debate about indigenous representation in Mexican government – in fact, the term representative bureaucracy is rarely or never used in the academic debates or by the media. Therefore, bureaucratic efforts aimed at promoting indigenous concerns and opportunities were focused on what is known as active representation of indigenous.[4] In the mestizo-nation imaginary, indigenous could not preserve their ethnic and cultural integrity if they really wanted to get included within the ranks of the post-revolutionary State.

Finally, we should mention that the development of the intellectual and academic debate in Mexico has been mostly structured around the contemporary liberal political philosophy and what has been named as "the multi-cultural persuasion."

The CDI was created as an autonomous organization in 2003 to replace the almost half-century-old National Indigenist Institute. The establishment of the CDI was a response to the amendments to article 2 of the Political Constitution of the United Mexican States (PCUMS) introduced 2 years earlier (2001), which recognizes the multi-culturality of the Mexican nation, and establishes that indigenous peoples – and the individuals within them – must be the main and co-responsible agents of public actions aimed at their comprehensive development (CDI, 2010, p. 15).

The CDI activities are focused on five topics: (1) indigenous rights; (2) overcoming socio-economic deficiencies and attaining development with identity; (3) recognizing cultural and linguistic diversity in the country; (4) participation and survey for an effective democracy; and (5) institutional management for a culturally and linguistically diverse country (CDI, 2010, p. 12). In fact, the Mexican public administration believes that a consensus exists concerning the need to recognize the indigenous population as a subject of public policies, not just within the CDI but within all of its organizations, comparable to establishing transverse evaluation standards for policies aimed at women and disabled persons:

> Improving the institutional management related to the care of indigenous populations requires an additional effort from within, as it encourages every [federal government] agency to perceive the indigenous population in administrative and statistical terms, focusing their actions with cultural and linguistic diversity standards, and with equity, including elements that provide their actions with cultural pertinence. (CDI, 2010, p. 13)

The Program for the Development of Indigenous Peoples 2009–12 (PDPI) was created for the same purpose, having as its legal foundation section B of article 2 of the Constitution, which establishes that overcoming the economic and social deficiencies of indigenous peoples and communities is a responsibility of the Mexican State agencies at their three levels of government.[5]

As part of the PDPI strategy for involving indigenous communities in development policies, the System of Indigenous Survey was created in 2005, consisting in a methodology that serves to guide public officials in the organization and implementation of surveys in indigenous villages and communities on a series of strategically relevant subjects. The main goal of the survey system is to include indigenous peoples as co-responsible agents of their development (CDI, 2010, p. 16).

Also, since 2003, an instrument named Federal Budget for the Attention of the Indigenous Population – also known as Consolidated Budget for Indigenous Peoples – has been developed with the aim of requesting accountability reports on the budget, actions, and programs each agency of the Federal Public Administration targets to indigenous development (CDI, 2010, pp. 20–21). A crucial aspect of this is that the Mexican bureaucracy's view on ethnic minorities is a clear example of an active representation where, however, the fact of taking into service indigenous public officials that have the ethnic and cultural traits of the constituencies they represent is considered irrelevant.

However, that oversight is important since according to different approaches, passive representation is *a democratic right in itself*. It is relevant not only in terms of increasing bureaucratic sensitivity vis-à-vis the constituencies they represent, but also because of its impact on the public space on the whole, in terms of democratic legitimacy and social and political mobilization (Lim, 2006). Thus, a major challenge is to identify and recognize legitimate and authoritative interlocutors within indigenous communities.

> However, as to the interlocution between the State and indigenous peoples for the design and implementation of public policies the practice of surveys represents a particularly delicate challenge, since those peoples constitute a diverse and heterogeneous group where it is not easy to identify a single representative for interlocution or a unified representation of each indigenous population or community. (CDI, 2010, p. 16)

There is an additional – perhaps elementary, yet crucial – hindrance for the representation of indigenous populations. Thus far there are no official statistics in Mexico on public servants having ethnic or cultural minority backgrounds. Certainly, there are individuals with these racial traits – that is, indigenous persons in public positions – not only in government offices as the CDI and their local branches, but also in other governmental agencies, in the treasury and tourism, for example. However, what matters is that the presence of minorities in public positions is not visible, being a symptom and blatant evidence of the absence of the issue of passive representation on the public agenda.

One major hindrance to developing indigenous populations and communities, is knowing how many and who they are, and how they live. The absence of statistics on indigenous officials in government – relevant per se – goes in hand with the complicated story of population censuses for estimating the indigenous population in the country:

> The 1895, 1900, and 1910 censuses grouped the population that spoke an indigenous language, while the 1940 and 1950 censuses introduced some cultural variables to estimate more accurately the volume of the indigenous population. However, the data obtained with those variables revealed a population four times larger than the number of monolingual and bilingual persons, so this proposal was abandoned, keeping the language as the only variable for identifying the indigenous population, until the criterion of membership was included in the extended questionnaire of the 12th Census of Population and Housing in 2000. (CDI, 2010, p. 19)

As we draw from this extract, the main problem was to find a relatively simple and friendly indicator – in this case, language – to differentiate indigenous and non-indigenous populations. But the problem was that language is not always an effective indicator of whether an individual considers himself or not a native, especially in a country like Mexico, where the *mestizaje* process has distrusted the narrowness of this category. Thus, someone may not speak an indigenous language and consider himself an indigenous, or vice-versa, he may speak an indigenous language and not consider himself a member of the native communities.

An additional obstacle to the estimation of the indigenous population is also related to language. It refers basically to the linguistic barrier between the staff conducting the census in scattered and remote localities – who often ignore the dominant language in the region they are working – and the indigenous populations.

Finally, we should recall that describing oneself as indigenous in an official census is something that some might consider negative or overtly humiliating (CDI, 2010, p. 19). This fact synthesizes a long history of discrimination and abuse that is not easy to obviate, and stands clearly beyond the scope of the statistical information. Besides the basic efforts to know how many individuals in indigenous communities there are in Mexico much more is needed in order to make this information socially useful for the country.

It was not until the late 1980s when the first efforts to link up data collected by the 1980 census to carry out socio-demographic analyses of municipalities with more than 70 percent of indigenous population were made (CDI, 2010, p. 20). Some years later the INI developed a proposal of socioeconomic indicators of indigenous populations, based on the 1990 census, that started by locating indigenous populations in their home municipalities, which were then classified according to the number of indigenous persons to assess the conditions of social backwardness of those municipalities. The last effort in this sense was carried out with the 2000 Census data, based on which and in coordination with the UN Development Program (UNDP), the CDI developed the National System of Indicators on Indigenous Population in Mexico, that includes statistical information on access to health services, water, electricity, communications, and housing.

As mentioned earlier, from this recent study it is noticeable that while there has been a visible improvement in the standard of living of the indigenous population in Mexico in the course of the last decades, there are still asymmetries associated with being a member of the indigenous population (CDI, 2006). For example, school attendance of 6- to 14-year-old indigenous children is slightly lower than in the rest of the country – 91.5 percent versus 94.7 percent, respectively. Within the indigenous population school attendance in this age range increased 4.5 percent in 2000–05, a rise that was slightly higher among women (5.2 percent). Differences between the indigenous population and the rest of the country in second-ary and higher education levels reveal, however, a more drastic contrast. In 2005, for example, the number of indigenous attending higher educa-tion institutions amounted only to 275 268 individuals, while for the rest of the country it reached 9 091 209 persons.

More fundamentally, the educational gap of indigenous population is also evident when we consider the number of illiterates 15 to 64 years of age. In 2005, while the illiterate share in this age rank represented 6.3 percent of non-indigenous-language speakers, the proportion escalated to 21.6 percent within the indigenous population. Also, the majority of the indigenous population – 72 percent – did not have access to public health services in 2005, versus 50 percent of the rest of the population.

The larger nuclei of indigenous population are still concentrated in the states of Chiapas, Oaxaca, and Yucatán, although states such as Aguascalientes, Coahuila, Nuevo León, and Zacatecas have higher growth rates – more than 10 percent – of indigenous peoples. While most of the indigenous do not live in the major urban centers, a considerable share – 17.1 percent – live in two of the largest Mexican cities, Monterrey and Guadalajara, as well as in the most important tourist resort in the Mexican southeast, Cancún, Quintana Roo. Also, the indigenous are moving out from their hometowns, changing the demographic pattern, the social order, and the reciprocity and authority relationships within those communities. This is particularly true for states such as Baja California, Baja California Sur, Nuevo León, Sinaloa, and Tamaulipas, with indig-enous growth rates higher than 15 percent relative to the local population.

Another revealing fact concerning official information on indigenous peoples is that the programs and public policies implemented by the Mexican public administration have no data required for counting, identifying, and distinguishing the indigenous populations that benefit from them. It is interesting to note that this omission affects only ethnic minorities; as we said, in the case of women and disabled persons every governmental agency has evaluation standards, which are included in the Performance Assessment System at the federal level. As the CDI acknowl-edges: "Currently we do not know exactly who and how many indigenous benefit from the social programs and whether changes in their life condi-tions are a result of actions by public institutions" (CDI, 2010, p. 20).

CONCLUSION

Within the Mexican public space it seems that two political languages coexist in a quite unclear way: the language of democratic transition – and civil society – and the language of multi-cultural persuasion. As a result, they seem to intermingle in a single language – that of citizenship. On the one hand, the boom of the NPM in Mexican public administration reforms has nurtured a notion of citizenship based on an inclusive democratic pact, which for this same reason trivializes major dissimilarities among different citizen sectors. Seemingly, this stance reflects another key piece of indigenous bureaucratic representation, in particular concerning their passive or descriptive representation. As Groeneveld and Van de Walle (2010) suggest, human resources management lies at the core of NPM as the main instrument to improve public sector performance. However, in this model of human resources, ethnic and cultural differences do not count as relevant factors for assessing personnel: "This individual worker [the public official, according to the NGP] has no body, gender, race or age" (p. 248).

Groeneveld and Van de Walle call this model of representative bureaucracy the model of representative bureaucracy as diversity, with no moral or political claims supporting the access of ethnic minorities to influential public positions, as diversity is understood merely (managerially) to increase the efficiency of the organization. This vision of ethnic and social dissimilarity is comparable with the language of citizenship mentioned before, where the distinctive though problematic trait is the substitution of the language of rights and citizenship by the language of mercantile relationships – the strictly speaking private language of efficiency and profitability (Escalante, 2006, p. 33).

Thus, two different logics of representation regarding the indigenous population seem to coexist – not always harmoniously – within the Mexican State. On the one hand, some organizations such as the CDI are explicitly concerned about including in the public agenda a "culturally pertinent" economic and social development that would allow for differences and opportunities of the indigenous population. On the other hand, the more widespread rhetoric of efficiency and profitability in the Mexican public administration – not only in terms of values, but also of daily material practices – seems to subsume cultural differences within a notion of citizenship not always aware of the real and systematic differences among indigenous communities and the rest of Mexican society.

ACKNOWLEDGMENTS

My gratitude to Hector Flores for the support that he gave me to write this chapter and to Lorena Murilo for her translation of the Spanish version.

NOTES

1. The calculation of the HDI is based on variables such as the life expectancy at birth, literacy and scholar matriculation rates, and the income per capita adjusted to the purchasing power parity (PNUD, 2010).
2. At the federal level, the municipality is the most bounded governmental domain in the Mexican Republic, both in territorial and legal terms. There are two additional domains: state power and federal power.
3. In the bureaucratic representation debate, the basic distinction refers to passive versus active representation of society. Passive representation consists of the degree of similarity between individuals and those they claim to represent in terms of social and economic class, or ethnic and cultural identity, for example. The key notion in this method of representation is that, given the correspondence of formative experiences, cultural values and social status of both public servants and citizens, the former will accurately represent the interests of the latter – the represented ones – once they assume a bureaucratic charge. On the other hand, active representation refers to how much the action and decisions of civil servants and bureaucracy as a whole protect and develop the benefits of the represented group, irrespective of its ethnic or cultural background (Groeneveld and Van de Walle, 2010).
4. Obviously, one should not discard the virtues of the active bureaucratic representation. Hong-Hai Lim (2006), for example, maintains that the dilemma between active and passive representation – and their impact on the merits of bureaucratic efficiency and neutrality – should take seriously into account the "costs" associated with the bias resulting from affirmative action policies within bureaucracy.
5. Thus, in 2007 a number of federal organizations were called to participate in the definition of strategies and lines of action that would later become the PDPI. The invited agencies were federal departments, such as the Government Secretary, the Social Development Secretary, the Labor Secretary, among others. Other participants included decentralized government agencies such as National Population Council, the National Council Against Discrimination, and public institutions like the Social Security Mexican Institute, and the Agrarian Attorney (CDI, 2010, p. 12).

PART II

Europe

5. Representative bureaucracy in Belgium: power sharing or diversity?

Steven van de Walle, Sandra Groeneveld and Lieselot Vandenbussche

INTRODUCTION

For a long time the question of representativeness in the Belgian administration has been dominated by the cultural–linguistic cleavage that divides the Dutch-speaking Flemings and the French-speaking Walloons. Since 1960 this cleavage has become, and still is, a central issue in the organization of the political and administrative structure of the Belgian state (Heisler, 1977). The polity of the current Federal Belgium is a result of different state reforms aimed at pacifying the relations between the two dominant language communities, the Flemings and the Walloons. Over time, the two language groups have received rights and protection in the different aspects of the public sector in Belgium. Various policy measures and a comprehensive Language Law regulate the representation of Dutch-speakers and French-speakers in the parliament, the executive, and public employment (Deschouwer, 2004).

Only recently has representativeness in the Belgian public sector got a wider interpretation. Since about 2004, the Federal government also has a diversity policy that is explicitly aimed at establishing a representative civil service, i.e. a representative bureaucracy. The policy includes a focus on equal opportunities and diversity for men and women, youngsters and elderly, persons with another nationality or ethnic–cultural background and handicapped persons in the Federal public sector. With this diversity policy the Federal government wants to respond to the growing diversity in the Belgian society and aims to mirror this diverse society in her public sector (Federale Overheidsdienst Personeel en Organisatie, 2006). Also both the Flemish and Walloon regional governments are concerned with reflecting the diversity of the regional society in the composition of the public sector (Région Wallonne, 2007 (see charter); Dienst Emancipatiezaken, 2010). However, the degree to which the regions explicitly take measures to build a representative bureaucracy in their administrations differs.

In this chapter we explain how the Belgian administration is confronted with a double challenge for building a representative bureaucracy. Representative bureaucracy is concerned with making bureaucracies more responsive to the public they serve (Krislov, 1974; Sowa and Selden, 2003). On the one hand, that public, i.e. the Belgian society, is characterized by an ubiquitous division between Dutch-speaking Flemings and French-speaking Walloons. An elaborate set of rules (Language Law) regulates the representation of the two language groups in the federal as well as in the regional public administrations. On the other hand, Belgian society is also dealing with growing ethnic–cultural diversity. Therefore the federal and regional governments have rules, policies, and instruments aimed at establishing a diverse federal and regional public administration. These policies all give, to a certain degree, attention to the representation of ethnic–cultural groups in the administration (Région Wallonne, 2007; Dienst Emancipatiezaken, 2010). Before discussing these rules, policies, and instruments, we first discuss the starting conditions. We illustrate how the two dominant language communities increasingly drifted apart and how this growing cultural–linguistic cleavage has determined and is still determining Belgian polity and policy. At the same time, Belgium is rapidly becoming more and more ethnically and culturally diverse. As such, representativeness in Belgian administration faces two kinds of diversity: (1) an old, deep-rooted cultural–linguistic diversity between Flemings and Walloons; and (2) a newer kind of diversity, the growing presence of ethnic–cultural minorities, i.e. immigrants and their descendants.

STARTING CONDITIONS

A Divided Country . . .

Belgium is a divided country. It covers a territory that is built on the ancient fault line between Romance and Germanic culture (O'Neill, 2000). The different cultural and language backgrounds of the Dutch-speaking Flemings and the French-speaking Walloons has been and is a leading principle for the organization of the Belgian state. After World War II, the cultural–linguistic divide became politicized and translated into a territorial definition (Deschouwer, 2004, pp. 1–9). The territorialization of the language issue divided Belgium into four linguistic areas: a Dutch-speaking area in the north, a French-speaking area in the south, a small German-speaking area in the east and a bilingual area in Brussels, the capital. The language border between the areas was fixed in 1963, and from 1970 on, the country gradually transformed into a federal state. This has, over time, resulted in a very complicated state structure, with a federal level, three communities and three regions which are all on an equal footing. The federal level holds a limited but still important number of competences in foreign affairs, defense, justice, social security, finance, law and order, and the police service. The three communities (French Community, Flemish Community and German-speaking Community) are delineated by language and their main powers and responsibilities are related to individuals and include education, culture and 'social matters' such as family, and aspects of healthcare. The three regions (the Brussels Capital Region in the center, the Flemish Region in the north and the Walloon Region in the south) focus on territorial issues and their powers extend primarily to considerations of a more economic nature. This double structure allows for the two major communities (Flemish and French) to both exercise powers in Brussels. The polity of the current Federal Belgium is a result of different state reforms aimed at pacifying the relations between the two language groups. To date, the cultural–linguistic communalism is the principal cleavage that characterizes and dominates Belgian politics (O'Neill, 2000).

The majority of the Belgian population is Flemish, i.e. 57.7 percent of the 10.1 million inhabitants live on the territory of the Flemish Region, 32.2 percent are inhabitants of the Walloon Region and 10 percent live in the Brussels Capital Region (Algemene Directie voor Statistiek en Economische Informatie, 2010). However, these data do not give a realistic insight into the distribution of the language groups in Belgium. Many Dutch-speakers live in the Walloon region and many French-speakers live in the Flemish region. Furthermore, quite a few families, especially in Brussels, are bilingual, or do not use French or Dutch as first language. Recent official data on the use of language are not available because the official language census was abolished in 1954 (Sieben, 1987).

... And a Diversified Country

Since World War II, Belgium has known three major immigration waves. The first wave of immigration concerned the labor immigration of guest workers from the Mediterranean area (Italy, Spain, Portugal, Morocco, Turkey). The first immigration wave resulted in a second wave of family reunification. The third more recent immigration wave is a more diffuse and diverse group of immigrants and consists of refugees, marriage migrants, people without documents and so on (Easton et al., 2009). From the first immigration wave on, Belgian society has become more and more ethnically and culturally diverse. Although the absolute number of the Belgian population increases only slowly, researchers agree that the ethnic–cultural composition of the population is diversifying rapidly (Easton et al., 2009).

However, the real diversity of the Belgian society can only be estimated since official data on ethnic–cultural origin is hard to find. Official administrative data and statistics only register a person's nationality and not his or her ethnic–cultural origin. According to these data, in 2008, the Belgian population consisted of 90.9 percent Belgians. The rest, or 9.1 percent, are foreigners (Algemene Directie voor Statistiek en Economische Informatie, 2008). However, because of a number of policy options, among which are adaptations in the Belgian nationality law, less strict naturalization procedures, and mixed marriages, data based on nationality are inadequate to map the presence of ethnic–cultural minorities in Belgium. In the period 1990–2004 about half a million citizens with foreign nationality were nationalized, most of them Italian, Moroccan or Turkish. These naturalized foreign citizens disappear in the official statistics. If foreigners and foreigners who obtained Belgian nationality are considered as one category, then the foreign population in Belgium is estimated at around 16 percent, far above the official 9.1 percent. The 1962 law on public statistics forbids Statistics Belgium, the national statistics agency, to do statistical research and studies focusing on race and ethnic descent (as well as sexual behavior, political and religious behavior and affiliations). The relevant article in the law (24 quinquies) even explicitly starts with 'under no circumstance'. While this ban remains in place, there have been frequent calls to allow ethnic registration in order to be able to design diversity policies. A number of public organizations have found ways around this law. With these difficulties concerning ethnic registration it is hard to estimate the real diversity of the Belgian society. However, the above suggests that Belgian society is far more diverse than can be estimated on the basis of nationality statistics (Easton et al., 2009).

TWO CHALLENGES FOR A BELGIAN REPRESENTATIVE BUREAUCRACY

The above shows that the Belgian administration faces a double challenge when it comes to representative bureaucracy in the public sector. On the one hand, there is a deeply rooted cleavage between Flemings and Walloons based on cultural and linguistic differences. On the other hand – on top of this cultural–linguistic cleavage – Belgian society is becoming more and more ethnically and culturally diverse, so Belgian administrations have to deal with representation of two 'diversities'. The first concerns the language diversity and is addressed in language policies. The second concerns ethnic–cultural diversity and refers to the presence of ethnic–cultural minorities in society, i.e. immigrants and their descendants.

The federal level in particular faces this double challenge. The Federal Administration aspires to be a 'representative bureaucracy' that recruits from all segments of society (Scheepers, 2007; Janvier et al., 2011). Both dimensions are present in the federal representativeness policy: The Federal Administration aims to balance power between the country's major language groups through an extensive language policy. Representativeness according to language is symbolic for the social struggle between Flemings and Walloons. The main concern of language policy is to ensure equal opportunities for the two language groups in government employment. Laws, rules and other measures are designed to stabilize the power relations between the two language groups (Hondeghem, 1999). But the federal government also aspires to be a diverse workplace (Scheepers, 2007). Various levels of government therefore developed various policies and instruments to stimulate "respect for the behavior, values, cultures, lifestyles, competences, and experiences of each member of a group" (own translation, Federale Overheidsdienst Personeel en Organisatie, 2005).

Since the division of Belgium in two unilingual regions, the social struggle between Flemings and Walloons has narrowed to the federal level and the Brussels bilingual region. As such, the issue of language representation is of less importance for the two major communities in Belgium: the Flemish and French communities. Although the Language Law also regulates the linguistic representation in Brussels Capital Region, there exists some contention about the composition of the Brussels regional administration. Brussels Capital Region has become a new cultural battleground (O'Neill, 2000). Both major regions, the Walloon and the Flemish, also aspire to mirror the diversity in the Belgian society (Région Wallonne, 2007; Dienst Emancipatiezaken, 2010) but there are some crucial regional differences concerning the policy options regarding diversity in the regional administrations.

LANGUAGE POLICIES AND REPRESENTATIVE BUREAUCRACY

In a multilingual country such as Belgium, debates about the composition of the government administration naturally focus on language issues. This debate, however, is hardly ever coined in terms of representative bureaucracy. Instead, it uses a discourse of power sharing, in which, surprisingly, the concept of "minority" is carefully avoided. The country has three official languages, and while language use is generally free, there are detailed regulations organizing the use of language in administrative affairs, courts, education, and employer–employee relations.

The Federal Level

Administrative regulations to some extent reflect the arrangements made for political representation in the Federal Parliament and Government and in the Brussels Regional Parliament. The Federal Government has an equal number of French- and Dutch-speaking ministers (parity rule), with the Prime Minister as a possible exception. In the Brussels Regional Government, out of a total of five ministers, two have to be Dutch-speaking and two French-speaking. Such a principle also applies to top positions in the Federal Administration, and, for example, the Council of State, the Court of Cassation, and the Constitutional Court. The overall legal framework for language groups' representation in the Federal Administration is the 1966 Royal Decree concerning coordination of the laws on the language use in administrative affairs (Language Law).

One of the main organizing principles in the effectuation of the Language Law and thus to ensure the language balance in the Federal Administration are the so-called language frames. These language frames are updated every 6 years and determine the percentage of functions assigned to each language group within the federal departments. The percentages, developed for all hierarchical levels, are based on the relative importance of Dutch- or French-language areas for that administration. Here mirror-image representativeness is aspired to (Hondeghem, 1999, p. 134). For top positions (director and above), however, the allocation of places to Dutch- and French-speakers is equal. Twenty percent of top positions are reserved for officials belonging to the bilingual group. This thus means that officials in management positions do not have to be bilingual. However, if a head of department is unilingual, a bilingual assistant ("adjoint") is added to ensure the uniform application of the law and jurisprudence across language groups. Where the size of the office and the nature of work allow it, Dutch- and French-language sub-departments exist within a department.

In order to implement the language frames, each public official is assigned to a linguistic role. The language in which public officials participate in the public sector recruitment exams or the language in which the public official received his or her education determines his or her linguistic role or group. So officials belong to a French or Dutch group. Officials can participate in exams to prove their knowledge of the other language in order to be admitted to the bilingual group. Bilingual officials are entitled to a financial language allowance. Table 5.1 shows the distribution of public officials according to language for the main Federal Public Services, both for level A (the highest level of employment, generally officials with a university degree) and for the entire staff.

While the general principles of the law are generally adhered to, detailed application is often quite uneven across departments, with language frameworks not being established, and departments operating along a parity system rather than adhering to a 58 percent Dutch/42 percent French division of positions that would reflect the wider composition of Belgian society. Indeed, the actual division is closer to 53 percent Dutch/47 percent French, with larger discrepancies in smaller agencies, e.g. certain federal scientific institutions. The extreme-right Flemish-nationalist party Vlaams Belang described this practice as a jobs transfer of approximately 20000 from Flanders to Wallonia.

There appears to be a widespread agreement about the language frameworks. Complaints and parliamentary questions are limited to a small number of political groups, or specific cases. Such cases include top-level appointments within the Ministry of Finance, yet this debate mainly concentrated on the Finance Minister's purported politicization of the department through appointing members of his own (French-speaking) political party to top positions, and less on representative bureaucracy issues per se. The army is another area where there has been debate about representation following complaints first about an overrepresentation of French speakers in the army (often attributed to the weaker economic situation in Wallonia), and later also about an overrepresentation of the Flemish in top positions. A Parliamentary Committee was established in 2011 to look into these allegations.

Another problematic area is the appointment of top officials. Whereas the parity rule operated well under the traditional system of appointments, the new mandate system and associated assessments sometimes returns as best candidate a person who speaks the 'wrong' language and thereby upsets the balance within the institution or a set of institutions. It may also happen that top managers outside the Federal Administration are not bilingual. In the pre-NPM system, this did not happen because top officials had been working in the Federal Administration their entire life before assuming a leadership position, and had thus acquired a functional fluency in both languages.

Table 5.1	*Public officials in the Federal Administration according to linguistic role on 1 January 2011*

	Level A			All levels		
	French linguistic role (%)	Dutch linguistic role (%)	Total (abs.)	French linguistic role (%)	Dutch linguistic role (%)	Total (abs.)
Ministry of Defense	47.4	52.6	456	48.5	51.5	2148
FPS Chancellery of the Prime Minister	47.9	52.1	73	50.8	49.2	189
FPS Personnel and Organization	47.5	52.5	244	49.4	50.6	532
FPS Budget and Management Control	49.5	50.5	91	51.6	48.4	157
FPS Information and Communication Technology	39.1	60.9	23	44.1	55.9	34
FPS Mobility and Transport	42.0	58.0	426	39.6	60.4	1347
FPS Economy. SME Middle-classes and Energy	50.3	49.7	819	47.7	52.3	2483
FPS Finances	44.6	55.4	6639	43.8	56.2	29298
FPS Foreign Trade and Development Cooperation	46.7	53.3	1052	47.8	52.2	1945
FPS Home Affairs	47.6	52.4	1406	43.4	56.6	5209
FPS Social Security	49.3	50.7	341	49.3	50.7	1230
FPS Food Chain Security and Environment	47.6	52.4	635	47.1	52.9	1317
FPS Justice (Central administration)	50.5	49.5	643	50.6	49.4	1771
FPS Justice (Justice Houses)	53.1	46.9	49	50.4	49.6	1181
FPS Justice (Penitentiary Establishments)	49.1	50.9	591	50.9	49.1	9783
FPS Labor and Social Dialogue	45.1	54.9	439	44.8	55.2	1402
PPS Sustainable Development	50.0	50.0	14	41.2	58.8	17
PPS Combatting Poverty and Social Economy	47.0	53.0	83	49.7	50.3	191
PPS Science Policy	51.4	48.6	175	53.0	47.0	302
Total	46.3	53.7	14199	46.0	54.0	60536

Note:	SME, small to medium-sized enterprises

Source:	Pdata, www.pdata.be. List includes all Federal Public Services (formerly ministries, FPS) and all Programmatic Public Services (PPS), but excludes agencies, federal scientific institutions and social security institutions. Officials at level A, the highest level, generally have a university degree.

The Regional Level

When considering language representativeness on the regional level, most of the language debate plays in the Brussels Capital Region, in the Flemish border municipalities and in a number of "facility" municipalities (27) straddled along the language border between the Dutch-speaking and French-speaking territories. The Brussels Regional Administration is subject to the same directives of the municipalities on the bilingual territory of the Brussels Capital Region. The regional administration has to proportionally spread positions over both language groups. Contention exists about the composition of the Brussels Regional Administration, whose composition reflects the amount of work done in a certain language. This situation is especially problematic because the rules are based on the assumption that Brussels is a French–Dutch bilingual city. However, in reality the city has become multilingual, with French often used as lingua franca. English has also become a frequently used language for daily communication; Dutch-speakers are estimated to be between 10 and 15 percent of the Brussels population. Furthermore, because of the large number of (Dutch-speaking) commuters into Brussels, the number of Dutch-speakers using public services is much larger by daytime than at night (Deschouwer, 2004). In the Flemish border municipalities the language law prescribes that administrators can only be appointed or promoted if they know Dutch.

In general, the language debate is of less importance in the Walloon and Flemish regions. Here the situation is much clearer since both are by and large homogeneous language areas. The official language of the Walloon region is French; that of the Flemish region is Dutch. So the question of linguistic representation in the Flemish and Walloon administrations is superfluous. However, there are a number of municipalities straddled along the language border where various arrangements regulate the linguistic representation of both language groups, although they officially belong to the unilingual French-speaking Walloon or Dutch-speaking Flemish territory. In these "facility" municipalities the top officials, such as the municipal secretary, the treasurer and the chief commissioner of police, have to be bilingual. Only candidates that pass a language exam that tests their knowledge of the second language (French in the Dutch-speaking territory, Dutch in the French-speaking territory) can apply for these functions (Deschouwer, 2004). These municipalities also enjoy language facilities, meaning that inhabitants can be helped in their own language.

One official language is conspicuously absent from this overview: German. While German can be used in the Federal Parliament or administration, in practice it hardly ever is, and many laws are not even translated. The legal framework for positions in the federal government and administration only distinguishes between French and Dutch speakers, not German speakers. An analysis of representative bureaucracy with regard to the German language would thus only make sense around the small German-speaking Community in the east of the country. German speakers enjoy a considerable autonomy.

DIVERSITY POLICIES AND REPRESENTATIVE BUREAUCRACY

The introduction of equal opportunities and diversity policies in the Belgian public sector is relatively recent compared to other European countries. It is the assignment of the responsibility of Equal Opportunities to the Minister of the Civil Service in 2003 that led to the creation of an internal diversity policy and only from then on the idea of equal opportunities became important for the functioning and the organization of the civil service (Decat and Scheepers, 2005).

The Federal Level

The diversity policy of the federal government is aimed at improving equal opportunities and diversity within the Federal Administration (Federale Overheidsdienst Personeel en Organisatie, 2006). In her policy letter ('beleidsbrief'), the Minister directly referred to representative bureaucracy by emphasizing the importance of a Federal Administration that mirrors society (Arena, 2003). On top of that, she points out that a diverse public service is also a more competent public service that is more sensitive to the expectations of the society. In the policy period that followed, the first initiatives and plans to improve diversity were launched.

The "internal" diversity policy of the federal government is framed by the general "external" equal opportunities policy. The external equal opportunities policy is oriented towards citizens, whereas the internal diversity policy is oriented towards public officials (Facon et al., 2004). The external equal opportunities policy is the responsibility of the Federal Minister of Employment and Equal Opportunities. The priorities in this external policy are, among others, ensuring the equality of men and women in working life as well as combating discrimination and improving diversity on the work floor. At the administrative level the minister of Equal Opportunities is supported by the Federal Public Service for Employment, Labour and Social Dialogue. One of the themes this federal public service works on is "non discrimination and diversity". Within this theme equal opportunities are seen as the basic principle and the aim of regulation against discrimination. Diversity policy is the means to realize these equal opportunities within organizations (Federale Overheidsdienst Werkgelegenheid, Arbeid en Sociaal Overleg, 2011). The internal diversity policy of the Federal Administration is the responsibility of the Federal Minister of Civil Service and aims to improve the diversity in the Federal Administration and to mirror the diversity in the Belgian society (Federale Overheidsdienst Personeel en Organisatie, 2006). This priority clearly refers to the concept of representative bureaucracy, in particular to passive or sociological representation (Groeneveld and Van de Walle, 2010).

Diversity policies are targeted at the representation of social groups that are being recognized as experiencing inequalities and discrimination in employment. In the European diversity literature six strands are generally recognized: gender, race/ethnicity, age, disability, sexual orientation, and religion (Kirton and Greene, 2010). The diversity policy of the Belgian Federal Administration is primarily targeted at the representation and integration of three target groups: ethnic–cultural minorities, women, and disabled people. Target figures are formulated for disabled people only: 3 percent of the influx in the Federal Administration should consist of disabled persons. Despite the fact that gender and ethnicity are central to the diversity policy of the Federal Administration, for these groups no specific targets are defined. The diversity policy is aimed at increasing the representation of people with a foreign background and at the equitable representation of women.

For the implementation of the diversity policy the Minister of Civil Service is supported by the Diversity Cells of the Federal Service Personnel and Organization, the selection agency of the federal government (Selor) and of the training institute of the federal government. The Diversity Cell of the Federal Service Personnel and Organization is responsible for the development, coordination and implementation of the diversity policy within the federal public service. The Cell also supports the development of diversity projects on the work floor. Selor is responsible for the diversity principle in the recruiting and selection of civil servants by "guaranteeing an objective selection procedure" (Selor, 2011). The training institute is mainly responsible for guaranteeing the diversity principle in its trainings and offers training specifically about diversity (Federale Overheidsdienst Personeel en Organisatie, 2010a).

In each Federal Public Service there are one or more diversity managers that are responsible for the development of a diversity policy specifically for their organization. Most of the diversity managers are members of the human resources (HR) staff. This is a conscious choice aimed at guaranteeing the integration of the diversity principle in the broader HR policy. In order to increase the representation of disabled people, women, and ethnic minorities, several policy instruments have been developed and implemented. Examples of policy measures enhancing the representation and integration of disabled people in the civil service are the adaptation of the work conditions, preferential treatment of disabled people in recruitment and selection, and specific attention for the situation of disabled people when entering the organization. The committee for the recruitment of disabled people supports the Federal Administration in achieving this goal and evaluates the actions undertaken. Examples of policy measures aimed at increasing the representation of women are adaptation of working conditions, in particular work family policies (part-time work, leave arrangements, etc.), recruitment campaigns targeted at recruitment of women for management positions and offering networking possibilities (Federale Overheidsdienst Personeel en Organisatie, 2010a). Policy measures aimed at increasing the representation of people with a foreign background are scarce. Recruitment campaigns targeted at people with a foreign background are one of the few examples. All in all, five categories of policy instruments can be distinguished: laws and regulations, target figures and quotas, publicity and recruitment campaigns, covenants, and HRM policies aimed at integration and an inclusive workplace.

The legal substructure for the internal equal opportunities (diversity) policy of the federal government can be found in the three Anti-Discrimination Laws of 10 May 2007 (Federale Overheidsdienst Personeel en Organisatie, 2010b). The first law is the General Anti-Discrimination Law that creates a general framework in combating discrimination based on 13 criteria: age, sexual orientation, civil status, birth, wealth, freedom of religion or freedom of consciousness, political affiliation, syndical adherence, language, disability, current or future health condition, a physical or genetic characteristic, and social origin. The second law is the Anti-Racism Law that aims to create a general framework in the fight against discrimination based on five criteria: nationality, race, skin color, descent, and national or ethnic origin. The third law is the Gender Law on discrimination between men and women (Federale Overheidsdienst Personeel en Organisatie, 2010b).

Apart from the (more general) anti-discrimination laws of 2007 since the mid-1990s, a number of legal measures exist to strengthen the participation of women in political decision-making (Valgaeren et al., 2008). For example, since 2002 several new laws (quota laws) require that the number of men and women on the lists of candidates for elections is equal and also include measures to avoid that the top of the list is populated by candidates from the same gender. The introduction of gender quotas on electoral lists in Belgium is seen as a key factor for strengthening the participation of women in politics (StemVrouw, 2007; Instituut voor de Gelijkheid van Mannen en Vrouwen, 2009). Apart from the above-mentioned gender quota for political decision-making, target figures and quotas are remarkably seldom used as a diversity policy instrument. We only found target figures with respect to disabled people in the Federal Administration: 3 percent of the influx in the Federal Administration should consist of disabled persons (Vervotte, 2009).

Publicity campaigns and recruitment campaigns are the third type of diversity policy instruments. "Diversity is an enrichment" ("Diversiteit is een verrijking") is a publicity campaign that was developed by the Federal Service Personnel and Organization in 2006. The campaign was targeted at improving the public image of the Federal Administration and recruiting specific groups in the workforce. Equal opportunities and diversity were communicated as the core characteristics of the Federal Administration. Along with this campaign for the general public, a campaign for target groups was also launched. With this campaign the Federal Administration tried to reach exactly those groups for whom diversity policies were actu-ally meant: people with disabilities and persons of foreign origin. In addi-tion, recruitment campaigns were launched that were specially targeted at improving the representation of women in the higher echelons of the Federal Administration. Both an internal recruitment campaign and publicity in the national newspapers were aimed at encouraging women to participate in the selection procedures for the higher management positions.

The diversity policy aims of the Federal Administration are further for-malized in a diversity charter. By signing the diversity charter the Federal Public Services are expected to improve the diversity of their workforce and to combat discrimination (Federale Overheidsdienst Personeel en Organisatie, 2010a). In recent years, the Federal Administration pays more and more attention to integrating diversity policies into the HR management policies and practices. In addition, methodologies and instruments are communicated and made available to every Federal Public Service in order to enable them to manage a diverse workforce (Federale Overheidsdienst Personeel en Organisatie, 2010a).

The recruitment campaigns appeared to be rather successful. For example, the Federal Service Personnel and Organization claims that as a result of the recruitment campaign targeted at disabled people the number of applications has doubled (Federale Overheidsdienst Personeel en Organisatie, 2010a). In addition, the share of female applicants for the higher job positions has risen as well. However, women are still underrepresented in the higher echelons of the Federal Administration

Table 5.2   Public officials in the Federal Administration according to gender on January 1, 2011

	Level A		Total Federal Public Services	
	Men (%)	Women (%)	Men (%)	Women (%)
Ministry of Defense	70.4	29.6	57.5	42.5
FPS Chancellery of the Prime Minister	58.9	41.1	42.3	57.7
FPS Personnel and Organization	42.2	57.8	37.4	62.6
FPS Budget and Management Control	68.1	31.9	50.3	49.7
FPS Information and Communication Technology	78.3	21.7	64.7	35.3
FPS Mobility and Transport	69.2	30.8	54.0	46.0
FPS Economy. P.M.E. Middle-classes and Energy	62.4	37.6	46.2	53.8
FPS Finances	63.4	36.6	46.5	53.5
FPS Foreign Trade and Development Cooperation	68.7	31.3	54.1	45.9
FPS Home Affairs	45.9	54.1	52.2	47.8
FPS Social Security	54.3	45.7	41.1	58.9
FPS Food Chain Security and Environment	52.1	47.9	40.6	59.4
FPS Justice (Central administration)	52.1	47.9	47.8	52.2
FPS Justice (Justice Houses)	28.6	71.4	18.5	81.5
FPS Justice (Penitentiary Establishments)	41.5	58.5	69.3	30.7
FPS Labor and Social Dialogue	56.0	44.0	44.1	55.9
PPS Sustainable Development	50.0	50.0	47.1	52.9
PPS Combatting Poverty and Social Economy	41.0	59.0	35.6	64.4
PPS Science Policy	66.3	33.7	54.3	45.7
Total	59.44	40.56	50.60	49.40

Source: Pdata, www.pdata.be. List includes all Federal Public Services (formerly ministries, FPS) and all Programmatic Public Services (PPS), but excludes agencies, Federal scientific institutions and social security institutions. Officials at level A, the highest level, generally have a university degree.

(see Table 5.2) (Federale Overheidsdienst Personeel en Organisatie, 2010a). Whereas the share of women in the Federal Administration can be monitored, there are no statistics available neither for the number of disabled people employed in the Federal Administration nor for the number of ethnic–cultural minorities. The latter is because there is no ethnic registration in Belgium. In addition to gender, there is personnel information available on age, language and nationality.

The Regional Level

The diversity policy for the Federal Administration can be considered as a conciliation between the more proactive approach of the Flemish Region and the more republican approach of the Walloon Region to diversity and integration policy. The interpretation of diversity on the regional levels shows some crucial differences in the way both regional administrations aim to build a representative bureaucracy. However, both regions do explicitly aim to mirror the regional society in their administrations.

The development of a Flemish internal diversity policy was triggered by the decree on the proportional participation on the labor market. This decree states that the Flemish employment policy has to be organized according to the principles of proportional participation and equal treatment. The principle of proportional participation contends that participation in the labor market has to reflect the composition of the labor force and that the proportional participation of minority groups has to be guaranteed. The principle of equal treatment contents the absence of any form of direct or indirect discrimination or intimidation on the labor market.

The Flemish Region launched a first internal diversity policy plan in 2005 aimed at the promotion and support of the equal opportunities and diversity in the Flemish Administration. Since (about) then the Flemish Government has an extended Service for Emancipatory Affairs. The Service is coordinated by the Flemish Emancipatory Officer and is specifically aimed at creating a representative bureaucracy. Its mission states: "The Flemish Government believes in the added value of a diverse workforce. This workforce has to be a mirror of the society" (own translation, Dienst Emancipatiezaken, 2010).

The Service takes several actions to promote more equal opportunities on the work floor – on all levels and for all positions – for men and women, foreigners, disabled persons or persons with a chronic disease, and homosexuals and transgender persons. To ensure the representation of these four target groups, a range of measures is taken. For each group, except for the target group homosexuals and transgender, the Flemish government formulates target numbers. In 2015 the Flemish government aspires to be composed of at least 4 percent foreigners, 4.5 percent disabled persons and 33 percent women in management positions. To follow up the representation of the target groups, the Service works with a voluntarily registration by its personnel.

Besides target figures, the Flemish government also tries to pursue diversity through recruitment and selection policies. For instance, there are certain positions that are reserved for disabled people, since disabled persons are now underrepresented in the Flemish administration. What is more, in some vacancies the Flemish government mentions that they preferably want to recruit a person of one of the target groups. The personnel statute of the Flemish government contains an article that states that when, in recruitment and selection, applicants are equal, priority will be given to the applicant of the underrepresented group. Target group employees can also appeal to a job coach that guides them through the first 6 months working at the Flemish administration. Finally, the Flemish government also launched a few diversity campaigns to promote diversity in the Flemish administration.

The range of interventions taken by the Flemish government strongly differs from the Walloon approach to ensuring representative bureaucracy in their administrations. Whilst the Flemish government focuses on measures to increase the diversity in the Flemish administration, the Walloon government focuses more on the idea of non-discrimination in its administrations without specifically taking measures for target groups. The first internal diversity policy plan is still to come.

The essential difference between the Flemish and francophone policy frames concerns the degree of interventionism considered to be necessary to achieve the objectives of cultural homogeneity or diversity. It seems that the different perspective on diversity and the different policy frames also have influence on the way both regions try to build a representative bureaucracy. The Flemish Region has a more direct and interventionist policy that is inspired by the policy approaches in the Nordic countries, whilst the Walloon Region rather opts for a laissez-faire approach that leans more to the policy model of France (Jacobs and Rea, 2005; Adams, 2010). These different policy frames are reflected in the internal diversity approach in the respective regional administrations. So, despite the fact that the cultural–linguistic issue is mainly depoliticized on the regional level through the far-reaching cultural autonomy of both regions and Language Law, it still is a determining factor for the regional approach to representing diversity in the public sector.

CONCLUSION: POWER, EQUAL OPPORTUNITIES AND DIVERSITY

The diversity policy of the Belgian Federal Government strongly echoes the equal opportunity discourses of the 1960s and 1970s (Groeneveld and Van de Walle, 2010). It emphasizes the sociological representation of the population by gender, ethnic origin, and disability. Given the current position of disabled people, women, and ethnic minorities on the labor market, the policy aims at improving their representation in the

Federal Administration. However, except for women, statistics for the number of disabled people and ethnic minorities employed in the Federal Administration are lacking.

The policy instruments are mainly legalistic in nature (laws, regulations, and covenants), which not only fits into the aim of increasing representation, but also contributes to the symbolic function for the government of having such policies at all (Groeneveld and Verbeek, 2010). Further, the policy instruments are primarily aimed at increasing the diversity of the Federal Administration workforce, and to a far lesser extent to managing the diversity that is already there. Only recently, some methodologies have been developed aimed at an inclusive work climate.

The divergence between the diversity policies of the regions can be explained by the specific regional perspectives on diversity that are inspired by two different policy frames (Jacobs and Rea, 2005; Adams, 2010). In the Walloon Region the discourse on integration and diversity is inspired by the French Republican model, whereas in Flanders it is more influenced by the policy frames of the Nordic countries (Jacobs and Rea, 2005; Adams, 2010). As such, the cultural–linguistic cleavage between Dutch-speaking Flemings and French-speaking Walloons seems to affect the diversity policies of the regions.

The most striking feature when studying representative bureaucracy in Belgium, however, is that language-related representativeness is generally not discussed as an issue related to representative bureaucracy or diversity, but as a power-sharing issue. Language is, in other words, the elephant in the representativeness room. The Belgian government's aim when designing rules for the representation of language groups were thus different from those generally mentioned in the public administration literature on representative bureaucracy. Diversity and linguistic representation are entirely unrelated debates, and the former is clearly subordinate to the latter. While most federal public officials are very sensitive to language-related issues of representation, and many policies and practices have been developed to safeguard such representation, broader diversity policies have been far less institutionalized.

Even the system for language representations shows a number of intriguing anomalies. The first is the quasi-absence of German speakers, or policies for German speakers, at the federal level. A second interesting anomaly in the Belgian context is that the country has not ratified the Council of Europe's Framework Convention for the Protection of National Minorities, because of its implications on existing arrangements in the country (Maertens, 2002). The Convention conflicts with Belgium's territoriality principle in the origination of language protection. For this reason, the country officially has, despite its elaborate power-sharing structure, no 'minorities'. The signing of this Treaty has been a recurring issue of contention. One of the (unintended) consequences of this situation and of the salience of the language issue is that it may have hindered the development of effective policies for stimulating the entrance of recent and second-generation immigrants into public service. Diversity policies directed at "new minorities" are furthermore hindered by the absence of – even soft – targets, and the absence of ethnic registration (and the accompanying sensitivity of such registration).

6. Representative bureaucracy in transitional bureaucracies: Bulgaria and Romania

Katja Michalak

INTRODUCTION

While good governance and civil service system have become the buzz words in Western policy research circles and the political establishments of post-communist countries, and the concepts involved have attracted strong interest on the part of economists, public administration observers, and international organizations that provide financial support for development (Abed and Gupta, 2002), there still remains conceptual and analytical confusion about what constitutes effective governance and, more importantly, what constitutes accountability of bureaucracy and to what extent it is representative of civil society itself. The mutual relationship between the bureaucracy and the public reflects a representative bureaucracy, which the literature defines as good governance. Representative bureaucracy literature argues that "[p]ublic bureaucracies must be representative of the people they serve" (Evans, 1974, p. 628). This broad definition of the concept of representative bureaucracy can be investigated through various means. Since passive representation can be rather easily achieved in emerging democracies, whereas active representation faces the challenge of patronage and clientelistic networks that are still present in both Romania and Bulgaria, the focus here is on this important distinction.

On examining representative bureaucracy, it becomes abundantly clear that both Bulgaria and Romania are still continuing to struggle within post-transition phenomena, such as cutting large public sector size, diminishing politicization, establishing rule of law, and fighting corruption, among others. These issues pose additional challenges that are typically less pronounced in non-transitional democracies. Thus an investigation of representativeness in bureaucracies in transition is particularly insightful.

The question arises: does representative bureaucracy, in fact, refer to representative democracy? Meier (1997), in 'Bureaucracy and democracy: the case for more bureaucracy and less democracy' attributes a higher weight to the bureaucracy, and characterizes this as a state in which bureaucrats "respond to political demands whether or not those demands are consistent and whether or not they are expressed through politically legitimate channels" (Meier, 1997, p. 196). Transitional bureaucracies focus primarily on strong bureaucratic capacity that serves the function of political stability. A significant purpose resides in the monitoring work of political appointees that serve the crucial function of accountability, especially in post-transition time. Also, in the fight against bureaucratic corruption, the role of political appointees takes on a rather prominent role (cf. Niskanen, 1971). This is particularly true in the context of de-stabilization that dominates the political landscape in transitional states. Here, the role of political appointees that keep the balance is very crucial, especially in countries such as Romania and Bulgaria, where the violation of meritocratic procedures was, and continues to be, a main problem in its implementation step.

The principal contribution of this chapter is both a theoretical and an empirical examination of representative bureaucracy in transitional bureaucracies. The cases represented are bureaucracies in emerging democracies, with special focus on Bulgaria and Romania. Both cases are representative of bureaucracies that are undergoing transformation as a consequence of regime change. While we can observe the experience of an emerging democracy as well as a possible shift to representative bureaucracy, conceptually they are distinct, though the two events are not mutually exclusive.

Four distinct, though interrelated, goals can be discerned in this context and are followed throughout the chapter. The first is a brief evaluation of what constitutes 'transitional bureaucracy' in the case of Romania and Bulgaria. The second is motivated by the key challenges of current bureaucracy in Bulgaria and Romania, which presents an attempt at interlinking both representative bureaucracies and transitional bureaucracies. Third, empirical support is provided to examine representative bureaucracy in Bulgaria and Romania, with a main focus on both the institutional settings for representative bureaucracy as well as the main push-and-pull factors for representative bureaucracy in Bulgaria and Romania. Finally, a brief normative perspective is provided, in which the key question is: what is the content of the concept of a perfect representative bureaucracy in a transitional democratic country? A related concern is, of course, as to what this conception of representative bureaucracy is, contrasted with what it ought to be.

TRANSITIONAL BUREAUCRACIES: CASE STUDIES OF ROMANIA AND BULGARIA – AN OVERVIEW OF THEIR KEY CHALLENGES

Analysing Bulgaria and Romania in the context of representative bureaucracy in transitional democracies is a unique opportunity, insofar as they are two young democracies that entered the European Union in 2007. Both countries are still struggling with their administrative capacity (European Commission (EC), 2010a, b) and at the same time showing some, but limited, attempts at an increasing representative bureaucracy. Whereas Bulgaria presents a small bureaucratic apparatus in terms of the total number of personnel, Romania presents the biggest bureaucratic apparatus in southeastern Europe, both in terms of personnel and with the largest number of ministries compared to all other countries in the region. In comparing Bulgaria and Romania, two additional distinctions are significant with regard to representativeness of their bureaucracies. First, on demographic characteristics, Bulgaria is more homogeneous whereas Romania exhibits a greater diversity in the proportion of minorities in the total population.[1] Second, in terms of operational influence, Bulgaria has greater representativeness at the central government level, whereas Romania ranks higher in influence of minorities at the regional or local government levels.

However, in overall East European comparison, Romania and Bulgaria are amongst the very few European Union member states that still provide very low levels of remuneration to civil servants. Hence, this chapter concentrates primarily on those similarities, rather than differences. As such, Romania becomes a unique case through which corruption, nepotism, the problem of transparency, and the general malaise especially of the Southeastern European (SEE) reform system can be observed. The low levels of salaries awarded to civil servants become a very important aspect of the overall governance of the country, as defined and measured by the World Bank (2010). This part tackles aspects referring to the overall incentive structure with which governments in emerging democracies try to stimulate civil servants' effectiveness through a reward system. Both Romania and Bulgaria are especially characterized by the problem of being politicized bureaucracies that are malfunctioning for objective reasons, arising from low remuneration and insufficient incentives to remain loyal to the public sector. In addition, Romania's is also oversized. "Politicization" and "oversized" bureaucracy relate indirectly to representative bureaucracy, because representative bureaucracy cannot emerge if the institutional settings are not sufficiently developed, which is a main characteristic of transitional democracies.

In this context, the bulk of the literature on representative bureaucracy concentrates on established democracies (democratic societies), where the main concern lies in the representation of the people. To this effect, the main assumption of representative bureaucracy is that "a bureaucracy which truly represents all segments of the population can best serve the interests of the people" (Evans, 1974, p. 628). Moving from conceptual form to specific content, the key problems with the Romanian and Bulgarian transitional bureaucracies, as outlined briefly below, are (1) patronage and corruption, (2) politicization, (3) transparency, and (4) remuneration, which will be addressed and briefly elaborated in the following parts.

Patronage and Corruption

It was not until 1999 that any change, however little, occurred in the state administration structures or indeed in the administrative practices of the Bulgarian (started in 1995) and Romanian bureaucracies. Pre-transition practices continued to have a very substantial lingering effect on the post-transition period, with virtually no civil service reform. The turnover rate of personnel remained stagnant overall, although some ministries expanded, whereas others contracted. As a consequence, there are some pre-transition era bureaucrats who remain in power today, making a lingering effect of old clientelistic networks still prevalent. Furthermore, the low turnover rate creates significant difficulties in the professionalization of ministerial staff, insofar as new, young professionals do not get inducted into the ministry in question. However, the key problem of low turnover is the small representation of the public in the bureaucracy, which provides it an additional negative characteristic to the already existing ones.

Corrupt practices of civil service staff in both Bulgaria and Romania remain a major stumbling block. Although convicted of offenses involving organized crime, some members of the civil staff continue to be employed. The 2008 and 2010 EU Monitoring Reports of the European Commission (2008, 2010b) have noted the EC's dissatisfaction with the Romanian government's failure to solve very many unsolved mafia killings. Romania thus risks facing EU funding withdrawal such as the ones clamped on Bulgaria in late 2008.

Thus, in the context of representative bureaucracy, there have been, and continue to be, serious nationwide problems of highly inadequate bureaucratic reform primarily in Romania.

Politicization

Civil service administrations in both Romania and Bulgaria continue to exhibit to date an absence of a line of demarcation that is supposed to separate bureaucrats from politicians. Autonomy of civil service staff from political control is effectively absent in both countries. Corruption and patronage are interrelated. There is a relationship of mutual benefit between politicians and bureaucrats that continues to haunt these countries. Therefore, detaching political pressure and influence on bureaucracy, so as to achieve greater representativeness, continues to be a significant problem for both Bulgaria and Romania.

Transparency

Romania exhibits a particular lack of transparency in the implementation of the Civil Service Reform Act, which was promulgated in 1999. This law has remained almost completely unimplemented, despite the requirement in the law that an independent agency be set up to oversee its implementation. While such an agency was established in 2000, it lacks the power of enforcement of the 1999 reform law. Moreover, political influence in the recruitment of civil servants continues to date. Arbitrariness pervades the practices of hiring and promoting new civil service staff by high-level civil servants. This problem is further exacerbated in Romania by a freeze on any new hiring due to the economic crisis.

With regard to general hiring criteria in Romania, general requirements in terms of language proficiency, nationality and qualifications are in place. Three institutions are in force, such as (1) the Contest Commission for senior civil servants, (2) the National Agency of Civil Servants for management positions, (3) and each administration, on a decentralized basis, for "executive positions" and office manager and department manager positions.

There are no centralized administrative competitive exams for recruitment purposes in place with regard to hiring criteria in Bulgaria, one must note that about an applicant. In spite of the requirement under Article 10 of the civil service law that stipulates that a competition procedure must be followed for all assignments exceeding 6 months, 80 percent of contractual hires and 35 percent of civil servants are recruited openly by the appointment.

The civil servants' union was created in 2004 to defend the rights of public sector employees, and between 25 percent and 40 percent of civil servants are unionized.

In the Romanian case, however, the administrative institutions and authorities concluded agreements with the union representatives on issues such as improving conditions of health, and safety at work. About 55 percent to 70 percent of the civil servants belong to a trade union.[2]

Remuneration

Another significant problem of the Bulgarian and Romanian bureaucracies is that they have so far failed to create a professional civil service. The administration depends, providing professional training, on existing civil servants out of existing cadres. This task of separation of new recruits from pre-existing bureaucrats is essential because attracting, retraining and developing new professional civil servants has been one of the main problems during the civil service reform in both countries. The biggest problem is that financial attractiveness of highly professional young civil servants lies mainly outside the control of the bureaucracy. It is the Romanian state's responsibility to recruit and keep young professionals. The strongest attractions for young civil service professionals are consulting offers, partly initiated by the European Union. These incentives make it especially difficult to build a representative bureaucracy in emerging democracies. The problem of wage compression vis-à-vis the private sector is rather serious, and it has become exacerbated over time, since the fall of communism. In fact, the ratio of the highest- to lowest-paid employees decreased from 4.5 in 1991 to 3.7 by 1994, almost entirely due to across-the-board cost-of-living adjustments in the public sector. The consequence was a further reduction in the incentive for talented young professionals to join the Romanian civil service, as Nunberg (1999, p. 76) points out.

INSTITUTIONAL SETTINGS FOR REPRESENTATIVE BUREAUCRACY IN BULGARIA AND ROMANIA

Turning from wage structure to the complexion of bureaucrats, both Bulgaria and Romania have yet to introduce any gender quota for the public sector. Nor indeed is there any ethnicity quota in force in either country. In fact, "the refusal of Roma persons to be included in the programs of Ministry of Labor and Social Policy for subsidized employment" (Vladimirova, 2010, p. 59) and their underrepresentation is a clear indication of discriminatory practices of representative bureaucracy in Bulgaria. This is despite the fact that numerous discussions took place, both at the national and local level government in this regard. In addition, research on employment in Eastern Europe shows that a majority of Eastern European women in the public sector have been negatively affected by the post-communist transformation due to "the rescind of former communist rights to political representation, employment, public services and different forms of social assistance" (Spehar, 2008, p. 1). There were, for example, arguments that women should be liberated from their 'forced' participation in the labor market under communism and retreat to domesticity. Those kinds of arguments were most often advocated by the extreme right-wing political parties and supported by fundamentalist wings of organized religion.

THE BULGARIAN CASE

In the Bulgarian example, equal rights and the principle of non-discrimination are embedded in the Bulgarian Constitution of 1991. However, the Constitution does not explicitly provide specific regulations on gender equality. Moreover, the National Action Plans on Employment (2002, April 2003, February 2004), that were developed and adopted by the Council of Ministers, include a section on the promotion of equal opportunities for women and men. In this respect, the National Action Plan for Employment for the last 3 years expresses the state policy, which introduces several consistent and special measures for encouraging the participation of women in the public sector. It is, however, crucial to note that most equal employment law and regulations were discussed with the EU entrance incentive, referring to the European Action Plan for Employment. Implementation of such directives has, in fact, not materialized to date.

Looking at the challenges of gender quota in the public sector, one cannot ignore the existing gender bias that is present overall in Eastern Europe. Referring to the World Values Survey Association (2000) question, "Do you agree that 'On the whole, men make better political leaders than women do?'" the answers show astonishing results, ranging from 46 percent (Slovenia) to 83 percent (Armenia). In the Bulgarian case, 61 percent and 67 percent in Romania, believe that men make better political leaders than do women. While looking at those results, one might argue that it needs stronger public support to enforce a discussion on gender quota in the public sector.

Looking at ethnicity in Bulgaria, one can observe a strong homogeneous society, with almost 84 percent "Ethnic Bulgarians". In addition, there are two main minorities, Turks (9.4 percent) and Roma (4.7 percent). The remaining 2 percent consist of 40 smaller groups, such as Russians, Armenians, Vlachs, Jews, and Crimean Tatars. With regard to religion, Bulgarians are primarily (82.6 percent) Eastern Orthodox followed by 12.2 percent Muslims and around 1 percent who ascribe to Western Christianity. The language aspects show similar patterns, with 84.5 percent speaking Bulgarian, 9.6 percent Turkish, and 4.1 percent Romany (see CIA Fact Book, 2010). Having in mind that Bulgaria is a strongly homogeneous society, the question arises as to what constitutes a representative bureaucracy? Are 16 percent of bureaucrats non-Bulgarian ethnically? The answer is clearly no. They are significantly fewer. In fact, there are less than 5 percent.[3]

Moreover, in the last two decades, Bulgaria has turned into a country that generates migration, which has a strong influence on Bulgaria's ethnic and cultural constellation. First of all, it is crucial to mention that Bulgaria's population has decreased by about 13 percent in the last 15 years. In fact, Bulgaria has had the slowest population growth of any country in the world since 1950. This issue is especially crucial for evaluating socio-demographic changes and its necessary adjustment in bureaucratic representation, which is a matter of particular significance to the notion of passive representative bureaucracy.

According to the Eurostat database (2010), Bulgaria has 83 000 employees in public administration. Moreover, in public administration (including defense and compulsory social security) work, there are 78 females to every 100 male employees (Bulgaria National Statistical Institute, 2010). Given the female:male ratio with its dominance of male employees, it is even more surprising that no effective gender quotas have been introduced to engender representativeness.

THE ROMANIAN CASE

According to the 2010 CIA Fact Book, Romania consists of 89.4 percent ethnic Romanians, with two main minorities, Hungarians (6.6 percent) and Roma (2.4 percent). With regard to religion, Romanians are primarily (86.8 percent) Christian Orthodox, followed by 7.5 percent Protestants, and 4.7 percent Roman Catholic. Language aspects shows similar patterns, with 91 percent speaking Romanian, 6.75 percent Hungarian, and 1.1 percent Romany.

Public Sector Employment

In 1995, Romania had 130 344 civil servants, and by 2000, there was a decrease of 30 percent in the total number of the civil servants. While some existing civil servants were shed, new hiring was virtually absent. In fact, until 1999, the state administration structures remained largely the same as before transition. While the size of the bureaucracy decreased in the first decade after the transition, there was significant variation in size across ministries (Michalak, 2008). Whereas employment in the Ministry of Foreign Affairs increased slightly from 1732 in 1990 to 1845 employees in 1994, the Ministry of Agriculture decreased from 1492 in 1990 to 845 employees in 1994, as noted by Nunberg (1999).

MAJOR PUSH AND PULL FACTORS FOR REPRESENTATIVE BUREAUCRACY: MIGRATION FLOW

This chapter identifies "emigration" as the main push-and-pull factor for representative bureaucracy in Bulgaria and Romania, which consequently led to the decreasing population rates. To be more specific, the key push-and-pull factors of a new social representation can be named as (1) fears and barriers to EU enlargement, and (2) the changing structure of migration.

Migration flows between Central and Eastern Europe (CEE) and the EU are characterized by the 'push-and-pull' model of comparative advantage of the EU-15 – not only economic but also political, social, and cultural factors for migration (Massey et al., 1993; Piracha and Vickerman, 2002). The OECD report (2009) shows Bulgarians to comprise 4 percent of all intra-EU migrants for the period 2004–08, which in absolute terms seems to be rather small, however, in the light of a decline of population through the last two decades, it represents a strong impact on the demographic picture.

In contrast to the strong emigration process in Bulgaria, as a ratio of a considerably smaller population than that of Romania, case-specific literature for Bulgaria confirms that a small percentage of emigrants return (Mintchev and Boshnakov, 2007). Political events that are worth mentioning are the facts that Bulgaria was included in a visa liberalization regime in 2001, and gained full EU membership in 2007.

As mentioned before, the return of skilled labor is a new observable event in recent years. According to Ilieva (2010), three categories of reasoning for the return of skilled labor to Bulgaria can be identified: (1) social factors, (2) career development, and (3) personal motivation. Ilieva (2010) shows in her study that the primary reason for return migration is family, where the skilled labor force returns primarily from Turkey, Spain, Greece and the United States. However, the economic situation in their land of emigration should not be overlooked in these cases, referring primarily to countries where the economic crisis remains a salient issue, most prominently Spain where the unemployment rate stood at 21 percent in May 2011.

Hence, the main question in this context is whether socio-demographic changes and political–attitudinal preferences are also reflected within the bureaucracy? Special reference must be made to the Turkish minority in Bulgaria (9.6 percent), as well as the strong Hungarian minority in Romania (6.6 percent). In addition, referring to the overall representation of civil society in bureaucracy, the Ministry of Foreign Affairs is a more representative case compared to all other ministries that reflects the homogeneity of the Bulgarian society in bureaucracy. In 2010, the Ministry of Foreign Affairs had a total number of employees of 1478, of which 776 were male and 702 employees were female. With regard to ethnicity, eight employees were of Turkish origin, two Armenian, two Jewish, and one of Roma origin (according to Human Resources). These data pertaining to Ministry of Foreign Affairs help provide a link between passive representative bureaucracy on the one hand, and the demographic makeup of the Bulgarian society in 2010 on the other.

In contrast to Bulgaria, Romania with a rate of -0.27 migrant(s)/1000 population in 2010, shows a strong difference compared to Bulgaria (-3.71) with regard to socio-demographic changes (see CIA Fact Book, 2010). Hence, the key issue is not the decreasing population or shift in socio-demographic changes, but the tremendous decrease of the public service sector. The main problem in Romania is that due to the main focus on decreasing the public sector, representation of society remains a secondary issue.

In summary, given negative net migration and the decreasing public sector, the issue of representative bureaucracy remains rather secondary in both Bulgaria and Romania. This observation can be supported by the fact that no quotas have been introduced. The mind set (especially during the first decade after the transition) rested primarily on decreasing the vast bureaucratic apparatus instead of "making" it more representative.[4]

Moreover, the international push for a stronger representative bureaucracy has an indirect impact on both countries. The European Union, for example, encourages both countries to achieve greater participation of minorities and to monitor the impact of specific measures devoted to increasing enrolment in public employment programs.

Lastly, a main shortcoming of the research in the area of representative bureaucracy is the lack of reliable and consistent statistical data (as required by the Freedom of Information Act). In both Bulgaria and Romania, there are some general data available but it is often not detailed enough, nor is it broken down by gender, age, or location. Hence, an attempt at deductive reasoning has been applied to this research.

CONCLUDING REMARKS

To summarize, this chapter presents an exploration into the transitional bureaucracies of Bulgaria and Romania in the overall context of representative bureaucracies. Both Bulgaria and Romania present an interesting case of how representativeness in a bureaucracy can or cannot be achieved while the country is simultaneously experiencing a political change of a very substantial nature. In fact, it is important to look at representative bureaucracies in transitional bureaucracies, because a successful transition cannot occur without representation of the public in the bureaucracy. While examining representative bureaucracy, it becomes glaringly apparent that both Bulgaria and Romania are still struggling within post-transition phenomena, such as cutting the large public sector size, diminishing politicization, establishing rule of law, and fighting corruption, among others. These issues pose additional challenges typically not faced by full-fledged democracies, which lend importance to an investigation of representativeness in bureaucracies in transition.

For instance, both Bulgaria and Romania still have a long way to go in introducing gender or ethnicity quotas in the public sector. However, with regard to representative bureaucracy, slow changes have indeed occurred over the last two decades in both countries especially in the form of demographic changes due to emigration, which can be identified as the main push-and-pull factor for representative bureaucracy.

The investigation undertaken here opens up a crucial question, to wit, does more representativeness – however construed – make for a more robust democracy? What is the ideal type that should be employed in this context? This is particularly relevant especially in a case where social trust towards the bureaucracy remains the main problem of the legitimacy of the bureaucracy itself. Hence, would a higher representativeness function as a driving force for a more democratic outcome? One might argue that both democratic performance and bureaucratic representation positively influence each other. Should this be a core value? This question is of great pertinence in the case of both Bulgaria and Romania.

Also, Sen (2009), in *The Idea of Justice*, proposes the approach of piecemeal reform, of achieving more justice instead of characterizing what would be construed as a perfectly just state, if, of course, one could agree on what that would constitute. This proposal ought to be taken seriously, since Sen's is the most authoritative work on the subject matter of achieving a superior state, in terms of a more just society. So, does a more representative bureaucracy lead to a more just society? Should greater representativeness be an end in itself? Not necessarily. In fact, it can be argued that the value of representativeness is solely of positive instrumental value insofar as it may lead to the greater good of society, which, by itself, would have positive constitutive value. The distinction between instrumental value and intrinsic, constitutive value of representativeness of a bureaucracy is not a trivial one at all, and deserves greater emphasis in investigation than it appears to have received in the literature. The contrast between Bulgaria and Romania expresses this issue sharply in the form that while the size of the Turkish minority is proportionately larger in Bulgaria than the proportion of the Hungarian minority in Romania, the operational political influence of these minorities is, in fact, not equally weighted in the two societies.

NOTES

1. In Bulgaria the proportion of minorities in total population is 16:100, but in Romania it is 11:100. However, it is crucial to notice that the total population of Bulgaria is 7 million, and that of Romania 21.9 million. Hence, the absolute number of minorities in Bulgaria is 1.12 million, and in Romania 2.4 million.
2. See EIRO (European industrial observatory online, http://www.eurofound.europa.eu/eiro/index.htm).
3. See http://www.epp.eurostat.ec.europa.eu.
4. An exception is the Hungarian minority in Romania that has a significant representation in the bureaucracy at the regional level, primarily in Transylvania (19.6 percent is proportion in population and below 5 percent in bureaucracy; see National Statistical Institute, http://www.nsi.bg).

7. Representative bureaucracy in Germany? From passive to active intercultural opening

Patrick von Maravić and Sonja M. Dudek

INTRODUCTION

One in five persons – 16 million – living in Germany today is an immigrant. Reacting to the labor shortage from the economic boom of the 1960s (*Wirtschaftswunder*), the German government invited people from Turkey, Yugoslavia, Portugal, and Spain to work in Germany. After the fall of the "iron curtain" in 1989 the majority emigrated from Turkey and the former Soviet Republic. Today, Germany is economically dependent on immigrant labor and the demographic situation is one of an aging society that lacks specialists for certain jobs.

Immigration has not always been commonly accepted but subject to fierce political debates; "multicultural" is often used derogatorily. Conservatives use the word to emphasize the alleged failings and illusions of the liberal left – the Green Party and some Social Democrats – and hold the latter responsible for today's integration problems. Although immigration is still a controversial political topic, the Citizenship Act (2000) and the Immigration Act (2005) are landmarks in a slow and incremental policy change that has lasted for more than three decades and led to more liberal immigration policies (Schönwälder, 2010).

Despite all this, Germany's civil service has seemingly remained unchanged. Is this image of a mono-ethnic, unrepresentative public service still valid for a civil service that employs more than 4 million people and delivers myriad services, including all types of functions of a fully developed welfare state? We argue that there are good reasons for redrawing the image. The composition of the public workforce has undergone considerable change, especially on local and state levels. Blue-collar jobs and the police force have led the way. Immigrants in higher-ranking planning and policy-making positions are, however, exceptions to the rule. Civil service has furthermore transitioned from a *passive* opening of the public service to non-natives for functional reasons in the 1970s to a more politicized *proactive* recruitment and personnel selection in the 1990s and since 2000 has aligned with the notion of a representative bureaucracy.

In total 2 to 4 percent (90 000–180 000) of the public service workforce is non-native (Liebig and Widmaier 2009). An exact quantitative breakdown of ethnic minorities in German public service is impossible due to strict legal principles of equality and individual data protection. The reason for such strict handling of ethnic data is a heritage of the racist public personnel policy of the Third Reich. The principles of bureaucracy as equal treatment and merit-based recruitment were "carved in stone" in the new Basic Law (*Grundgesetz* Art. 33 §2) as well as the Public Service Law (*Bundesbeamtengesetz* §8) after the end of the Nazi regime. Section 8 of the Public Service Law explicitly states that public personnel recruitment must adhere to the principles of qualification, adequacy, and merit without regard to gender, ancestry, or race. The protection of individual data enjoys a privileged status in Germany, further prohibiting the collection of ethnic personnel data.

To ground the empirical observation of a transformation of the civil service since the 1970s theoretically we briefly sketch the major political discourses on the issue of migration and show why we can talk of an "intercultural turn" (Schönwälder, 2010) in the 1990s. We then turn to classical functional theory and illustrate the main difference between *active* and *passive* intercultural opening strategies in the civil service. We sketch a more differentiated picture of the civil service in terms of its ethnic representativeness by considering the different levels of government and tasks. We end by describing briefly the situation of gender equity in Germany and point out some of the major challenges within and hindrances towards a more multicultural civil service.

FROM IMMIGRATION TO INTEGRATION POLICY SINCE THE 1970s: A BRIEF HISTORICAL OVERVIEW OF THE INTERCULTURAL TURN

In the past decade a consensus among the political elite emerged to improve integration of Germany's immigrants. The "push" toward integration found expression in 2006 by, for example, holding the first high-level roundtable with representatives of immigrant groups (National Integration Summit), issuing the first National Integration Plan (2007), the promotion of a Minister of State for Migration, Refugees, and Integration in the Chancellery under the conservative Chancellor Merkel, and offering mandatory language and political education courses for immigrants.

These examples demonstrate the notion that something has changed in the way immigrants are perceived and treated in German politics.

The new style illustrates a brief historical account of immigration policies since the 1970s. The focus of past federal governments was, after a recruitment offensive in the 1960s, to revise immigration processes. The term *Gastarbeiter* (guest worker) implied a temporary stay; no substantial integration was intended. The end of the German *Wirtschaftswunder* (economic miracle) that set in with the oil crisis of 1973 led to a recruitment ban that included financial incentives for guest workers to return to their countries of origin. The policy was guided by the aim of keeping immigration at a minimum level and counteracting the inflow of guest workers (Schönwälder, 2010, p. 153). Germany would not have a migration background[1] population of about 20 percent if the policy had been extremely successful. The high living conditions in Germany and the often unattractive economic situation in their home countries and – in the case of political refugees – the possibility of asylum caused many to stay.

The conservative Chancellor Kohl took cautious steps towards reversing the policy around 1990, inching toward accepting guest workers as permanent residents but not citizens. The attitude of the German population towards ethnic minorities after reunification in the 1990s was, however, hesitant, if not hostile. Despite the fact that the conservative–liberal government and Social Democrats introduced severe restrictions to the right of asylum in 1992, the trend towards a slow liberalization of immigration policy was not reversed.[2] The new coalition of Social Democrats and the Green Party elected in 1998 introduced a harshly debated new citizenship law that combined elements of the traditional *ius sanguini principle* with the *ius soli principle.* The main driver that triggered the policy change was the growing awareness among politicians and businesses that the German economy needed highly qualified personnel, especially in the field of IT services, which German universities could not provide in the near future.[3] Although the Conservative party gave up its "no-immigration stance" (Schönwälder, 2010, p. 153), struggles remain in acquiring German citizenship.

The incremental policy transformation since the 1970s and the intercultural turn of the 1990s illustrate the ambivalent relationship between the German majority and ethnic minority. Employment of foreigners was for many years primarily a matter of private companies granting low-skilled jobs. Civil service as employment for ethnic minorities was neither discussed nor was discussion felt necessary in most areas. Section 7.1 of the Public Service Law states that only German or EU citizens can become public servants. Additionally, legal restrictions prevented employing non-EU nationals in public bodies and certain areas such as

the Secret Service (§7.2, Public Service Law). An interesting exception is
an advance made by the minister of the interior in Berlin in 1979, who suggested having people of Turkish heritage on the police force, even without
German citizenship. He argued from an integration perspective and had
strong opposition within and outside of the police sector. He characterized
the discussion as follows: "Behind the question if a Turk can work as a
police officer lies the more general question how tolerant we are towards
minorities. This especially shows itself in this discussion. The question at
stake here is – and one should be allowed to say this in public: are black
people allowed to arrest white people?"[4]

CONCEPTUALIZING PASSIVE AND PROACTIVE MODES OF INTERCULTURAL OPENING

As we are interested in how the German Civil Service adapted its personnel systems to cope with the challenges of a multi-ethnic society and
what rationales underscored the process, we now take a closer look
at institutional changes accompanying different modes of intercultural
opening. In doing so, we may be able to identify the tipping point from
a *passive* or *reactive* opening of local personnel systems to a more *proactive* mode of recruitment in line with a representative bureaucracy. We
base our empirical analysis on a heuristic that marries elements of the Old
Institutionalism (e.g. Barnard, 1968; Selznick, 1996; Stinchcombe, 1997)
with certain traits of the sociological Neo-Institutionalism that allows us
to differentiate between the *regulatory*, *normative*, and *cultural–cognitive*
pillars of institutions (Scott, 2001; see also Campbell, 2004).

   We follow Scott in conceiving institutions as "multifaceted, durable
social structures, made up of symbolic elements, social activities, and
material resources" (Scott, 2001, p. 49). According to this understanding,
institutions have formal and informal dimensions. Important ingredients
are rules, norms, and cultural beliefs, which encompass material and
behavioral resources. Furthermore, institutions are resistant to change,
transmitted across generations, and reproduced (Scott, 1994). The *regulatory* pillar concerns processes and structures designed to constrain
and regulate behavior such as rule-setting, monitoring, and sanctioning.
The *normative* pillar emphasizes the prescriptive dimension of social life
relating to norms and values that tell us what is (not) desirable, define
goals, (e.g. tolerance towards difference or profit making), and prescribe
legitimate or appropriate means to pursue specific goals. Because action is
social insofar as actors attach meaning to behavior, the *cultural–cognitive*
pillar looks at factors that shape the meaning attributed to objects and

action. Symbols, gestures, words, and signs are therefore central elements of institutions. They are the basis of the unconscious, culturally formed, and taken-for-granted assumptions about reality. The pillars are not mutually exclusive but three overlapping elements on a continuum moving from "the conscious to the unconscious, from the legally enforced to the taken for granted" (Hoffman, 2001, p. 36). Together they form an integrated conception of institutions, and allow differentiated analysis and institutional change.

Passive and Active Mode of Opening: Traits and Explanations

Against this theoretical background, we argue that there are two dominant rationales for 'opening-up' government services: one is driven by functional requirements and operational needs of public sector organizations; the other exists in antidiscrimination legislation combined with external pressure from organized interested groups and normative-philosophical considerations of ethnic group rights. The two may often mix and overlap, but are distinct analytical categories.

A *functionality-driven* strategy, which has *reactive* and *proactive* variants, suggests that ethnic diversity largely reflects the supply and demand of desirable labor at any given time. A functional reason for recruiting personnel would pertain solely to the internal operational *needs* of the organization, which could be intercultural competencies or multi-linguality. Such needs are rationally determined by their function in the administrative production process and influenced by factors such as the labor market. A tendency towards an ethnically and culturally diverse workforce can in this case be an accidental side-effect of certain labor market necessities. From this vantage point, local government employers show no regard for the ethnic, linguistic, or cultural background of applicants, but seek purely to fill staff positions according to their operational job requirements.

A characterization of the *passive mode* along the distinction between the regulatory, normative, and *cultural–cognitive* institutional pillars shows that none is changed: the organization does not see factors such as ethnic diversity affecting its operations. Even general laws on anti-discrimination and equal treatment are rarely represented on the organizational level, which would eventually affect the regulatory pillar. If institutionalization exists at all, it is to a low degree. External actors like political parties, immigrant organizations, and commissioners for integration are not involved in recruitment decisions. A *passive* or *reactive* stance on diversity issues might in fact unintentionally lead to a sizeable influx of foreign-born employees, particularly at the lower end of the pay scale where employment is least attractive for the established middle classes that serve as the archetypical talent pool for public sector employment, and specific top-paying expert positions that often cannot be filled by the local labor market. For example, software companies use programming languages based on international standards; they are interested in employing people who can fulfill job requirements regardless of nationality.

In contrast to the passive mode, a more *proactive* strategy towards ethnic diversity in public organizations values the contributions of new entrants to organizational performance based on their cultural background, making it an inherent part of institutionalization. According to Selznick institutionalization is "to infuse with value beyond the technical requirements of the task at hand" (1957, p. 17). His main point was that such a process takes time and is influenced by factors such as the history of the organization, the character of the actors, established interest groups, and how they adapt to environmental changes. "To infuse with value" means that to become a stable element within an organization a process needs to go beyond technical and operational requirements and make sense in a way that corresponds with other organizational goals and values. This definition helps to draw the line between a functional, passive opening of public service and a proactive, intercultural opening that sees multiculturalism as a value in itself. A proactive mode eventually affects all three institutional pillars of the organization. While the underlying rationality is still entirely based on the organization's functional and operational needs, a proactive stance on diversity recognizes the value of having a multi-cultural staff to improve their performance. Its openly normative or political considerations affect the *normative* institutional pillar. Terms like 'diversity' and 'multicultural' are often in the organization's mission statement or management explicitly defines diversity as an organizational goal.

The *regulatory* pillar is affected when quotas, positive measures, or other requirements aim to increase immigrant employment. Stating intercultural skills as a job requirement can be a sign that an organization actively promotes diversity;[5] installing a diversity manager with an annual budget, staff, and formal authority places the institutional adaptations beyond the creation of an image. The proactive mode eventually affects the *cultural–cognitive* pillar by having employees participate in intercultural communication seminars, a management that promotes diversity in its own ranks, and the maintenance of concepts or ideologies of multiculturalism. The latter then forms the ideological superstructure for an organization that affects the way terms are used. To a certain extent this politicizes the topic and starts to drift away from purely functional criteria. Recent experience has shown a politicization of the entire issue and therefore a stronger role for external actors pressing towards an open civil service. Factors in this category are not necessarily inherent to the functioning of the organization, but externally driven by coalitions of representatives of minority groups, political parties, non-governmental organizations, or so-called "integration commissioners." They have a primarily political dimension as they infuse non-managerial norms, values, and interests into the decision-making process. Political and normative considerations find a common focal point when the argument in favor of representative bureaucracies follows the discourse of the "politics of identity" or "politics of recognition" debate (Taylor and Gutman, 1994; Bauböck, 2004; Parekh, 2006; Kymlicka, 2009). In such a (philosophical) line of thought, the inclusion of cultural minorities is not contingent on functional necessities or politically opportunistic behavior but rather a manifestation of minority rights per se. From this flows a politically powerful symbolic meaning attached to pressures to open public sector organizations because working for "government" can be interpreted as a strong signal of a successful integration of minority groups into statehood and society majority.[6]

A MULTICULTURAL TURN? FROM PASSIVE TO ACTIVE OPENING OF THE GERMAN CIVIL SERVICE

How is all of this linked to developments in the German public service? We will try to give a balanced answer by taking into account the different layers of the federal German polity and different functional areas. The majority of persons with an immigrant background in German public service are employed in areas of low discretion and policy relevance, such as garbage collection, street cleaning, and elderly care. These are typical functions of municipalities, which are responsible for policy implementation with the State. The federal level, with its small personnel body, is mainly responsible for policy-making; some exceptions are unemployment, the military and federal police service.

For more than three decades employing minorities has been primarily functional and linked to German socio-demographic development, a classic economic outcome of demand and supply of public sector personnel. The management of an organization addresses "generic needs" (Selznick, 1948, p. 29) to secure the fulfillment of organizational functions and eventual organizational survival. In most cases, we would argue, decisions have long been blind to the cultural background of a potential employee as they have not been relevant to the function. Whether the street cleaner is German or Turkish is irrelevant.

The wider socioeconomic development during the last 50 years has strongly affected this development. During that time most Germans have been able to increase their personal wealth, accompanied by higher levels of technical or academic education. Increasing salaries and the growingly unattractive blue-collar jobs in the public sector led to a situation in which municipalities increasingly depended on immigrant employment. At the same time, minorities were highly attracted to the job security and relatively high income. Nor should the symbolic attractiveness of working for "the State" be underestimated for those coming from Turkey or the Maghreb countries. The increasingly multicultural workforce in lower levels of the public service during the past three to four decades has largely been unnoticed by the public, administrative specialists, and policy-makers. This is typical for the passive mode of intercultural opening, which is not accompanied by considerable institutional change along our three pillars. Apart from some general anti-discrimination laws, the *regulatory* pillar has not adapted, nor has the *normative* pillar – core normative values of an organization – been actively affected. The *cultural–cognitive* dimension has not been subject to active policy change although we can assume that an organization with a considerable immigrant population experiences some cultural change. We cannot, however, see a general trend towards active change such as diversity management workshops or courses.

The last decade has, however, shown a more proactive intercultural opening of the public service, especially for police services (e.g. Dudek, 2009). Many State police forces have begun to recruit minorities actively. The city-states of Hamburg and Berlin, which embrace the typical functions of a municipality-state, have been forerunners in doing so. Bavaria, Hessen, Northrhine-Westfalia have started to actively recruit personnel with immigrant background and "intercultural skills." According to Hessen's Ministry of the Interior of the State, its workforce (including police officers) consists of roughly 152000 persons, 3081 (2 percent) of which are non-native (Hessen's foreign population is 12 percent) (Hessischer Landtag, 2007). Berlin presents its new multicultural public workforce as a kind of image campaign, with real consequences at least in the area of vocational training. Berlin explicitly states since its *Verwaltungsreform-Grundsätze-Gesetz* (Principles of Administrative Reform Law) in December 2005 and the aforementioned law on integration and participation that "intercultural competencies" must be considered when hiring and promoting. One institution that has explicitly tried to attract young migrants is the police force. The Police Authority of Berlin has introduced requirements regarding German language skills to enter the Police service. Its vocational administrative program minority-trainees increased from 1.2 percent (2003) to 8.6 percent (2006) and 13.2 percent (2007) (Ludwig and Vogel, 2005/06; BQN, 2007).

In contrast to countries such as Switzerland or Austria, the recruitment of persons of foreign origin to the police force has not led to a harsh political debate about the undermining influence of foreigners in the field of security. Rather the opposite seems to be the case as politicians increasingly campaign for a more proactive stance towards immigrants in public service. The former Mayor of Hamburg, Ole von Beust, set 20 percent as a goal for multicultural staff in the senate of Hamburg (Hamburg-Personalamt, 2009). In an interview with the *Rheinische Post* in January 2010, the Federal State Minister of Integration, Maria Böhmer, was quoted as demanding an increase of multicultural public service personnel in the fields of police, firefighting, and schools and even preferring a quota for immigrants. Immigration organizations immediately applauded the idea but not all politicians, who claimed that an arbitrary quota system would not lead to a better public service. One argument was that an insufficient number of young immigrants would pass the entrance test. Although this argument exaggerates the problem of educational backwardness – especially for young male immigrants – it points towards a severe problem of the German educational system, which still seems unable to cope with the demands of a multicultural education system. Germany is still far from introducing such a quota and the federal government urged denial of such a strategy. A discussion on the role and responsibility of the public service in a growingly multicultural society will, however, be difficult to ignore.

Different parties in the Länder parliaments have nourished the discussion by requesting information about immigrants in public service (e.g. Hendricks, 2008). Two recent parliamentary interpellations by the Linke and the FDP urged the Ministry of the Interior to respond to similar requests (Stadler, 2007). The Ministry's answer was strictly "Weberian" by referring to the merit principle in recruiting and to non-existent data (Federal Government, 2007). Despite such a formalistic denial, interest seems to have grown. Several federal agencies such as the Federal Agencies of Migration and Refugees have begun inquiries about the ethnic background of their employees.[7] In cooperation with the Federal Census Bureau the Ministry of Interior issued a survey from November 2008 to January 2009 asking all trainees of all agencies of the Federal Ministry of the Interior (e.g. the Federal Police) to report (voluntarily) on their ethnic background.[8] Due to low response rate (26.3 percent) the Ministry did not publish the results.

The negative demographic development of the German population in the next 30 to 40 years, the large number of baby-boomer retirees who entered the civil service in the 1970s, and increasing competition between the private and public sectors for the best university graduates will all lead to a decreased recruitment basis for civil service and emphasizes the need to increase the attractiveness to non-traditional personnel. This argument especially has led the OECD to call German politicians to care more about the specific demands of children, prepare them for a potential career in the public service, and set a symbolic signal by recruiting more non-natives (Liebig and Widmaier, 2009).

With regard to the three institutional pillars described at the outset, we can observe a timid institutional change towards a more pro-active opening of public service, but hardly on all state levels and in all functional areas.

GENDER EQUITY IN THE CIVIL SERVICE: A BRIEF OVERVIEW

Since the mid-1990s, there have been more women than men in the civil service – 50 percent in 1998, 52 percent in 2006, and 54 percent in 2010 (Statistisches Bundesamt, 2007, p. 1084; 2011, p. 116). This does not mean that there is an equal distribution along all hierarchical levels and functions of the civil service. We find a strong representation of women in the lower and middle ranks of the civil service and in the areas of social security (73 percent), health (63 percent), and education (62 percent) in 2006. Women are less represented in the area of defense (17 percent) and security (36 percent; Statistisches Bundesamt, 2007, pp. 1084–1085). Although the proportion of women in higher positions of the civil service, compared to their male colleagues, is lower one can observe an increase during the last 10 years in certain areas: especially in the area of higher education and justice, the proportion of women has significantly increased. The proportion of female professors has increased from 10 percent in 2000 to 18 percent in 2010 and the proportion of female judges or state attorneys has risen from 30 percent to 41 percent in the same period (Statistisches Bundesamt, 2011, p. 1116). Researchers observed that it still makes a difference whether a woman works in East or West Germany. Women working in the East have a higher chance of getting into higher positions of the civil service than women in West Germany (Institut für Arbeitsmarkt und Berufsforschung (IAB), 2011, p. 2). While 46 percent of all higher positions in the East German civil service were filled with women in 2007, the proportion of women in West Germany is significantly lower (29 percent). The researchers see a number of factors that explain this difference: combining work and family is much more accepted in East Germany due to the legacy of the full employment policy in the Germany Democratic Republic. Second, a better infrastructure of daycare institutions allows women to reenter their job earlier than West German families, and third, women in East Germany are younger when they have their first child. Compared to the situation of young migrants in Germany, the level of formal qualification is equally high in East and West Germany and does not serve as an explanation for the observed differences. Despite the trend towards a higher proportion of women in the civil service, pushed by the creation of new positions in childcare institutions and public schools, one should be quick to point out that this trend has been slowed down by privatization and cut-back policies on all levels of government in the 1990s and 2000s. Overall, the number of positions in the German civil service went down from 6.7 million in 1991 to 4.5 million in 2010. These reductions have taken place in areas where the proportion of women is traditionally high.

CONCLUSION

The diverse set of actors, discussions, and strategies leads us to argue that we are far from a passive representation of ethnic minorities, but the current demographic development, international standards, anti-discrimination laws, ideas of multiculturalism and diversity management, and functional pressure will eventually lead to a more multicultural public service along with the problems accompanying such a process. The transition will probably be especially strong in municipalities and state governments where public services have direct client contact and in which intercultural competencies are needed. This is particularly the case in security forces where intercultural opening seems fully underway. Other areas, such as planning, policy-making, and more high-ranking positions now depend too much on higher educational degrees, especially in law, and it is doubtful that we will see a considerable increase of immigrant personnel in such areas in the near future. The German public service is nonetheless in the process of change, which will, despite our thought and research, certainly bear some surprises.

NOTES

1. "Migration background" is commonly used as a concept in German discourse and refers to the origin of the parents of a person living in Germany. A person is considered to have a migration background when at least one parent is of non-German origin (see Statistisches Bundesamt, 2005).
2. Restricting the asylum law despite the public's attitude underlines the fact that functional reasons rather than a human rights perspective on immigration dominated the discussion.

3. The former Chancellor Schröder even made trips to India to attract specialists to Germany, see e.g. http://www.spiegel.de/wirtschaft/0,1518,165375,00.html, accessed on September 23, 2011.
4. Frankfurter Rundschau, September 6,1979.
5. In the case of public administration, this might also be due to laws. Berlin, for example, passed a law on Integration and Participation in 2010, which makes training on intercultural skills mandatory for certain positions and promotion.
6. As with many political and administrative power-sharing arrangements, such as ethno-federalist systems or consociational democracies, including cultural minorities is believed to increase system trust and legitimacy of politico-administrative institutions. From a different angle, of course, the interest of minority groups to be represented in official positions can also be in seen in light of rent-seeking (Krueger, 1974) or as a struggle for collective goods provided by government and being able to influence, change, or get them (Wimmer, 1997).
7. Interview, May 25, 2008.
8. Personal conversation with Ministry of the Interior, June 17, 2008, and April 4, 2011.

8. Representative bureaucracy in Italy

Giliberto Capano and Nadia Carboni

INTRODUCTION

In 1944, J. Donald Kingsley coined the term "representative bureaucracy" in a study of British civil servants (Kingsley, 1944). Observing gender and class distinctions within the British civil service, he noted that as British society became increasingly middle class, the composition of its civil service could also reflect this middle-class shift. Kingsley specifically argued that "representational participation" should lead to "functional effectiveness." His observations encouraged the launching of a new field of inquiry – representative bureaucracy.

The concept of "representative bureaucracy" as such implies a civil service in which each and every economic class, caste, region, and religion to be found in a given country is represented in exact proportion to its numbers among the population.

With regard to bureaucracy, the representative argument has gradually embraced various different perspectives, such as:

1. Equal chances: different groups in a population need to be offered equal opportunities to be recruited to administrative posts;
2. Political legitimacy: if different groups within a population are represented on administrative bodies, then they will identify with public actions;
3. Responsiveness/accountability: if the civil service is composed in a representative manner, it will respond to the diversity of political values within society.

Hence, bureaucracies are representative when they reflect the structure of the population in terms of the demographic, ethnic, and gender composition of that population, together with the opinions and interests of its members.

In this chapter we are going to consider the question of demographic representation, that is, gender, education, social class, and region of origin, in the Italian case. Of the representative-related dimensions, religion has not played any significant role (due to the dominance of the Catholic Church in Italy), while gender has been partially dealt with (although in an unconscious way), and ethnicity was until recently of very limited importance, but will become extremely important in the very near future.

Italian bureaucracy, especially at the senior level, emerges as very unrepresentative. We argue that this can be traced back to the original model of Italian public administration, the main features of which have substantially contributed towards the unrepresentative nature of Italian bureaucracy. This genetic imprinting has strongly influenced the adaptation of Italian bureaucracies to external changes (democratization, modernization, and gender equalization).

The material we present here, in chronological order, is descriptive since there are very few quantitative figures available concerning the main aspects of representative bureaucracy. There is no established research tradition in the field of representative bureaucracy among Italian scholars. Most of the available information on representative-related factors is almost exclusively confined to senior civil servants at the central level; officials working at local and regional government level have been almost totally neglected.[1] This lack of significant data is, in fact, a clear sign of the limited importance afforded to the question of representative bureaucracy by both social scientists themselves and the general public.

Thus, we will use the only available data, which are drawn from the annual national statistics produced by the Italian National Institute of Statistics (ISTAT), from the annual statistical handbook on public employment published by the Treasury Directorate General (DT) and General Accounts (the "RGS") department, from the database of research carried out in 2002 by the Cattaneo Institute,[2] and from previously published studies by the present authors.

THE ORIGINAL MODEL OF ITALIAN BUREAUCRACY

In this section we are going to examine the original model of public administration in Italy dating from the end of the nineteenth century. We are going to trace it back to its historical origins by outlining the main features of its structure, organizational ethos and personnel.

Structure

The organizational structure of Italy's public administration is rooted in the reform implemented by the statesman Camillo Benso Cavour, in the Kingdom of Piedmont in 1853. The administration, conceived of as a machine, was entrusted with the execution of those directives issued by political decision-makers; the organizational structure was therefore strongly hierarchical and centralized, and was characterized by a notice-able Napoleonic imprinting, filtered by the Belgian experience. Cavour aimed to incorporate the majority of administrative activities, previously carried out by a variety of organizations, into one homogeneous organizational model based on a system of ministries, which in turn were to be subdivided into *direzioni generali*, that is, divisions and departments. This format was extended to the rest of the country after the creation of a unified Italian state in 1860.

As far as the relationship between the center and the periphery of the administrative system was concerned, the Italian State has traditionally been highly centralized. While the post-war Republican Constitution gave considerable importance to local governments,[3] and created a new political level represented by regional government, in practice, however, local authorities were closely controlled by a series of legal and financial instruments until the beginning of the 1990s; Italy's regions, on the other hand (with the exception of a few special cases[4] with strong linguistic minorities and/or independent movements), had limited powers before 1970. Numerous contradictions characterized the nature of power, functions, competencies, and resources at different levels of government (Lewanski, 1997). While sub-national governments were granted legislative powers in important areas provided for by the Constitution, the discrepancies between taxing and spending powers tended to limit considerably regional autonomy and accountability. It was not until the 1990s that the roadmap of decentralization began to be effectively implemented. Regional and local governments (thanks also to the 2001 constitutional reform) have then been provided with new instruments of governance, and strong institutional partnerships (both horizontal and vertical), social partnerships and updated administrative models based on the principles of New Public Management (NPM), have emerged.

Personnel and Organizational Culture

The number of civil servants has grown considerably since the creation of a unified Italy, both in absolute terms and in relation to the population. When the country was unified in 1860, there was 1 public employee for every 145 inhabitants (Lewanski, 1997); now there is 1 for every 18 inhabitants (Ragioneria Generale dello Stato (RGS), 2009). The growth in their numbers, however, has been linear: there have been phases of rapid expansion (1910–20, and in the 1930s during the fascist regime), and others of limited increases (Capano, 2006).

The greatest increases occurred during the twentieth century; since 1900 the population of Italy has doubled, whereas the number of public employees has increased 30-fold (Sepe, 1995, pp. 292–293). Unlike in other European nations, "administrative revolution in government" (Melis, 1996, pp. 12 and 181) - i.e. its increase in terms of functions, organizational dimensions, and personnel – did not coincide with the creation of a unified national state, as the result of a policy of nation building; rather, it took place slowly, from the 1930s onwards, as the State gradually took responsibility for welfare, infrastructure, and productive activities (Cassese, 1980; Capano, 2006). In fact, during the 1930s and '40s, numbers grew considerably (527000 in 1930, 722000 in 1937, 1 140000 in 1943) as the regime attributed new functions to the State, and thus to the administration, especially in the welfare and economic fields (Melis, 1996, p. 330).

In the war's aftermath, numbers rose once again (in 1946 there were 1 054000 civil servants, while 20 years later their number had risen to 1 581000); in the face of the economic crisis, Italy's public administration acted as a kind of "social shock-absorber," offering jobs in order to integrate various different groups, especially the southern middle classes who had not benefited from the country's economic development (Melis, 1996, p. 535). As a consequence, Italy's governing parties have often used civil service posts in a clientelistic manner, that is, as goods to be assigned in exchange for political support.

Numbers continued to grow until the late 1980s, when consistent efforts were made to curb the extension of the public sector, with a wave of red-tape cuts as part of the administrative reform process.

The main features of the personnel and organizational culture within the public sector definitely emerged at the beginning of the twentieth century. Two key processes helped shape Italian bureaucracy (Capano, 2006):

1. The process of "giuridicizzazione": the almost total dominance of administrative law in molding bureaucratic action.
2. The process of "meridionalizzazione": the "southernization" of jobs (above all in central administrative bodies) and of the organizational culture pervading the public sector.

Specifically, 1904 saw the establishment of a degree in law as the principal job requirement for senior civil service posts (Melis, 1996). This meant that the Italian civil service became the "monopoly of jurists," whereas technical capabilities were deemed of marginal importance. This process had two main consequences: (1) it favored a legally oriented bureaucracy, whose approach and style of action were based on the principle of legality, that is, the conformity to law, rather than on the concepts of efficiency and performance; (2) it led to a drain of technical experts, who moved on to the private sector, thus isolating Italy's bureaucracy from the rest of society.

Moreover, civil service employees were predominantly male and recruited from the South, particularly in the ministries and within the education system (Aberbach et al., 1981; Cassese, 1999). As far as *gender* is concerned, women started to enter the public sector en masse after World War I, although they were confined to the lower ranks and had to make do with the repetitive carrying out of orders from their male superiors (Melis, 1996, p. 267). After World War I associations of public employees and war veterans mounted a strong campaign against women working in general, arguing that they should return to their homes and take care of their families (Melis, 1996, p. 290). Fascism, with its male-oriented ideology that saw women as nurturing children for the good of the regime, cut the number of women working in the public sector. After World War II, there was a steady increase in female numbers among Italy's civil servants and public service employees: 26 percent of public employees (in central and local government) were women in 1969, 33 percent in 1980, 51.4 percent in 1985, and 49.9 percent in 1991 (Presidenza del Consiglio dei Ministri, 2003). However, women generally occupied middle- or lower-level positions: out of a total of 6660 managers in 1989, only 9.7 percent were women (Pipan, 1992, p. 130).

If we look at the geographical origins of Italy's public employees, it is very clear that from the beginning of the twentieth century onwards there was a gradual increase in the percentage of employees from the South of Italy within the public sector (Cassese, 1999). When the then Kingdom of Piedmont succeeded in unifying Italy in 1860, the new State's administration was mainly in the hands of personnel from the previous Piedmont administration (Melis, 1996, pp. 37–41; Sepe, 1995, p. 307). Their common roots helped maintain internal cohesion of civil servants during the nation-building phase. By the beginning of the twentieth century, however, recruitment drives shifted towards Italy's southern regions; the process began at the lower levels, and gradually rose up the hierarchical ladder (Sepe, 1995, p. 307). By 1930 the process of "meridionalizzazione" (the occupancy of posts by southern Italian workers) was well advanced, and it became even more so during the 1950s and '60s,[5] especially at national state level, whereas it was much less evident at the level of the country's local authorities. Moreover, since southerners were often hired for positions in the north, and approximately one fourth of State civil servants working in the north were originally from southern Italy (Cerase,

1994, p. 34), Italian bureaucracy became increasingly unrepresentative in territorial terms:

> While people from the north have been involved in the conquest of the economy and the market, those from the south have dedicated themselves to the conquest of the State. This has produced the paradox of a senior civil service that administers the nation, but which is not national. (Cassese, 1999, p. 56)

The underlying reason for this historical phenomenon is rather simple: the lack of alternative jobs in Italy's southern regions, which had not benefited from industrialization and economic growth like the north (Lewanski, 1997). Even though salaries were generally lower than in the private sector, a position in the civil service was often perceived as an opportunity of social betterment. Employment in the public sector was used, more or less "knowingly," as a means by which to contain restlessness and win over the consensus of the educated middle classes from Italy's south, who had been excluded from the benefits of economic growth, which was substantially concentrated in the North (Melis, 1996, p. 185), by offering them a form of "compensation" for their plight (Cassese, 1984, p. 96).

The "meridionalizzazione" of the public administration has had a number of significant consequences: First, it has affected the prevailing belief among public sector workers, whereby job and career security is held at a premium compared with other possible values (responsibility, high earnings, power, professional satisfaction, service to the public, etc.), whereas a modern, results-based, explicitly productive culture is absent. This situation contributes to determining low levels of professional motivation among civil servants, since they very often enter the civil service due to the lack of alternatives, rather than as a result of any deliberate career choice.

Furthermore, the difference in social–cultural background and cultural values in general created a significant gap between the private and public sectors, and led to a reduction in the social and cultural representativeness of bureaucrats in general – and in particular of senior civil servants – within the nation as a whole (Guarnieri, 1988). In this respect, the rise and success of the Northern League (Lega Nord),[6] a political party that brought questions of national unity and identity to the fore of Italian politics during the 1990s, can be seen as an expression of the dissatisfaction of the productive strata of northern Italians with the inefficiency of the country's public administration. Civil servants, by and large coming from the less developed southern regions, have permeated the administration with a pre-industrial culture that is unrepresentative of the more advanced areas and sectors of Italian society (Lewanski, 1997).

In conclusion, this historical overview of Italian bureaucracy does not paint a picture of a genuinely representative body. The civil service, especially at the senior level, has been characterized by the marked underrepresentation of women, and by the substantial presence of middle-class law graduates. For a long time, personnel were recruited mainly from Italy's south. The prevailing organizational culture within the public administration has developed a highly formalistic-juridical character, with scarce concern for results and problem solving. Religion and ethnicity[7] have been not an issue at all.

Hence, the original model of Italian bureaucracy reveals the following:

1. The civil service is not a homogeneous entity, and especially at the senior levels, reflects the division of the country into north and south, with the country represented in an asymmetric manner.
2. Senior civil servants mainly come from the south, and thus the service itself tends to reflect certain intrinsic characteristics of southern Italy: coming from an area characterized by high levels of unemployment, job security is considered much more important than efficiency or service, and thus the prevailing mentality is anything but a managerial one.
3. Bureaucracy suffers from a lack of legitimacy in the eyes of many citizens, due in particular to its perceived ineffectiveness, which in Northern Italy is very often seen as the result of the overrepresentation of Southern Italy (this argument is partially false, since the majority of those employed in local administration are from the local area in question; however, this factor has undoubtedly been of some political importance).

Nevertheless, the systemic crisis of the 1990s ensuing from the *Tangentopoli* scandal – which exposed the deep corruption within the political–administrative system and confirmed the majority of Italians' negative views of Italy's public administration – coupled with the reform process which, supported by international institutions, aimed to cut public expenditure and increase the effectiveness of the public sector, led to mounting pressure for substantive change. As a result, several attempts were made to reform the administration in general, and the civil service in particular.

Administrative Reforms

Italy's bureaucracy has been considerably affected by the reforms that have been implemented from the early 1990s onwards. Formally speaking, the reform introduced in 1999 not only set up separate administrative agencies for the supply of services, but also reorganized Italy's ministries by replacing the old directorates general with larger "departments" organized on a product basis (Gualmini, 2007). However, the subordination of the agencies to the ministries, and the maintenance of directorates general in certain ministries, means that the degree of bureaucratic decentralization has been much weaker than in other western democracies.

As far as employment policy is concerned, the Italian government has tried to dismantle the existing system of public law regulation. The 1993 reform reviewed the powers of senior officials, while senior civil servants were given both greater autonomy over expenditure, and increased responsibility for the technical and administrative implementation of policy (Carboni, 2010a). In the field of human resource management, a number of major innovations were made which marked a significant break with the past. First, the special public law regime for civil service employment was replaced by collective bargaining. Civil servants' employment conditions and wages were now regulated on the basis of centralized collective bargaining with the trade unions. Decentralized and individual forms of bargaining, designed to link salaries with productivity/performance were part of the reform. Special assessment bodies were set up to evaluate performance. Openness to external recruitment[8] was actively promoted, as was mobility both within the public sector and between the private and public sectors. The procedural dimension was the one most significantly affected by change; from the latter half of the 1990s onwards, managerial techniques have been incorporated into government documents and programs concerned with improvements to service efficiency and customer satisfaction (Gualmini, 2007).

Last, the current administrative reform being introduced by the Minister of Public Administration, Renato Brunetta, focuses mainly on the redefinition of senior civil servants' roles by increasing the autonomy and power of senior bureaucrats in human resources management and by introducing measures designed to promote management skills and professional expertise (Carboni, 2010b). Italian law no. 15/2009 specifically emphasized the importance of meritocracy by focusing on individual and collective performance and on the accountability of public officials. It has been gradually introducing the principle of transparency into the country's public administration, with the evaluation of both administrative structures and individual civil servants, by a new central, independent evaluation agency (Drumaux, 2009).

However, the effectiveness of administrative reform in Italy has been somewhat discontinuous. While a more managerial approach has been adopted wholesale within local and central bureaucracies, certain features of Weberian bureaucracy continue to pervade the nation's public administration (Gualmini, 2007). Such features include: a limited degree of bureaucratic cohesion among the administrative class; a lack of mobility between public and private sectors; the predominance of a legalistic bureaucratic culture; and the largely unrepresentative nature of the senior ministerial class, as we shall see in the following section.

REPRESENTATIVE BUREAUCRACY IN ITALY

A comparative study conducted by Aberbach et al. (1981) regarding the attitudes, values and patterns of behavior of governmental élites in western democracies, shows that Italy's senior executives are predominantly male, recruited from the south, middle class and of a certain age. A previous study by Aberbach et al. during the 1970s declared that the Italian administrative élites were "distinctively unrepresentative." However, such characteristics, which prevailed until the 1980s, have partly changed since then according to recent studies of Italy's senior civil service (Capano and Vassallo, 2003; Carboni 2008, 2010a, 2010b).

We are now going to look at the distribution of public employment by gender, education, social background and geographic origin. We have not taken religion or ethnicity into account as they are not subject to debate in the Italian case.

Gender

At the end of 2008, as Table 8.1 shows, Italy had about 3.6 million public sector employees – slightly down from the 2003 figure (−1.1 percent) – which represents almost 15 percent of all employees registered in Italy that same year (Zamaro et al., 2009). The percentage has gradually fallen with the social security and insurance sectors (−11.5 percent) and within municipalities (−7.4 percent), whereas in regional and local governments, the number of employees has increased by 21 percent and 13 percent, respectively (that is, by approximately 50 000).

One interesting aspect of change within the social system, and thus with the public sector itself, has been the increasing participation of women (see Tables 8.1 and 8.2). Despite the fall in the total number of civil servants, the number of women employed in Italy's public administration reached 2 million in 2008, an increase of 5 percent on the equivalent figure for 2003, that is, 100 000 more female public sector employees (see Table 8.2). Percentage increases have been particularly marked in regional government (+43.7 percent), local government (+22.6 percent) and provincial

Table 8.1   *Distribution of public employees by level of government*
            (2003–08)

	2003 (% of women)	2005 (% of women)	2008 (% of women)	2008/2003
Ministries	1 940 643 (50.35)	1 922 669 (51.76)	1 891 157 (53.36)	−2.6
Other central administrations	108 652 (44.38)	111 260 (44.60)	108 152 (47.46)	−0.5
Regions	78 367 (49.30)	77 374 (50.97)	94 581 (58.71)	20.7
Provinces	61 070 (40.01)	63 018 (41.12)	62 929 (43.05)	3.0
Municipalities	513 499 (48.61)	503 972 (49.82)	475 427 (51.52)	−7.4
Health organizations/ services	703 964 (60.69)	712 089 (61.69)	718 845 (63.43)	2.1
Other local administrations	174 012 (44.86)	184 256 (45.71)	197 371 (48.49)	13.4
Social security and insurance bodies	56 498 (53.20)	55 468 (54.25)	49 987 (55.71)	−11.5
Total	3 636 705 (51.51)	3 630 106 (52.75)	3 598 450 (54.67)	−1.1

Source: DT and RGS (2010)

government (+10.9 percent). It should be pointed out that the percentage of women employed in the public sector (55 percent) is slightly higher than the percentage of women within the Italian population as a whole (52 percent).

Gender has become an issue in recent years, and significant changes have been made in order to try and create equal career opportunities for both men and women (Presidenza del Consiglio dei Ministri, 2003).

In the senior ranks of the public administration women now account for some 306 000, thus constituting a growing population (see Table 8.3). Between 2003 and the end of 2008, their numbers grew by 7.6 percent (almost 22,000 jobs). The largest increases were seen in the ministries (+8.8 percent) and local institutions (+14.0 percent). Conversely, the number of senior executives in regional and municipal government, and in social care institutions, fell during that same period (−20.5 percent, −6.1 percent and −10.2 percent, respectively).

The number of women employed in managerial posts has risen by

Table 8.2   Distribution of women by level of government (2003–08)

	2003	2005	2008	2008/2003 (%)
Ministries	977 228	995 262	1 009 137	3.3
Other central administrations	48 229	49 626	51 329	6.4
Regions	38 640	39 441	55 537	43.7
Provinces	24 436	25 919	27 094	10.9
Municipalities	249 631	251 082	244 959	−1.9
Health organizations/services	427 251	439 320	455 988	6.7
Other local administrations	78 066	84 239	95 710	22.6
Social security and insurance bodies	30 057	30 095	27 852	−7.3
Total	1 873 538	1 914 984	1 967 605	5.0

Source: DT and RGS (2010)

Table 8.3   Number of top executives by level of government (2003–08)

	2003 (% of women)	2005 (% of women)	2008 (% of women)	2008/2003 (%)
Ministries	45 755 (21.38)	46 368 (22.14)	49 775 (25.71)	8.8
Other central administrations	13 211 (33.97)	13 977 (35.16)	14 163 (39.99)	7.2
Regions	4480 (25.29)	4111 (28.07)	3560 (33.42)	−20.5
Provinces	1844 (24.07)	1912 (25.10)	1865 (28.41)	1.1
Municipalities	6575 (27.77)	6652 (29.17)	6172 (31.05)	−6.1
Health organizations/ services	138 376 (35.01)	142 045 (36.57)	146 489 (39.85)	5.9
Other local administrations	72 540 (32.48)	80 619 (33.81)	82 723 (35.77)	14.0
Social security and insurance bodies	2246 (31.47)	2274 (33.28)	2017 (37.33)	−10.2
Total	285 027 (31.71)	297 958 (33.13)	306 764 (36.12)	7.6

Source: DT and RGS (2010)

Table 8.4   Women at the top, by level of government (2003–08)

	2003	2005	2008	2008/2003 (%)
Ministries	9783	10268	12798	30.8
Other central administrations	4488	4915	5664	26.2
Regions	1133	1154	1190	5.0
Provinces	444	480	530	19.4
Municipalities	1826	1941	1917	5.0
Health organizations/services	48450	51957	58383	20.5
Other local administrations	23565	27258	29592	25.6
Social Security and insurance bodies	707	757	753	6.5
Total	90396	98730	110826	22.6

Source: DT and RGS (2010)

about 20000 (Table 8.4), representing a remarkable rise of 22.6 percent in 5 years. This means that of every 17 new posts created, 16 went to women and only 1 to men. However, the figures show that women are still under-represented at senior administrative levels compared to their overall share of the employed population. In fact, only one third of senior civil servants are women, while more than a half of all public sector jobs are held by women.

Education

Figures for the distribution of senior executives according to education (Figure 8.1) show that:

- The percentage of senior government officials with an academic background has increased considerably in recent years: almost two-thirds of all managerial staff now have a university degree.
- A significant number of managers now have postgraduate qualifications (around one-third), and their numbers are rising (up from 30.9 percent in 2003, to 32.8 percent by 2008).

As far as concerns the type of higher education of senior civil servants (Figure 8.2), law degrees still prevail, especially within Italy's central administration. However, the percentage of people with different educational backgrounds has significantly increased: almost 50 percent of top executives employed by regional or municipal government now possess a technical or scientific degree (Institute Cattaneo, 2002).

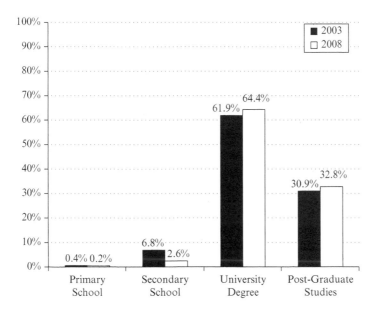

Source: Zamaro et al. (2009)

Figure 8.1   Level of education of top executives in percentages (2003–08)

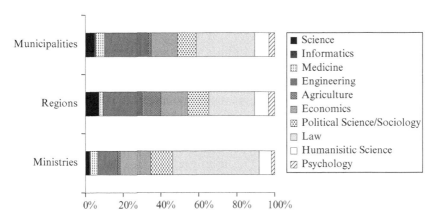

Source: Author computations

Figure 8.2   Educational background by level of government

Table 8.5 Social origin of top executives by level of government

	Ministries	Regions	Municipalities
Working class	19.3%	29.4%	25.5%
Middle class	69.5%	62.3%	62%
Upper class	11.2%	8.3%	12.5%
Total	100%	100%	100%

Source: Author computations based on Institute Cattaneo data (2002)

SOCIAL AND DEMOGRAPHIC ORIGINS

With regard to civil servants' social background, Table 8.5 confirms the middle-class nature of Italy's bureaucratic élite. Senior bureaucrats at all levels of government are prevalently from the middle-classes.

According to the last population census conducted in 2001, 51 percent of those employed in the public sector were born in the south of Italy, where only 36 percent of the total population live in the south; this compares with the 26 percent from Northern Italy (which, on the other hand, accounts for some 54.4 percent of the total population), and with 23 percent from Central Italy (19.6 percent of the total population). This imbalance is even more marked in the case of senior executives: 65.7 percent are from the south, compared with just 10.3 percent from Central Italy and 13.7 percent from the north (Carboni, 2008).

This geographical bias within Italy's bureaucracy is reflected in the composition of those public bodies located in the country's southern regions, where no less than 75 percent of public employees were born in the same region in which they work (91.5 percent in Campania, 91.3 percent in Sicily, 89.2 percent in Puglia, and 87.3 percent in Sardinia). Things are somewhat different in the northern regions, such as Lombardy, Piedmont, and Friuli, where the percentage of locally born civil servants stands at 57.4 percent, 58.5 percent and 59.3 percent respectively (Istat, 2001).

There is a clear "migration" of civil servants from the south to the center-north, whereas the south is the only part of the country with a negative balance between the percentage of public employees born there and those currently living there. However, it must be said that the greater part of this difference is represented by the migration of schoolteachers from south to north.

These figures are confirmed by the demographic origins of senior executives employed at different levels of government (Figure 8.2). While the predominance (79.1 percent) of Southern Italians in the ministries can be largely explained by the location of those ministries in Rome, which is very

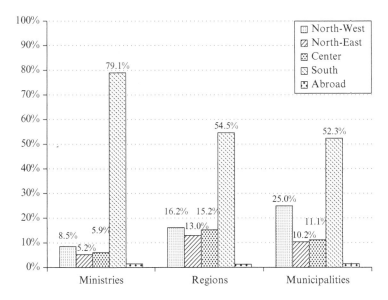

Source: Author computations based on Institute Cattaneo data (2002)

Figure 8.3 Geographic origins of top executives by level of government (%)

close to the Southern Italy, they also continue to constitute the majority of employees in regional and municipal governments (54.5 percent and 52.3 percent, respectively); and this can only be partly explained by the fact that, in relative terms, there are more senior executive positions in local and regional government in Southern Italy than in Northern Italy.

Summing up, then:

- Women are now better represented within Italy's civil service than before, especially at the more senior levels; however, this is a trend common to all Western democracies, since large numbers of women have entered the labor market for the first time since the late 1970s.
- Educational background reveals an increasing proportion of managers with university degrees not only in law or political science, but also in other subjects as well.
- The Italian civil service is still predominantly middle class.
- The major issue pertaining to representativeness concerns the geographical origin of civil servants, that is, the fact that there is an overrepresentation of public sector employees who were born in Southern Italy.

Thus we may conclude that the Italian civil service is still not a representative body, as was in fact the case in the previously described original bureaucratic model. With regard to the three aspects of civil service employees analysed here (social background, gender, and geographical origin), the representative fit has only been attained, in fact, with regard to gender, whereas social and geographical representativeness is still characterized by previous traits.

THE MISSING DIMENSIONS OF REPRESENTATION

Unlike in other Western countries, the analysis of the representativeness of Italy's civil service has still not dealt with ethnic or religious issues. This is because for a long time, immigration was largely an irrelevant phenomenon in Italy. In fact, at the beginning of the 1990s there were only around 800 000 immigrants in Italy. However, in the last two decades their numbers have risen dramatically. In 2011, there are around 4.5 million registered immigrants in Italy (one half of whom are from Eastern European countries), accounting for some 7.5 percent of the overall population.

Of these 4.5 million, 2 million are Christians, while the remaining 2.5 million belong to other religions, including 1.5 million who are Muslims. Thus these remaining two dimensions of representative bureaucracy are going to be of critical importance in future decades, when second and third generation immigrants will be integrated into Italian society to a far greater degree, and will further their social standing considerably. At the moment, however, these two critically important aspects of representative bureaucracy are totally missing from both public debate and academic analysis. Increasing ethnic and religious heterogeneity is still not perceived to be a socio-political problem at all. Thus, there is a risk that when this process of integration eventually produces structural effects, the country may well be unready to deal with such effects.

CONCLUSIONS

Representative bureaucracy is not really perceived as an important issue in Italy, expect with regard to the "southernization" problem. Historically, Italy's public administration has represented only one geographical area of Italy, namely the south, and this represented an expression of a complex process leading to the so-called "southern-style" bureaucracy. This original pattern of public administration thus explains the limited degree of analysis of representativeness within Italy's civil service, as it tended to overshadow any consideration of the other representative-related dimensions of the Italian case. However, slowly but surely this feature is changing. On the question of gender, Italy has now modernized completely, and more than half of public employees are now women.

The real challenge for Italy's public administration is going to be that of the potential impact of immigration. As things stand, Italian society does not yet perceive itself as a multicultural, multiracial, multireligious society based on equal rights, notwithstanding the fact that a substantial percentage of the population now comes from other countries and holds different cultural and religious values. What this means is that religion and ethnicity are not yet key subjects of debate: Italy continues to be dominated by the Catholic Church, and has yet to experience any really significant problems of immigration.[9] However, various different factors have already started to impinge on this model.

First, recent administrative reforms have undoubtedly led to cultural change within Italy's bureaucracy, through a shift away from the Weberian hierarchical model to a more entrepreneurial, accountable, results-oriented model. Customer satisfaction, pay-for-performance, management by objectives, diversity management, gender mainstreaming have all become working tools absorbed into administrative practices, at least in the more avant-garde public administrations (especially at local level and in Central-Northern Italy).

Second, international and European actions designed to create greater awareness of the representative issue represent a forceful, albeit indirect, factor.

Third, societal changes deriving from immigration, increased female participation in the labor market (i.e. the shift from the "male breadwinner" to a "dual earner" model), an aging population, and so on, call for a rethinking of the role and functioning of the country's public service sector.

Last, but not least, the current process of political decentralization, coupled with the increasing empowerment of local and regional government could finally create the preconditions for representative bureaucracy to become a nationwide issue.

However, we should all be aware that substantial public indifference to the representative bureaucracy issue – with the exception of the "southernization problem" – could represent a negative factor when the effects of recent immigration clearly emerge and impact the public administration itself. When new generations of immigrants demand a greater degree of representation within Italy's public administration, the country may well not be prepared to address this demand.

NOTES

1. The following studies are of particular interest here: Cassese (1980), D'Auria and Bellucci (1995), Lippi (1998), Dente (2001), Lewanski and Vassallo (2002), Capano and Vassallo (2003), and Carboni (2008).
2. This constituted one of the broadest studies of the Italian Civil Service carried out over the last few years. It analysed the Civil Service in terms of different institutional models of administrative competence and managerial skills: interviews were conducted with senior civil servants representing about 12–13 percent of those managers employed by central (758), regional (740), and local (217) governments. The results of the study were published in Capano and Vassallo (2003).
3. Local government is subdivided into two distinct levels: that of Italy's municipalities (dating back to the medieval period), and that of its provinces (introduced by Napoleon).
4. Up until the early 1970s, only five "special regions" (Regioni a Statuto Speciale) had been created (Sicily, Sardinia, Valle d'Aosta, Trentino-Alto Adige, and Friuli). The formation of the remaining "ordinary regions" required specific legislation, and as such was delayed until 1975–77. The "special regions" benefited from much greater autonomy, at least as far as legislative powers and competencies were concerned.
5. In the 1950s, in the central administrative bodies, 78 percent of senior bureaucrats came from the South; in the 1960s the numbers of southerners rose to 84 percent (Cassese, 1999).
6. The fundamental political aim of the Northern League is to protect Northern Italy's economic and cultural interests, and in order to do this the party proposes the creation of a federal Italian state, which would give greater autonomy to the north.
7. The only case characterized by a problem of ethnic representativeness was that of the SudTirol/Alto Adige Province (bordering Austria); in order to halt a situation in which political differences in the 1960s were degenerating into genuine acts of terrorism, an agreement between the Italian and Austrian governments ("De Gasperi-Gruber") provided for a division of all public resources (including posts in the administration) in proportion to the entity of each linguistic group (German, the predominant language in the area, Italian, and Ladino); knowledge of German is required in order to get any job in local government. Although certain problems do arise regarding application of the agreement, generally speaking the solution has brought about a "workable" peace among the different linguistic groups.
8. Competitive training courses have been introduced and are open to all those passing an initial test (which may be sat not only by those already employed in the public sector, but also by persons under 35 possessing a university degree). Those candidates who pass the initial exam are to attend a 1-year training course at the Higher School of Public Administration (SSPA), including 6-months internship in a public or private organization.
9. For example, in Italy there is no minister appointed to deal with immigration policy.

9. Representative bureaucracy in the Netherlands

Frits M. van der Meer and Gerrit S.A. Dijkstra

INTRODUCTION

In the current Dutch political and societal climate, a discussion on representative bureaucracy and diversity in the public sector workforce focusing on ethnic minorities could be considered controversial, to say the least, by some in Dutch society. Since the early 2000s, discussions on the pros and cons of multiculturalism in society have become highly polarized mostly along left/center and right-wing dividing lines. We will return to this appreciation of representativeness and diversity management later on in this chapter.

Nevertheless, during the last decade representativeness and its current manifestation diversity (management) have become integral parts of the HRM agenda of most Dutch public sector organizations. Given the scope of the topic, the aim of this chapter is to present an overview of, examine the changing discussions, and debate on representative bureaucracy and diversity relating to the dimension of ethnicity in the Netherlands. In addition, we will present relevant empirical data. We will examine the shift from representative bureaucracy to diversity (management) and try to assess to what extent formulated ambitions have produced tangible results. In order to do so, we will highlight both the normative/policy and empirical dimensions of representative bureaucracy and diversity management with respect to the Dutch civil (public) service. Less emphasis will be put on the techniques of managing diversity. We will however review evidence to which extent the objectives as formulated in government diversity policies have become realized. Two central aims will be examined: the supposed enhanced organizational performance and the improved labor market position for diversified public sector organizations. For this assessment, in the third section, empirical evidence regarding the changing composition of the public service in the Netherlands will be presented. The issues under discussion include religious background, gender, ethnicity, and age. Given the scope of this project we will concentrate on ethnicity. From the information given in this section it will become known that the composition of the civil service is still not a mirror image of society but increasingly the representation of target groups as women and ethnic minorities is growing into this direction. Finally, in our concluding remarks "things" will be wrapped up.

CONCEPTUAL ANALYSIS OF REPRESENTATIVE BUREAUCRACY IN THE DUTCH CONTEXT

In this section, the normative and policy aspects will be examined as they have developed in the Netherlands over time. We argue that although the term representative bureaucracy has seldom been used in the public and scholarly debate, issues of representation and the normative underpinnings have popped up repeatedly. The issue of religion first reached the public agenda given its significance to Dutch society during the nineteenth and the greater part of the twentieth century. Next, attention is drawn to what can be called the process of a conceptual reframing entailing a transition from representativeness to diversity (management) in the late 1990s and 2000s. In particular, we will concentrate on the rationale behind this process. Finally, in this chapter, we will examine the content and ambitions formulated in recent policy intentions regarding enhancing representativeness and diversity management.

From Representative Bureaucracy Towards Diversity (Management)

In current Dutch policy documents and the academic output of Dutch Political Science and Public Administration the term of representative bureaucracy is rarely used. The actual concept of representative bureaucracy was imported from American political science by the Dutch academic community in the 1970s. In the Netherlands that time was also characterized by an increasing level of polarization within society. This polarization accompanied the (start of the) collapse of the pillarized organization of society and government. Discussions on who owned real power in society and government gained in popularity. The role of bureaucracy was also scrutinized but for the most part in terms of politicization.[1] It is rather surprising that this power dimension has hardly returned in Dutch debates on the necessity of a more representative bureaucracy. Recently, representative bureaucracy as an issue for policy-making has resurfaced under the seemingly less laden concept of diversity. We will return to the change in terminology later in this section.

Nevertheless, discussions on the composition of the public service really do have a venerable tradition in Dutch society. The actual term used in the nineteenth and early twentieth century was "underrepresentation." Disadvantaged groups (or their supporters) have thus argued the case for more equal representation given the fragmented nature of Dutch society. Underrepresentation was mainly used in relation to religious background quite understandable given the diverse religious and political make-up of the Netherlands at that time. At first, this discussion primarily pertained to the underrepresentation of Roman Catholics and some orthodox Protestant denominations (van IJsselmuiden, 1988; Raadschelders et al., 1991). It should be noted that a number of additional issues were concealed under the flag of religious representation such as political background and regional representation. These issues were highly interrelated until the 1960s when the pillarized system began to disintegrate. The issue was used by these groups as a part of a struggle for social and political emancipation of these (minority) groups which led eventually to in Lijphart's term the pillarized society (Lijphart, 1975) Demands were made for improving the level of passive (demographic) representation. The idea of active representation was really an (informal) argument by some to resist, for instance, the inclusion of Catholics. Nevertheless, formal policy aimed at improving the level of representativeness dates to 1970s as part of a wider emancipation policy mainly improving the position of women and from the 1980s, it also includes ethnic minorities. To a certain degree, it is often considered almost a new taboo. For many political parties and segments in society, it is also a more principled issue. Often the separation between church and state is invoked to put emphasis on the stance that religious convictions should be clearly left out of the work place. This applies to convictions manifest either in symbols (head scarves, crosses, etc.) or in expression. Again, there is a discussion how this attitude is at odds with the freedom of expression and religion. However, much unknown to public and politics, there are groups of civil servants who have organized (prayer) groups along religious lines. There is a link between this taboo on active representation related to the topic of religion in the workplace and multiculturalism. The rise of a multicultural society and in particular the increase of the Muslim share in society has opened a debate triggered by more right wing and populist parties with respect to Muslim civil servants. To a certain degree, misgivings could be considered identical to the fear of Roman Catholics in the nineteenth and twentieth century. A major difference with the old debate on religious representation is that nowadays there is no demand for equal representation from either the groups themselves or policy-makers. Nevertheless, it returns under the surface of the ethnicity dimension.

Since the end of the 1990s, the term "representative bureaucracy" in terms of emancipation of underprivileged groups has more or less been replaced by the concept of diversity and from the 2000s, we find the introduction of diversity management (Ministerie van Binnenlandse Zaken en Koninkrijkrelaties, 2008b). It is necessary to examine this transition from representative bureaucracy to diversity (management) in more depth. That move can be explained by a reframing of concepts that have proved not only to be controversial in political and societal debate but also to produce rather disappointing result for the supporters of such policies or concepts. At the same time, it also signifies a new approach to personnel issues. There is a clear similarity with a similar transformation in personnel management from personnel policies to human resource management. The shift from power, democracy, issues of morality, equity, and social emancipation that in one way or another is in the forefront of the various conceptualizations of representative bureaucracy towards the organizational performance and labor market perspective dominant in diversity management symbolizes the managerialization of the approach on civil service systems (Groeneveld and Van de Walle, 2010).

Dimensions of passive and active representation are relevant to both representative bureaucracy and diversity concepts. Within the notion of representation a distinction can be made involving demographic (always passive), opinion, and interest forms of representation (Van der Meer and Roborgh, 1996b). The latter two can have both passive and active forms (Mosher, 1968). Already before the introduction of formal diversity policy plans and programs, ample attention has been paid to this theme particularly in implementation and street level bureaucratic agencies. For instance, in the police force representativeness and diversity schemes were introduced at a relatively early stage. One could speak of passive opinion and interest representation thus widening the antennae of the agency in order to become more effective in executing the primary tasks. Thus using diversity management terms the performance of the organization can be improved. We return to this issue in our concluding section when evaluating evidence concerning its success or failure.

Recent Diversity Policy Programs in the Netherlands: the Case of Central Government

Before central government, many other public organizations such as the police have developed programs using diversity concepts. That early start is not surprising given the street-level bureaucracy character of these organizations. As early as 1996, the police have formulated a diversity program (Politie en diversiteit, 1996–2000). Given the extensive size of programs developed by the various governments, we will concentrate on policy plans developed by central government. For central government a major turning point was 2005 with the publication of the white paper "Central government and diversity" (Rijk en diversiteit: geen voorkeursbeleid maar professionaliteit). The emphasis was put on integral diversity management plans with the emphasis to improve organizational performance and to attract human resources from the labor market given the estimated labor market shortages in the near future. In addition, the aim was to develop diversity management policies to stimulate retaining newly recruited staff members from the target groups, stimulating career moves up the hierarchical ladder and enhancing interorganizational cooperation. In 2006 the Minister of the Interior informed the Second Chamber of Parliament that the Cabinet (Balkenende IV) planned to have an integral diversity policy (brief aan de Tweede Kamer 5 December 2006). In policy documents published by the Cabinet Balkenende IV (2007) this has been described as being essential for advancing a more representative government in what is considered an essential multicultural society. Arguments provided by this cabinet in favor of diversity policy include:

- increasing the labor market potential;
- enhancing social justice/equity; thus increasing the image and legitimacy of public institutions;
- improving internal performance of an organization. In a multicultural organization synergy effects can improve the problem solving capacity of government;
- and increasing customer satisfaction.

There are three basic goals:

- More civil servants with ethnic minority background in policy-making and management.
- More women in management.
- Maintain diversity (also in age groups).

This catalog of arguments also contains the old arguments given in favor of representative bureaucracy with the exception of the argument of increasing the labor market potential. Missing though is the control argument. With some effort, this can be read as increasing customer satisfaction involving a higher level of responsiveness. Even specific targets were formulated in the policy program of Cabinet Balkenende IV for 2011. Fifty per cent of new recruitment should be women and 30 percent of new recruits in top positions should be filled by women. The share of non-Western minorities should increase by 50 percent and the exit figure of civil servants in senior age groups (50 plus) should decrease by 2 percentage points. It is important to take notice that these figures relate to targets and not to quota or positive discrimination schemes. Recently a senior position in a northern police force was advertised and it was stated that white males should not apply. There was a public outcry and the Equal Opportunity Commission doubted its legality. Nevertheless, the representative of the force said the job description would remain intact because it was sanctioned by the (former) minister of the Interior, Ter Horst of the Labour Party, who is considered a staunch supporter of affirmative action. At the end of this chapter in our concluding remarks, we will briefly contemplate material differences. These targets were formulated for the whole of the public sector. As labor relations and personnel management in the Netherlands is sectorized, central government employers are only responsible for the implementation in central government departments, defense, and the judiciary and police sectors. Within local government, provinces, the water boards, universities, hospitals, and education sectors, the individual organizations are responsible for developing and prioritizing policy proposals and implementation plans (Ministerie van Binnenlandse Zaken en Koninkrijkrelaties, 2008a).

Representativeness and Diversity in the Dutch Public Service: The Case of Ethnicity

Ethnicity as a topic for special attention with government personnel policy reached the political agenda in the 1980s. Ethnic background relates to so-called non-Western minorities who are considered persons living in the Netherlands who have one or both parents born abroad. Ethnic background as an issue was defined in the late 1980s after the big influx of labor migrants from the Mediterranean area, in particular Morocco and Turkey, starting in the late-1960s and 1970s. The original idea was that these migrants were here on a temporary basis. For the categories mentioned above, it proved less transient than for labor migrants from, for instance, Spain, Portugal, Italy, and Greece. Apart from the labour migrants, there were migrants from former colonies such as Surinam particularly around independence in 1975 and the Dutch Antilles and Aruba. Earlier there was a big migration flow from Indonesia to the Netherlands after its independence in 1950; though these immigrants were never included in a minority policy. Given family reunion schemes and the arrival of refugees, the percentage of non-Western ethnic minorities did increase very rapidly; changing the composition of at first inner city areas.

Due to the economic crisis and the rising number of so-called second-generation ethic minorities, unemployment within these groups did rise substantially, as they were particularly vulnerable given a relatively low educational level and for some groups (mainly the Moroccan and Turkish immigrants) Dutch language deficiencies hindering an easy access to the labor market. In this context ethnicity as a policy issue did develop in both the public and private sectors. Given the high unemployment rate a more general policy was developed in 1994 (Law on Equal Participation Minorities or Wet Participatie Evenredige arbeidsparticipatie Allochtonen or WBEAA). In 1998 the WBEAA was changed to the program the Law on Labor Participation Minorities (Wet Stimulering Arbeidsparticipatie Minderheden or Wet Samen) to run until January 1, 2004. Participation and a (regional) equal representation were key themes. For a long time central government policy had as a main ambition to provide a best practice example to private employers. In 1987 a policy plan called Employment for ethnic minorities with the Central Government (Werkgelegenheid voor ethnische minderheden bij de rijksoverheid) was adopted (Van der Meer and Roborgh, 1993). Though progress was made, the ambitions of all these programs were not realized. A major change concerning the objectives for central government came in 2005 with the white paper Central government and diversity (Rijk en diversiteit: geen voorkeursbeleid maar professionaliteit). Instead of (regional) equal representation as a way of emancipating defined minority groups the emphasis was laid on diversity as a norm both with respect to enhancing organizational performance as well as being more able to attract human resources from the labor market given the estimated labor market shortages in the near future. As described. the police had made earlier steps in this direction.

In order to get an overview of the situation in 2003 and 2008 in the public sector the figures for several branches of government are presented in Table 9.1 with respect to both actual percentages of total staff and the percentages of new entrants into the public service. In addition the percentage of non-Western migrants within the labor force in both years is given.

In all sectors, with the exception of primary education, we encounter a substantial rise, but the variation again is substantial. The highest percentage is to be found in the public administration sector with as most prominent examples central government and the municipalities. There is also a high figure for research institutions, but this can be explained by recruitment of non-Western scientists and PhD students. For instance, the judiciary and the water boards have a comparatively low level of minorities employed. To a lesser degree, the same applies to provinces, police and defense. Still the level of participation is much lower than we might expect on the basis of the share of ethnic minorities in the labor force. Partially

Table 9.1   *The percentage of ethnic minorities in public sector employment (F) and the percentage of ethnic minorities in recruitment to public sector positions (R) in 2003 and 2008*

	F		R	
	2003	2008	2004	2008
Public administration	6.6	7.6	10	12
PA sectors:				
Central government	6.2	8.2	12	15
Municipalities	7.4	8.0	10	12
Provinces	3.1	3.7	7	5
Courts	1.5	1.9	1	2
Water boards	1.5	1.8	3	3
Education (general)	4.4	5.0	6	9
Education sectors:				
Primary education	4.4	3.7	4	5
Research institutions	4.8	6.8	9	15
Defense	4.3	4.5	6	6
Police	4.5	5.2	8	9
Total:				
Public sector	5.2	5.9	7	10
Labour force	9.4	11.2	9[2]	11

Source: Ministerie van Binnenlandse Zaken (1976)

the underrepresentation can be explained by educational levels (see for instance the judiciary, provinces and the water boards) and the effects of a time lag. The share of ethnic minorities amongst new entrants to the public service is much higher and more compatible to the situation in the total labor force. In the case of central government, the municipalities and the research institutions it is even higher. In particular the rise in the police sector is considerable as in this area much attention has been paid to ethnic recruitment and diversity management. Nevertheless, there are again marked differences.

From Table 9.2 we can read that civil servants with a non-Western ethnic background are still working in the lower ranks and scales. There is an upward movement but this is very slow. Among the managers on the Senior Public Service (Algemene bestuursdienst or ABD) only 2 out of the 900 in 2005 belonged to non-Western ethnic minorities or 0.22 percent.

Part of the recruitment problem has to do with a discrepancy in the required educational qualifications for government. In Tables 9.3 and 9.4 data are provided with respect to the educational background of civil

Table 9.2   *Non-western ethnic minorities according to scale levels*

	2007	2008	2009
Low (1–2)	14.1	26.3	20.3
Middle Low (3–5)	16.0	15.9	16.1
Middle (6–8)	10.6	11.0	11.4
Junior High (9–11)	4.9	5.3	5.9
High (12–14)	2.6	2.8	3.1
Senior (15+)	1.1	1.3	1.3

Source: Ministerie van Binnenlandse Zaken en Koninkrijkrelaties, Arbeidszaken Publieke Sector (BZK-DGBK-APS) (2008b, 2010)

Table 9.3   *Educational background of civil servants (CS), Turkish (T), Moroccan (M), Surinam (S), and Antillean (A) minorities according to the educational background, 2006*

	CS	T	M	S	A	Other
Lower/middle	22.1	45.7	38.7	29.4	23.4	17.4
Middle level	30.4	40.5	37.6	46.7	59.6	36.8
Higher professional	28.3	1.7	4.3	13.2	19.2	2.4
University	19.3	2.6	5.4	3.0	0	13.0
Unknown	–	4.3	3.2	1.8	–	2.0

Table 9.4   *Educational background of total labor force (TL), autochthon (AUT), Turkish (T), Moroccan (M), Surinam (S), Antillean (A), and other non-Western minorities according to the educational background compared to that of the civil service, 2006*

	TL	Aut	T	M	S	A	Other
Lower/middle	1.07	1.05	2.07	1.75	1.33	1.05	0.79
Middle level	1.48	1.47	1.33	1.24	1.54	1.96	1.21
Higher professional	0.67	0.72	0.06	0.15	0.46	0.50	0.08
University	0.60	0.57	0.13	0.28	0.28	0.11	0.46

Source: Ministry of the Interior, 2007, 2008–09

servants, which can be considered the necessary and required level of education needed for a civil servant position. It should be added that a higher professional and university education is needed for a higher position within the civil service.

Within the Turkish, Moroccan, Surinam, and Antillean groups the level of education is still lower than that of the native Dutch population and much lower than the civil service. Regarding education the civil service is not representative of the Dutch labor force or the native Dutch part of the labor force. Nevertheless, the discrepancy with the non-Western minorities is substantial. It should be added that currently the number of students with a non-Western minority background at higher professional and universities has risen substantially. In addition to educational deficiencies with respect to some groups of non-Western minorities, there are sometimes cultural problems particularly with respect to those working in street-level bureaucrat functions, making retaining staff with a non-Western ethnic background difficult. These cultural problems have external and internal dimensions. The dominant (autochthon) organizational culture is often held responsible for difficulties in retaining staff. In addition, for instance among some groups many of the new non-ethnic recruits are women (who have generally a much higher level of education than men) who have to leave their jobs after getting married. Second, sometimes peer-group pressure makes it difficult for some civil servants of non-Western minorities to stay.

CONCLUDING REMARKS

Even before the discussions on diversity and wider inclusion of women, ethnic minorities, and age groups have been part of public sector discussions given labor market pressure, the improvement of organizational performance or the supposed rise of a multicultural society has been present in the social and demographic composition of civil service systems. Though some Dutch observers might loathe the idea, from this point of view the Netherlands has always been in essence a multicultural society. This has all to do with the fragmented nature of Dutch society as elaborated in the dominant system of pillarization that existed at least to the last quarter of the twentieth century. Until fairly recently the concept of the pillarized version of the decentralized unitary state was considered a prime instrument to function as a constitutional meeting ground and exchange house for these different groups in society. The tradition of a theme of representative bureaucracy and diversity is thus quite substantial as has been said when we discussed the history of representative bureaucracy in the Netherlands. On the other hand, representativeness and diversity have always been controversial. This has not been the case so much with respect to equal opportunity expression but much more with the mirror image idea. The notion of equal opportunities is widely accepted where it pertains to creating right conditions for entering the public service. The mirror image conceptualization is far more controversial and more specifically with respect to instruments such as positive discrimination and quota measures. The latter though have been replaced by target figures. In reality, recent nominations to top positions in the central government, civil service and the police force by the then Labour Minister of the Interior have stirred controversy when she appointed, seemingly at her own pleasure, female and non-Western candidates. Likewise, suggestions that only members of target groups would be able to apply for some top positions have been criticized and are reputed to have led to an exodus of white male candidates.

Different phases in the debate on representative bureaucracy can be distinguished. Even a shift in terminology has taken place as currently the term diversity has gained in popularity. The HRM perspective now prevails with its emphasis on organizational performance and the organizational labor market position. Even before the introduction of formal diversity policy plans and programs, particularly in implementation agencies and with respect to street level bureaucrats, ample attention has been paid to widening the perspective of the agency members through more representativeness in the composition of staff. For instance, within the police force, representativeness and diversity schemes were introduced at a relatively early stage. One could speak of passive opinion and interest representation thus widening the antennae of the agency in order to become more effective in executing the primary tasks thus using diversity management terms improving the performance of the organization can be improved. There is actually no substantial and hard evidence that these aims have already been achieved. The same applies to the proof of the existence and the effects of active opinion or interest representation with public service decision-making and service delivery (Hupe, 2007). Again, it should be argued that active interest representation would not be acceptable in wider political and societal quarters given constitutional principles as mentioned above. The neutrality and impartiality of government bureaucracy action is still valued highly. Policies based on representative bureaucracy and diversity management concepts are still controversial where they concern affirmative action plans and quotas. In particular, right-wing and center parties are highly critical. Proponents are to be found in left-wing parties as the Labour Party, the Socialist Party and the Greens. Though highly controversial, the use of positive discrimination and quotas (in the form of target figures) is perceived to have become stronger in recent years. Basic to this controversy is the definition and appreciation of merit criteria. These are seen as a fundamental expression of the constitutional rule of equality as expressed in Articles 1 and 3 of the Constitution. Particularly relevant is Article 3 proclaiming equal access to public positions. Thus, merit was and is still considered as vital principle on a constitutional symbolic and practical level. Nevertheless the ambition to attract and equally important to retain more recruits from wider segments in society has become a necessity given the aging of the civil service and the growing labor market shortages in the near future.

With respect to the empirical side, the composition of the civil service still is not a mirror image of society, but increasingly the representation of target groups, in this case ethnic minorities, is growing in that direction. With respect to new entries, we have provided information that almost presents a mirror-image representativeness. There is a time differential effect given the recruitment and in the case of the ethnic minorities also an educational backlog. The percentage of higher civil servants with a non-Western background is only slowly increasing. Here one of the main problems is still a deficiency in educational level compared to what is required for a civil service position particularly at a higher rank. This especially pertains to civil servants of Moroccan or Turkish origin. Nevertheless, in recent years at the institutions of the higher profession education in particular, (female) students with a non-Western background have increased substantially. As described above, we should also point to the so-called cultural dimension with respect to retaining civil servants with a non-Western background within this complex of cultural factors, external and internal dimensions can be distinguished. In diversity management literature, the dominant (autochthon) organizational culture is often blamed for difficulties in retaining staff. Externally among some groups, it is customary for women to leave their job after marriage. Second, sometimes group pressure makes it difficult for some civil servants of non-Western minorities to stay. The retaining aspect demands some effort as is seen to be crucial in diversity management programs.

NOTES

1. From a societal and party political control perspective, politicization could be seen as a part of the representativeness discussion. See for instance Sally Coleman Selden (1997) and the writings of Kingsley (1944), Van Riper (1958), Mosher (1968) and others in the classical tradition. The difficulty, however, is to separate the control from clientilistic and nepotism perspective.
2. 2003 figure.

10. Representative bureaucracy in Switzerland

Daniel Kübler

INTRODUCTION

In the international debate on representative bureaucracy most of the work has focused on issues related to administrative performance. Scholars of public administration have been preoccupied with the question of whether representativeness of public bureaucracies hampers or rather improves administrative performance – empirical evidence tends to show that the latter is more likely the case (see Meier and Stewart, 1992). A second, although less developed strand of research in representative bureaucracy relates to state legitimacy. This kind of work focuses on whether the representation of different social groups within public bureaucracies contributes to making the wider state apparatus, as well as public policy-making more acceptable to these groups. In Switzerland, the issue of representative bureaucracy touches upon both of these aspects, as the public administration faces the double challenge of a multi-ethnic state and a society that, mainly for labor market reasons, increasingly depends on immigration.

As in other multilingual societies (McRae, 2007) national cohesion in Switzerland strongly depends on finding the "right" balance between different ethno-linguistic communities. As we will see in this chapter, achieving adequate representation of the traditional linguistic communities – German, French, Italian, and Romanche – in the federal public administration is a crucial element in the web of power-sharing so characteristic of Swiss "consensus democracy" (Lijphart, 1999). Nevertheless, representative bureaucracy has also started to be discussed as a matter of administrative performance, mostly at the level of sub-national bureaucracies seeking to cope with demands of a clientele which, as a result of immigration, has become increasingly diverse. The federal public administration is much less exposed to such new demands, as it has only few direct contacts with citizens: the rules of Swiss federalism indeed delegate implementation of most federal policies to cantonal and communal governments.[1] Hence, it is mainly sub-national bureaucracies that are exposed to demands and needs related to increasing ethnic and cultural heterogeneity, especially in the large cities. As a response, some of them have deployed strategies to increase ethnic and cultural diversity of their staff, as part of a strategy to improve intercultural competence in their service provision. However, these new diversity strategies however fit uneasily with the Germanic tradition of public administration that prevails in Switzerland (see Painter and Peters, 2010), and often also face opposition from national-conservative political parties.

DIMENSIONS OF MULTI-ETHNICITY IN SWITZERLAND

Given its age-old religious and linguistic diversity the Swiss society has always been characterized by cultural segmentation. Lijphart, for instance, emphasizes Switzerland's "multi-ethnic" (1999, p. 33) nature that has contributed to shape institutional rules, political practice, and administrative culture. Since the 1960s however, global migration flows have added a new dimension of multi-ethnicity to the Swiss society, as immigrant communities have grown in number and size. Multi-ethnicity in Switzerland today therefore entails these two dimensions of a traditional (mainly linguistic) diversity, as well as a more recent diversity related to immigration.

Proportionality as a Principle for Accommodating Traditional Conflicts

Mainly shaped by nineteenth century history, nation-building in Switzerland depended on overcoming the two most significant lines of social division then present: the opposition between Protestants and Catholics, as well as the segmentation of the society by language into a German-, a French-, and an Italian-speaking community. The design of Swiss federalism with its built-in protection of religious and linguistic territorial communities is a first important element of the "solution to conflicts in multicultural societies" (Linder, 2010). Two additional constitutional elements have contributed to durably de-conflictualize societal divisions. First, there are a number of statutory rights guaranteed to the linguistic communities (Article 70 of the Federal Constitution). German, French, and Italian were defined as the official languages of the Federation,[2] and inhabitants have the right to communicate with federal authorities in any of these official languages. Official trilingualism, however, does not extend to sub-national authorities, as cantons decide on their official language and thereby must respect the traditional territorial distribution of languages. This so-called territoriality principle ensures the protection of indigenous

linguistic communities from pressures to change language in their own traditional territory. Second, there are a number of rules leading to political
quotas for territorial (i.e. religious and linguistic) communities at various
levels of government. As regards the Federal Council (the cabinet), the
constitution stipulates that the various geographic and linguistic regions
need to be adequately represented (Art. 175). This rule has been quite well
observed in the past: the ratio of German speakers in the cabinet normally
does not exceed five out of seven ministers, and Protestants and Catholics
have had an equal share. Furthermore, linguistic and geographic proportionality is a rule for the composition of parliamentary committees
or commissions of experts who advise the government, and also for the
federal public administration.

The terms of reference for linguistic proportionality are established via
the decennial population censuses. The figures of the 2000 population
census (Bundesamt für Statistik, 2005) show that first languages spoken
by the overall resident population are 64 percent for German, 19 percent
for French, 8 percent for Italian, less than 1 percent for Romanche, and 9
percent for other languages. The distribution with respect to the territorially defined linguistic regions is as follows: 72 per cent of the population
lives in the German-speaking region, 24 percent in the French-, 4 percent
in the Italian- and 1 percent in the Romanche-speaking regions. This
disparity between the share of first languages spoken and the population
share of the four linguistic regions is mainly a consequence of the strong
immigration from Italy, resulting in an increase in the number of Italian
speakers living in the German- or French-speaking regions.

Immigration and the New Multi-ethnicity of the Swiss Society

As in other Western European countries, international immigration has
been a significant phenomenon in Switzerland. Starting in the 1960s, a
period of fast economic growth steeply increased the demand for labor.
As a consequence, workers from Italy, Germany, France, and Austria,
and later from Spain, Portugal, Yugoslavia, and Turkey have migrated
to Switzerland. In the first period, immigrants were mainly low skilled
and found employment in unattractive and badly paid jobs. Thanks to
bilateral treaties with the European Union, the free movement of persons
was extended to Switzerland in 2002, thereby facilitating migration of
EU-27 nationals to Switzerland. As a consequence, immigration of high-
skilled workers has increased in recent years. In European comparison,
Switzerland is a country with a very high share of immigrants. In 2008,
22.6 percent of the resident population were foreigners, and, if we include
those who have obtained Swiss citizenship, 30 percent of the inhabitants in

Switzerland have an immigration background.[3] There are quite important deviations to this overall mean, as the share of immigrants is generally lower in the peripheral regions and higher in the large urban centers of the country. In Geneva, for instance, 38.7 percent of the population are foreigners, in Basle, 31.5 percent and in Zurich 30.5 percent.

From the 2000s onwards, a debate was started on how the public administration could appropriately react to this new dimension of ethnic diversity in Switzerland (Prodolliet, 2005). In 2005, the Federal Commission on Foreigners – a body of experts consulting the federal government – published a number of recommendations for what they called "opening up of institutions" (Eidgenössische Ausländerkommission, 2005). Most prominently, public administrations at all levels of government were recommended to reduce explicit and implicit barriers to recruitment of individuals with an immigration background. In an article on equality before the law (Art. 8), the federal constitution rules out discrimination on grounds of origin and race. Foreigners are thus not discriminated against legally, albeit they do not have the right to vote.[4]

Politically, however, issues related to immigration and to the presence of foreigners in Switzerland are very high on the agenda. Already in the 1970s "xenophobic parties and groups have emerged and brought pressure to bear on the political authorities to restrict immigration and prevent the 'alienation' of Swiss society" (Linder and Steffen, 2006, p. 236). And in the past two decades, the right-wing Swiss People's Party has nearly tripled its share of voters in national elections with a program that highlights Swiss national traditions and is directed against immigration and against the integration of Switzerland into the EU. Besides the left–right cleavage, the cleavage between losers and winners of globalization processes is currently the second most relevant line of conflict in Swiss politics (Kriesi et al., 2005). It is no wonder, thus, that the role of immigrants in government bureaucracies is often debated in this frame.

REPRESENTATIVE BUREAUCRACY IN SWITZERLAND

In Switzerland, most of the public sector employment is located at the sub-national levels, i.e. the federate states (the cantons), as well as the communes. The latest available figures show that, in the year 2005, the federal public administration offered roughly 32 000 jobs, whereas the 26 cantons together account for roughly 131 000 jobs and communes offer nearly 107 000 jobs in public administration.[5] Hence, the federal bureaucracy accounts for less than 15 percent of all public administrators in Switzerland.

Representative Bureaucracy at the Federal Level

In his review of the very few studies that have examined the representative-ness of the federal public administration in Switzerland, Varone (2007, p. 295) identifies five main themes on which the scientific debate has focused so far: religion, parties, social origin, gender, and language. In terms of religious denominations, the numbers loosely correspond to the figures in the general population, where Protestants and Catholics have traditionally had an almost equal share, but the number of those without any religious affiliation has sharply increased since the 1970s (Bundesamt für Statistik, 2004). With respect to the affiliation to one of the four major parties the Liberal Party tends to be overrepresented, but the Christian Democrats and Socialists are catching up, while the share of the right-wing Swiss People's Party has remained stable over much of the twentieth century. In terms of social origin, upper classes were shown to be over-represented at the level of senior civil servants, but their share has been decreasing over time. The gender gap is also important, as women are clearly underrepresented among federal public administrators – even if this situation has improved thanks to new measures for the promotion of gender equality taken in 2003. With respect to linguistic proportionality, the figures show that first languages spoken by federal employees corre-spond very closely to the distribution of the first languages spoken by the citizens.

The extent to which the federal administration pays attention to the adequate representation of these various groups parallels the political mobilization of the related issues over time. The religious cleavage has lost its salience during the twentieth century and confessional representa-tiveness of the federal personnel is a non-issue today. Stable large coali-tion governments and power sharing between the main parties over long periods have ensured that most major parties have access to top-level positions in the federal bureaucracy; the distribution of party affiliations among federal public administrators is only occasionally a matter of concern. Similarly, the public schooling system ensures access to educa-tion resources independently from social status, and public sector recruit-ment is generally not perceived as excessively biased with respect to the social origin of candidates. Two issues of representative bureaucracy are currently high on the political agenda: while the gender gap has become a hot topic since the mid-1990s, the proportionality of language groups has been a matter of concern since World War II. The more recent dimension of multi-ethnic representation – namely the representation of immigrants – is much less debated.

Traditional Multi-ethnicity: The Linguistic Proportionality of the Federal Employees

The question of linguistic representativeness of the federal personnel was first raised towards the end of the 1940s, when MPs from the French and Italian speaking regions asked the government to remedy the under-representation of French and Italian speakers in the federal bureaucracy, especially at senior positions (see Widmer, 1987). As a response, the government formulated, in 1950, a list of recommendations inviting human resource managers in the federal bureaucracy to pay better attention to linguistic proportionality at all hierarchical levels. However, the problem of underrepresented linguistic minorities persisted, as did MPs questioning the government about this topic. The recommendations and measures decided by the government to tackle the issue were developed and strengthened in subsequent revisions in 1965, 1983, 1997, and 2003 (Weil, 1995; Office fédéral du personnel, 2009). In addition to the measures aimed at improving the linguistic representation of the federal personnel, the 1983 revision also aimed at facilitating the effective use of minority languages in internal communication. This entailed the right of each federal employee to work in his or her preferred official language, as well as a number of recommendations with respect to language use and translation resources. Since then, the approach pursued by the federal government to improve linguistic representativeness of its public administration rests on two main goals, namely (1) to achieve adequate representation of the linguistic communities at all hierarchical levels of the bureaucracy, and (2) to promote effective use of all three official languages, and especially of minority languages, in internal and external communication.

Over the years, the measures taken to achieve these two goals have developed into a quite sophisticated set of rules, instruments, and recommendations of human resource management in the fields of personnel recruitment and development, communication, sensitization, as well as monitoring and reporting (see Kübler et al., 2011). However, most of these measures are of a voluntary nature, and aim at establishing symbolic pressure on the administrative units, rather than to install legal obligations that could be challenged in court. This is also true for the linguistic quotas that have been defined, and that come in the form of "target values" of linguistic representativeness. Article 7 of the federal ordinance on languages[6] defines the adequate representation of the linguistic communities in administrative units of the federal bureaucracy as 70 percent German, 22 percent French, 7 percent Italian and 1 percent Romanche speakers.[7] However, these target values are not compelling and, besides "blaming and shaming" in the yearly human resource reporting, no further sanctions can be taken against administrative units that do not achieve these targets.

What is the state of the situation regarding these two goals of linguistic proportionality and language use? Systematic reports on the first languages spoken by the federal employees have been compiled by the Federal Personnel Office since 1996. These reports tend to show that the linguistic profile of the federal employees corresponds quite well to the target values, not only overall but also at the level of management functions. However, recent and more fine-grained analyses showed that the German speakers are clearly overrepresented at the very top positions (Office fédéral du personnel, 2009, p. 4). All of the seven ministries' top executive functions are held by German speakers, as are 78 percent of the heads of the main administrative units. Looking at management functions within these administrative units, 95 percent of the financial officers are German speakers, 88 percent of those responsible for IT, and 82 percent of human resource directors. An independent analysis (Kübler et al., 2009) recently confirmed this picture of the Swiss federal bureaucracy where linguistic representativeness is achieved globally, but where the management positions of the single administrative units are disproportionally dominated by German speakers, mostly at the expense of Italian speakers (Table 10.1). Using multivariate statistics, Kübler et al. (2009, pp. 7–9) identified two factors that are positively associated with the representation of linguistic minorities among the personnel of an administrative unit. First and quite intuitively, the geographic location of the unit proved important. Decentralized units, i.e. those located in either the French- or the Italian-speaking region of the country had a much higher proportion of employees from the linguistic minorities than those offices located in the capital – German-speaking Berne. Second, and most importantly, the share of French or Italian speakers in higher management positions of an administrative unit turned out to have a significant influence on the share of French or Italian speakers among the overall personnel of this unit. This finding points to a linguistic effect in personnel recruitment, i.e. that senior officials as recruiters tend to give preference to candidates of the same linguistic origin.

Regarding the effective use of the three official languages, evidence available so far has suggested that, while communication in German and French is generally quite satisfactory,[8] Italian speakers have a difficult stance and are often forced to work in one of the other two official languages. A recent analysis of the original language used to elaborate federal legislative acts (Kübler, 2009; Kübler et al., 2009) shows that German is "over-used", mainly at the expense of Italian which does not appear as a real working language (Table 10.2). Indeed, less than 2 percent of all

Representative bureaucracy in action

Table 10.1   First language spoken by federal employees (excl. non-national languages) in the seven ministries, overall and in higher management positions (salary classes 32 to 38), means for administrative units in percent, 2001–2008

Ministries		German	French	Italian	Romanche	Total
Foreign affairs	All employees	79.62	16.82	3.41	0.13	100
	Higher mgmt.	75.88	18.44	6.31	0	100
Interior	All employees	69.88	22.03	7.74	0.32	100
	Higher mgmt.	64.63	29.05	6.31	0	100
Justice and	All employees	68.16	25.98	5.73	0.11	100
police	Higher mgmt.	77.72	20.04	1.72	0.50	100
Defense	All employees	81.60	12.74	5.45	0.19	100
	Higher mgmt.	86.14	13.80	0.04	0	100
Treasury	All employees	76.27	17.49	6.10	0.12	100
	Higher mgmt.	74.78	20.58	4.00	0.62	100
Economy	All employees	73.47	22.97	3.34	0.20	100
	Higher mgmt.	71.16	28.44	0.06	0.32	100
Infrastructure &	All employees	78.38	17.92	3.45	0.23	100
environment	Higher mgmt.	78.09	19.61	2.29	0	100
Chancellery	All employees	61.88	24.21	13.55	0.34	100
	Higher mgmt.	81.11	0	13.88	5.00	100
Total	All employees	73.66	20.02	6.10	0.21	100
	Higher mgmt.	76.19	18.75	4.33	0.81	100

Source: Adapted from Kübler et al. (2009)

legislative acts are elaborated in Italian, and a closer analysis reveals that these acts are often of lesser importance and mainly concern communications between the federal state and authorities located in the Italian speaking region of the country. In addition, if we look at the legal category of the various acts, it appears that the higher the political importance of an act (e.g. acts relating to the constitution, federal laws or acts of parliament), the more German is used for their elaboration. However, it is interesting to note the relatively high proportion of international treaties elaborated in French. This is linked to the status of French as a working language of diplomacy (e.g. in the realm of the United Nations), where the use of French reduces translation costs. However, independently from the category of the act, the linguistic profile of an administrative unit plays a role for the language used, but mainly for German and French (Kübler, 2009, p. 33–34). The use of Italian, however, is not correlated with the share of Italian speakers within a unit – thereby illustrating that Italian speakers often work in either French or German.

Table 10.2   Language used for the elaboration of federal legislative acts, according to category (means for 1998–2008)

Category of legislative acts	German (%)	French (%)	Ital. (%)	Total (%)	N
Constitution, federal laws, acts of parliament	92.99	6.85	0.16	100	642
Government and parliament ordinances	90.17	9.79	0.04	100	2381
Government messages and reports	88.96	10.80	0.24	100	1259
Popular initiatives and referenda	92.88	7.12	0.00	100	576
International treaties	61.23	37.74	1.03	100	1950
Administrative ordinances	93.99	6.01	0.00	100	1962
Miscellaneous	74.71	22.39	2.90	100	9778
Total	79.48	18.85	1.66	100	18 548

Source: Kübler (2009)

THE NEW MULTI-ETHNIC DIMENSION: IMMIGRANTS IN THE FEDERAL PUBLIC ADMINISTRATION

In 2002, a new Act on Federal Personnel was adopted. Very much in line with the tune of the time, it mainly aimed at facilitating public sector modernization via flexibilization of employment conditions. Simultaneously, the new law stated that employment in the federal public administration was in principle open to persons of any nationality – except in a restricted number of so-called 'sovereign tasks': the army, the federal police, tax administration, diplomacy, as well as the border guard. In the previous law, it was the other way round: public sector employment was restricted to Swiss nationals, exceptions could be granted. As a consequence of this new rule, the share of federal employees who do not hold a Swiss passport increased from 2.9 percent in 2002 to 4.1 percent in 2008. Nevertheless, immigrants are still under-represented in the federal public administration.

The debate about this underrepresentation of immigrants in the federal public administration is, however, very limited. The rationale for opening up the federal public administration to non-Swiss nationals basically was the pragmatic search for increasing the potential recruitment basis in times of a tight labor market.[9]

INTERMEDIARY CONCLUSION: REPRESENTATIVE BUREAUCRACY AT THE FEDERAL LEVEL

In the federal government's quest for representative bureaucracy, the old dimension of multi-ethnicity is clearly dominant. While the recruitment of immigrants pragmatically follows the goal of increasing the number of potential recruits, the adequate representation of the traditional linguistic communities is a very sensitive issue, whose salience has even increased during the twentieth century. Raised after World War II, the question of linguistic proportionality of the federal personnel has been a continuing point of public attention, mobilized essentially by politicians representing the minority regions, i.e. French- and Italian-speaking Switzerland. The linguistic cleavage is not organized in the Swiss party system (Kriesi, 1996); in contrast to other multinational states such as Belgium or Canada, Switzerland has no ethno-linguistic parties. Nevertheless, latent divisions between the linguistic communities have become accentuated since the 1990s, when the French-speaking minority was repeatedly outvoted in a number of political choices in the fields of foreign policy (e.g. isolationism with respect to the EU) and public education (e.g. preference of English over French as a second language taught in public schools of German-speaking Switzerland). As a consequence, language issues became increasingly salient on the political agenda (Grin, 1997). The increased attention paid to linguistic proportionality in the federal bureaucracy at the beginning of the twenty-first century must therefore be seen as a response to the political mobilization of the linguistic divide.[10]

The measures taken to promote language proportionality and multilingualism in the federal bureaucracy in Switzerland focus on the improvement of representativeness – rather than the promotion of equal treatment of language groups, such as in Canada for example (Gagnon et al., 2006) – and quotas for minority groups are a core element (Kübler et al., 2011). This approach must be seen in the larger context of Swiss consociationalism, where segments of the society entitled to participate in mechanisms of power-sharing are territorially delineated (Linder, 2010). The territoriality principle in language policy, indeed, has given rise to a conception of language rights not only as rights of the individual, but also as collective rights of linguistic communities (Papaux, 1997), which can therefore legitimately aspire to an adequate access to state power. This is not the case of immigrants, who not only are no electoral constituency, but whose presence is even actively put into question by strong nationalist parties.

REPRESENTATIVE BUREAUCRACY AT THE SUB NATIONAL LEVEL: THE NEW DIMENSION OF SWISS MULTI-ETHNICITY

We have seen that linguistic proportionality is a major issue of representative bureaucracy at the federal level, while the new dimension of Swiss multi-ethnicity is in retreat. At the sub-national level, the situation is the exact opposite.

At the sub-national level, the question of language proportionality among public administrators is also important in those four cantons that encompass more than one linguistic community. These are the cantons of Bern (German-speaking majority, French-speaking minority), Fribourg and Valais (French-speaking majority, German-speaking minority), and Grisons (German-speaking majority, Italian- and Romanche-speaking minorities). Most studies on linguistic diversity at the sub-national level focus on general aspects of language policy (see Grin, 1997) or political representation (see Stojanovic, 2006), but not multilingualism in the public administration. Those who do (a rare example is Altermatt, 2005) tend to find problems similar to those identified in the federal bureaucracy. But these, again, are limited to the four multi-lingual cantons, or the two major bilingual cities (Biel/Bienne and Fribourg).

However, the role of immigrants as public sector employees has become an increasingly relevant issue in sub-national units of public administration. Especially in urban centers, public administrators face increasing difficulties in their daily work, related to the growing cultural diversity of the resident population they are called to serve. These difficulties, for instance, result from mutual incomprehension, be it at the level of language, or are due to differences in religious beliefs or cultural habits. Some administrators therefore have actively searched to recruit employees with a migration background, in order to increase intercultural competences within their administrative units. In addition, the increasing share of foreigners among the resident population – especially in the younger age groups – makes it likely that immigrants or persons with a migration background aspire for a career in the public administration. There is thus an issue of equal opportunity and discrimination, if migrants continue to be underrepresented in the public sector.

As yet, there is no systematic overview to what extent public administrations in Switzerland have responded to this idea of opening up the institutions, and what issues this has raised. In the following, we will synthetically present the results of an exploratory case study on the canton of Basle city, where some sectors of the public administration have developed an active strategy of recruiting administrators with an immigration background

(Kübler and Piñeiro, 2011). With its high share of immigrants among the resident population (31.5 percent foreigners) Basle city provides a paradigmatic case for the challenges that public administrations face in managing Switzerland's new multi-ethnic dimension.

"OPENING UP OF THE INSTITUTIONS" IN THE CANTON OF BASLE CITY: TWO SERVICES EXPLORED

The canton of Basle city, located in the North where three countries meet (Switzerland, France, and Germany) is one of the smaller Swiss cantons, but the most urbanized. In 2009, it counted roughly 190000 residents, of which one-third held were non-nationals, and 13522 full time jobs in its public administration.[11] Already in 1999, the cantonal government had explicitly defined the goal to increase the share of employees with an immigration background and/or foreign nationality. The reasons given explicitly referred to principles of adequate representation ("the composition of the population should be reflected in the State's personnel"), but also to the hope of increasing linguistic skills and intercultural competence of Basle's public administration ("specific linguistic skills and intercultural competences [of foreign job candidates] are seen as qualifications") (Regierungsrat des Kantons Basel-Stadt, 1999, p. 18, translated by the author).

Case study evidence on two selected services of the cantonal public administration – the police force and the child protection agency – suggests that the goal of recruiting administrators with an immigration background is well supported by human resource managers and even preceded the governmental act (Kübler and Piñeiro, 2011). In the cantonal police force, the legal requirement of Swiss citizenship as a precondition to entering the police force was dropped in 1996, and the human resource department recently strengthened its efforts to appeal to candidates with an immigration background. The hope is mainly to widen recruitment potential, as the police force had recently struggled to find suitable candidates. Additionally, there are expectations that police officers with an immigration background will bring linguistic and intercultural competences that can be useful to police work in the context of a culturally diverse society, e.g. in interventions that involve immigrants. Similarly, the child protection agency has started to recruit social workers with an immigration background systematically since 2000, in order to facilitate communication with its clientele, of which nearly two-thirds are immigrants. Thanks to specific linguistic skills of the new recruits, costs for translation and interpretation have been reduced. Additionally, it is expected that, due to their own personal migration experience, social workers with an immigration background will have a better grasp of the situations and problems of their immigrant clientele, which will enable them to find better solutions.

Interestingly however, the expectations expressed by human resource managers – especially those related to increased intercultural competence – are not necessarily shared by the rank-and-file employees. In the police force, there are doubts whether the notion of intercultural competence is compatible with the principles of neutrality and equality in police work, that are also part of the oath that each police officer solemnly swears prior to entering the police force. Although police officers themselves tend to acknowledge intercultural competence as something useful, they mention potential loyalty conflicts in situations when officers with immigration background have to intervene against individuals who have the same cultural origin. In the child protection agency, language skills and inter-cultural competences of social workers who have personal immigration experience are appreciated as additional resources for the services that facilitate the work process. However, and as an unintended consequence, the presence of social workers with an immigration background favors a segmentation of the clientele according to ethnic–cultural criteria – for instance, clients of Turkish origin will be assigned to social workers with Turkish roots. Although this may appear as a pragmatically acceptable strategy in the perspective of the public service, such segmentation could ultimately reinforce the self-closure of immigrant into communities and thereby further reduce the chances of immigrants to integrate into the host society. In both services, thus, an increase of the bureaucracy's cultural diversity seems to increase risks of what we call "dysfunctional identification" (Kübler and Piñeiro, 2011), where cultural affinities get in the way of public administrators' professional behavior. Both services are conscious of these risks, and some responses have been found. Whereas the police force seems to rely on the normalizing power of the "esprit de corps" (i.e. peer pressure to act professionally), the child protection agency has started to debate the issue of other cultural client segmentation in internal train-ing, and the supervisors try to counter excessive segmentation through adequate case triage.

The example of Basle city shows that the increase of cultural diver-sity within a public bureaucracy can strengthen the capabilities of the bureaucracy to deal with an increasingly diverse clientele. Thereby, rep-resentative bureaucracy can indeed be seen as contributing to administra-tive performance. However, increased cultural diversity may also trigger situations and processes that put bureaucratic professionalism at risk, and therefore threaten administrative performance. Nevertheless, the evidence from the case study suggests that these risks can be reduced by adequate action.

CONCLUSION

Switzerland has always been a multi-ethnic society. The consociation-alist institutions, rules and practices embodied in the political system clearly reflect the quest to compensate (Ossipow, 1994) or accommodate (Lijphart, 1999) the tensions resulting from cultural diversity. The issue of linguistic proportionality has traditionally been the dominant theme of representative bureaucracy in Switzerland, and reflects the necessity of ensuring an adequate equilibrium between language communities in the consociationalist pattern of Swiss politics. The ensuring of linguistic pro-portionality in the federal public administration therefore aims at secur-ing the legitimacy of the wider state apparatus. And the strengthening of strategies to ensure linguistic proportionality has been an answer to polit-ical mobilization of the linguistic cleavages since the 1990s, challenging national cohesion and the legitimacy of the polity as such. The quest for legitimacy is the push factor for increasing bureaucratic representativeness in terms of language and gender.

More recently, the debate on representative bureaucracy in Switzerland has begun to integrate the question of how the public sector can and should adapt to the new dimension of multi-ethnicity resulting from immigration. Strategies of representative bureaucracy have been implemented, mainly in order to raise intercultural competence of administrative units, and therefore their abilities to deal with a culturally heterogeneous clientele. These are pull factors within the public administration that, independ-ently from issues of legitimacy towards the outside, explain the emergence of such strategies. As we have shown, this aspect is more confined to the sub national bureaucracies, who are also more "at the front" than the federal administration. The intellectual debate on this "intercultural opening" of the public sector is just beginning. As we have seen from the evidence on the Basle case, an increase of cultural diversity might come at some costs for administrative professionalism. Representative bureau-cracy, especially with respect to ethno-cultural diversity, therefore might pose significant challenges to the functioning of public administration in Switzerland in the near future. Theoretical reflection and empirical research on the ways in which these challenges can be met are, as yet, still underdeveloped.

ACKNOWLEDGMENTS

This article draws on research on issues of multilingualism in the federal public administration in Switzerland supported by the Swiss National Science Foundation (grant # 4056-113240), as well as on public administration and international migration in the canton of Basle, supported by the University of Applied Sciences of Northwest Switzerland.

NOTES

1. Even in centrally regulated fields such as immigration or military service, citizens are in contact with cantonal or communal administrators who act on behalf of the federal government. The only significant exception from this general rule is customs management, where there are no sub-national intermediaries and citizens directly deal with federal administrators. On the structure of the federal public administration in Switzerland, see Germann (1996) as well as Varone (2007).
2. Besides the German-, French-, and Italian-speaking Swiss, there is also a tiny minority of speakers of Romanche – a Rhaeto-Romanic language believed to have descended from Vulgar Latin. At the federal level, Romanche is used only in the (very limited) communication with Romanche-speaking citizens. Romanche thus does not have the same status of official language as the other three. The issues related to the promotion and use of Romanche as an official language are therefore not considered in this article.
3. Source: Federal statistical office (www.admin.ch/bfs, accessed in January 2011).
4. There are, however, a number of cantons in French-speaking Switzerland, where foreigners have the right to vote at the cantonal and communal level (Jura and Neuchâtel), or at the communal level only (Geneva and Vaud).
5. Figures represent jobs (full-time equivalents) in public administrations of the cantons, the cantonal districts, and the communes (excluding jobs in independent public sector agencies). Source: www.badac.ch, accessed in January 2011.
6. Ordonnance sur les langues, RS 441.11.
7. These target values correspond to the distribution of first languages spoken by Swiss citizens (thus excluding residents with a foreign passport).
8. The established practice is that of passive bilingualism, where German speakers communicate in German and French speakers communicate in French. In either group, the (passive) linguistic skills of the other language is generally sufficient to allow communication across languages.
9. See the answers given by the government on questions lodged by MPs (postulates Lumengo 08.3598 and 09.4114, as well as postulate by the Green Party group 08.3815; www.parlament.ch, accessed July 13, 2011).
10. This motivation of compensating the increasing mobilization of ethno-linguistic divisions has also propelled the reformulation of language policy more generally (Grin, 1997).
11. Source: Basle cantonal statistical office (www.statistik-bs.ch, accessed in January 2011).

11. Representative bureaucracy in the United Kingdom

Rhys Andrews

INTRODUCTION

To date, comparatively little research has evaluated the representativeness of UK public organizations. Although researchers in the UK have surveyed equal opportunities in the national workforce (e.g. Mason, 2003), debated the effects of New Public Management (NPM) on female workers in public services (e.g. Newman, 2002) and considered ways in which public organizations can manage diversity (e.g. Miller, 2009), workforce representativeness has received scant attention. Thus, although equality and diversity in the public sector workplace has been of high salience in the policy and politics of the UK for more than a decade (e.g. Office of the Deputy Prime Minister, 2003; Civil Service, 2008), little is actually known about the levels of representation of women and minority ethnic groups within public organizations; still less about the potential determinants of variations in the levels of representation.

In this chapter, variations in the representation of women and ethnic minorities across UK central government departments and English local governments are examined. At the central level, the civil service now has a long history of concern with policies to promote equal opportunities in employment (Brimelow, 1981). Nevertheless, little systematic empirical research has been conducted on the extent of workforce diversity in major central government spending departments (though see Margetts, 1996, for a preliminary analysis of gender representation). In fact, most studies of gender and minority ethnic people's representation in the UK public sector have focused on local rather than central government (e.g. Andrews et al., 2006). Indeed, much has been made at the local level of equality policy implementation (Young, 1997), which may reflect the perception that local governments are model employers and perhaps more open to political pressures to mirror the communities that they represent (Halford, 1988). Aside from the absence of published research on rates of gender and minority ethnic representation, organizational influences on the representativeness of central and local government are little studied. These too merit extended attention given the strong expectation in the UK that public organizations are responsible for enhancing gender and minority ethnic representation.

The aim in the chapter is to provide a preliminary profile of levels of gender and minority ethnic representation in central and local government in the UK. This will be accomplished by studying rates of representation in the workforce of the major central government spending departments, such as the Departments of Health, Education and Work and Pensions, as well as all the local governments in England. In the next part of the chapter, equality and diversity policy and practice in the UK is outlined and recent data on representativeness at the national level in central and local government are presented. Following that, prior research on gender and minority ethnic representation is examined and potential organizational influences on variations in representation considered. Next, data on gender and minority ethnic representation within UK central government departments are described along with the empirical methods and results of statistical models predicting variations in employment rates. The subsequent part of the paper repeats that analysis for all the local governments in England. Finally, theoretical and practical implications of the findings are discussed.

EQUALITY AND DIVERSITY POLICY AND PRACTICE IN THE UK

During the past four decades, the UK government has introduced wide-ranging legislation that covers equal opportunities employment practices for women, ethnic minorities, disabled people, and people of varying ages, sexual orientation, and religion or belief. The political pressures from rights activists, interest groups, and equal opportunities bodies (such as the Equal Opportunities Commission) which spurred this legislation eventually led the Labour Party to propose a single consolidated equalities legislative framework in its 2005 general election manifesto; a framework that also reflected EU Equal Treatment Directives. On taking office again in that year, the Labour government then drafted an Equalities Bill which required equal treatment in access to employment as well as private and public services, regardless of age, disability, gender reassignment, marriage and civil partnership, race, religion or belief, sex, and sexual orientation. The Equalities Act 2010 was eventually passed in Parliament just prior to the general election of 2010 in May, with its provisions coming into force in October 2010.

One of the most important parts of the Act is the public sector Equality Duty, which is intended to ensure that fairness is at the heart of public authorities' work and that public services are designed to meet the needs of different groups. To this end, the Act gives central government the power to impose specific duties to ensure public organizations meet their obligations to actively promote equality of treatment.

In large part, the Act reflected the work of Harriet Harman, Head of the Labour government's Equality Office. At the same time, the civil service has increasingly moved away from a reliance on an internal labor market, populated by white, male Oxbridge graduates, to draw on a much broader talent pool, including post-experience and private sector executives, as part of a drive to widen its managerial expertise (Greer and Jarman, 2010). Indeed, central government policies in this area increasingly regard enhancing representativeness as key to delivering the core tasks of government more effectively, reflecting the so-called "business case for diversity" (Rajan et al., 2003). The civil service equality and diversity strategy highlights, for instance, that there is a positive link between "workforce representation, service delivery and knowledge of customer population" (Civil Service, 2008, p. 8). These developments also reflect the wider influence of consumerism in the public sector, which places an onus on government to "be effective in delivering services in an increasingly personalized way" (p. 24). At the same time, under the Labour government, they have reflected a wider commitment to building a more inclusive society in response to the challenges posed by growing social diversity (Kearns and Forrest, 2000).

According to Newman and Ashworth (2008) the equality and diversity agenda in the UK has moved beyond notions of administrative justice towards a broader concern with social justice. For instance, the Gender Equality Duty (GED), which came into force in April 2007, placed a legal obligation on public authorities to actively promote equality of opportunity between women and men (www.equalityandhumanrights.com). At the same time, during Labour's period of office numerous public services became subject to targets designed to drive up the representativeness of the workforce. For example, the Fire Service Equality and Diversity Strategy (Fire and Rescue Service, 2009) set out a goal of ensuring that by 2013 minimums of 15 percent of new fire fighters were women, and that minority ethnic staffing rates were in line with local populations.

Recent data suggests that rates of gender representation across central and local government appear to be higher than within the UK economy as a whole. Table 11.1 shows that in 2008, women were better represented in the workforce and senior management of UK central government and English local government than in the working population. However, the

Table 11.1 Representative bureaucracy in the UK (2008)

	Population	UK central government	English local government
% Women in workforce	46	53	75.1
% Women in senior posts	12	31	34.1
% Minority ethnic people in workforce	8.9	8.4	5.4
% Minority ethnic people in senior posts	6.3	3.6	3.4

Source: Audit Commission (2008), Office for National Statistics (2009a, b)

representation of minority ethnic groups in government appears to lag behind that of the working population, especially in terms of their occupation of senior management posts. Perhaps surprisingly, local government in England does much worse than UK central government on these measures of representativeness.

The growth of the "equality architecture" in the UK has placed a strong requirement on public organizations to demonstrate that they are (at the very least) representative of the population that they serve (McLaughlin, 2007). Making organizations accountable for the rate of representation, in turn, implies that organizational influences on variations in representation rates may play an important role in determining the success with which the equality and diversity agenda can be pursued across the public sector.

ORGANIZATIONAL INFLUENCES ON GENDER AND MINORITY ETHNIC REPRESENTATION

The recent promotion of gender and minority ethnic representation in the UK has reflected a policy of "passive representation," focused on demographic representativeness, which some commentators criticize as mere tokenism (e.g. Ball, 1987). Yet since public employment is especially attractive to underrepresented groups (Perrott, 2002), passive representation remains a key policy goal and one that some organizations are likely to do better than others. Indeed, it is probable that any given set of public organizations will "differ on many dimensions which potentially influence minority and female employment prospects" (Kellough, 1990, p. 557).

The relative size of public organizations may influence the prospects of female and minority ethnic representation within the workforce. Bigger organizations may find it harder to become more representative. Put simply, the employment of additional women and people of minority ethnic origin in larger central government departments and local governments makes less of an impact on the overall rate of gender and minority representation than in smaller ones. Grabosky and Rosenbloom (1975), for instance, find that the largest US federal agencies had the lowest minority ethnic representation rates – a finding that is replicated in Kellough's (1990) subsequent study of the representation of women and minority ethnic groups in federal agencies. Although larger organizations are more likely to pursue proactive equality policies (Walsh, 2007), such policies alone are unlikely to overcome the scale of the challenge those organizations face in seeking to become more representative.

Another important potential influence on the representation of women and minority ethnic groups within bureaucracies is organizational growth. According to Krislov (1967), expanding agencies are more responsive to issues of equality and diversity because they "can be more easily accommodated within the goals of the organization" (p. 139). If there are more employment opportunities within an organization, then (in theory at least) it should be easier to increase the proportion of new positions being allocated to underrepresented groups. Moreover, the potential effects of expansion and contraction on representation in a pro-equalities policy context may be especially strong. Grabosky and Rosenbloom's (1975) study of US federal agencies in the 1970s does not support this argument, but Kellough (1990) furnishes evidence of a weak positive relationship between growth and minority ethnic representation in the same organizations in the 1980s. Thus, it is anticipated that organizational growth in UK public organizations may also have benefits for representation.

The proportion of positions that are occupied part-time is a further potential organizational influence on levels of representation. On the one hand, it may be easier for organizations to address issues of underrepresentation by employing women and people of minority ethnic origin on a part-time basis. On the other, it may also be the case that part-time employment reflects the lower status of underrepresented groups within some public organizations. In either case, it seems probable that bureaucracies find it easier to employ women and minorities part-time because resistance amongst existing (and potentially unionized) full-time staff is likely to be lower to individuals perceived to represent less of a threat to their own employment status (Ricucci, 1990). In terms of gender representation, it is also highly probable that women may be more likely to occupy part-time roles due to their often being the primary carers of children (Sirianni and Negrey, 2000). Thus, the connection between part-time employment and representation is likely to be especially strong for this aspect of representativeness.

REPRESENTATION IN CENTRAL GOVERNMENT

To evaluate levels of representation in central government, variations in the employment of women and minority ethnic groups within the workforce of major spending departments are examined. These organizations are headed by cabinet ministers appointed by the prime minister of the day, with the administration of departments carried out by permanent secretaries. Central government departments employ a wide range of professional career staff and are responsible for policy formulation and implementation at the macro level. Departments vary greatly in size and budget, depending on their functions and responsibilities, with those responsible for large policy fields, such as the Home Office, often being composed of multiple smaller functional units and executive agencies. In 2009, there were 21 major spending departments within UK central government (see HM Treasury, 2009).

Gender and minority ethnic representation in each major central government spending department is measured by calculating what proportions of the total number of employees in each department are women and what proportions are of minority ethnic origin. Data on the representation of these groups in the civil service is now collected and made publicly available on an annual basis. The representation figures were calculated for each year between 2007 and 2009 – the time period for which the most comprehensive set of organizational data were available. Post-hoc tests following one-way analyses of variance for the 3-year period reveal statistically significant differences in gender and minority ethnic people's representation between almost every department.

To explore potential organizational determinants of variations in representation across departments, it is necessary to identify relevant measures of departmental size and growth, and of the proportion of part-time employees within the workforce of each department. Department size is measured as the total number of full- and part-time employees within each spending department. Departmental growth is measured as the ratio of new entrants to leavers. Part-time positions are gauged as the percentage of employees within each department classified as part-time. Descriptive statistics for the departmental characteristics are shown in Table 11.2.

Seemingly unrelated regressions (SUR) are used to model the influence of organizational characteristics on rates of representation. SURs control for correlations between the error terms across separate Ordinary Least Squares (OLS) regression models (in this case a positive correlation between separate models of gender and minority ethnic representation of 0.36). In Table 11.3, the independent variables are regressed on to female representation and the measure of minority ethnic representation.

Table 11.2   Central government department characteristics

	Mean	Min	Max
Department size	24 730.2	120	121 210
Department growth	1.0	0	9.3
% Part-time posts	13.9	3.1	34.3

Source: Office for National Statistics (2008, 2009a, 2010)

Table 11.3   Determinants of representation in central government departments 2007–09

Variable	% Women		% Ethnic minority	
	B	s.e.	B	s.e.
Department size	−0.0001**	0.00003	−0.0001**	0.00002
Department growth	−0.240	0.562	1.056*	0.517
Part-time posts	1.296**	0.136	0.172+	0.125
Chi^2 statistic	103.49**		11.27*	
R-squared	0.62		0.15	

Notes: Number of observations = 63; + $p \leq 0.10$; * $p \leq 0.05$; ** $p \leq 0.01$ (one-tailed tests). Coefficients for year dummies not shown.

The data are homoskedastic and are not distorted by multicollinearity. Dummy variables for the first 2 years of the analysis control for the possible effects of idiosyncratic events within individual years.

The statistical model explains a high proportion of the variation in gender representation across departments (about 60 percent), but much less of the variation in minority ethnic representation (about 15 percent). The results provide support for the arguments on potential organizational influences on variations in representation. A smaller total workforce and a high rate of part-time positions are both associated with greater representation of women and minority ethnic groups within a department. However, departmental growth is only associated with a higher level of minority ethnic representation. Further analysis revealed that the inclusion of dummy variables for the type of department (i.e. the core executive (e.g. the Cabinet Office), distributive (e.g. department of health), regulative (e.g. department of transport)) made no contribution to the statistical power of the model. We turn now to representative bureaucracy at the local level.

REPRESENTATION IN ENGLISH LOCAL GOVERNMENT

Due to data availability, variations in the employment of women and minority ethnic groups within local government are examined solely in England, which covers over 80 percent of the UK's population. English local governments are elected bodies, which operate in specific geographical areas, employ professional career staff, and receive approximately two-thirds of their income from central government. They are multi-purpose organizations and deliver public services in the areas of education, social care, land-use planning, waste management, public housing, leisure and culture, and welfare benefits. At the time the data presented here were gathered, there were 386 local governments in England of five types. Thirty-two London boroughs, 36 metropolitan boroughs and 46 unitary authorities are primarily found in urban areas and deliver all of the services listed above; in predominately rural areas, a two-tier system prevailed with 34 county councils administering education and social services, and 238 district councils providing mainly regulatory services, such as local development planning and street cleaning.

Gender and minority ethnic representation in local governments is measured by calculating what proportions of the total number of employees in each government are women and what proportion is of minority ethnic origin. Until 2008, data on the representation of both these groups in local governments were collected and made publicly available on an annual basis. The representation figures were calculated for each year between 2007 and 2008 to match as closely as possible the time period for which representation in central government is studied. There is some variation in the rates of representation of women and minority ethnic groups across types of local government. Indeed, post-hoc tests following one-way analyses of variance for the 2-year period reveal statistically significant differences in gender and minority ethnic representation between each type of government, with the representation of minority ethnic people especially high in London borough councils.

To explore the potential organizational determinants of variations in representation across all local governments, organization size is measured as the total number of full- and part-time employees within each government. The logarithm of this measure is taken to correct a non-normal distribution. Organization growth is measured as the ratio of employees in the current year to that in the previous year. Part-time positions are gauged as the percentage of all employees within each government classified as part-time. Prior studies suggest that minority ethnic representation in the relevant labor market is an important predictor of

Table 11.4   Local government characteristics

	Mean	Min	Max
Organization size	5463.1	131	62 291
Organization growth	1.0	0.4	1.5
% part-time posts	38.8	8.0	75.2
% local workforce BME	5.8	0	59.3

Note: BME, black and minority ethnic.

Source: Local Government Association (2010); Audit Commission (2007)

representation within the workforce of public organizations (Mladenka, 1989). A measure of the proportion of the population of working age of minority ethnic origin is therefore included within the minority ethnic representation model. Dummy variables for each type of government (except unitary authorities) are also included to control for variations in representation potentially attributable to their different service responsibilities and context. Descriptive statistics for the characteristics of local governments are shown in Table 11.4.

Seemingly unrelated regressions (SUR) are again used to model the influence of organizational characteristics on rates of representation. A positive correlation between the error terms from models of gender and minority ethnic representation (0.11) was observed on this occasion. Table 11.5 indicates that the first SUR model regresses the independent variables on to female representation, while the second regresses the same variables on to the measure of minority ethnic representation. The data are homoskedastic and are not distorted by multicollinearity. A dummy variable for the first year of the analysis controls for year-specific effects.

The statistical model explains a very high proportion of the variation in both gender (82 percent) and minority ethnic (90 percent) representation in the workforce of English local governments. The organizational influences on variations in representation in local government are in some respects similar to those found for the analysis of central government spending departments. In particular, local governments with a larger workforce and with more part-time positions are associated with greater representation of women. However, in this instance size makes no difference to, and part-time working is negatively associated with, minority ethnic representation. Most women employed in local governments occupy part-time positions (on average 61.7 percent across the sector in 2008), while minority ethnic groups tend to be more likely to occupy full-time roles, perhaps reflecting gains made from the focus on promoting diversity in the public sector.

Table 11.5 *Determinants of representation in English local governments 2007–08*

Variable	% Women		% Ethnic minority	
	B	s.e.	B	s.e.
Organization size	−9.988**	0.946	−0.504	0.512
Organization growth	4.411*	1.992	−0.264	1.052
Part-time posts	0.315**	0.020	−0.050**	0.011
% local workforce BME			0.717**	0.018
District council	−25.452**	1.231	−1.499**	0.651
County council	7.507**	0.939	0.713+	0.509
Metropolitan borough	3.183**	0.866	0.236	0.457
London borough	−0.141	0.871	8.238**	0.575
Chi^2 statistic	3437.46**		6676.14**	
R-squared	0.82		0.90	

Notes: Number of observations = 772. + $p \leq 0.10$; * $p \leq 0.05$; ** $p \leq 0.01$ (one-tailed tests). Coefficients for 2007 dummy not shown. BME, black and minority ethnic.

Finally, departmental growth is not associated with gender or minority ethnic representation, and, as anticipated, the percentage of people of minority ethnic origin in the local workforce is an especially strong predictor of minority representation in local governments.

The results also indicate that inclusion of the local government type measures makes an important contribution to the explanatory power of the model. In particular, district councils, which provide fewer distributive services, such as education and social care, and more regulatory ones, such as environmental health and waste collection, employ fewer women and ethnic minorities. By contrast, county councils, which are more focused on the provision of distributive than regulatory services, employ more women and ethnic minorities. London councils, as one might expect given the size of the minority ethnic labor pool in the capital, have a much larger minority ethnic workforce than other types of local government.

CONCLUSION

This chapter has provided a profile of representative bureaucracy in the UK. It began by examining public sector policy and practice on equality and diversity issues, and then explored the potential impact of organizational influences on gender and minority representation in central and local government. The empirical evidence suggests that the workforce of central government spending departments may, on average, be more representative of the UK population than local governments. Although women are presently overrepresented within the workforce of local governments, a commitment to a social justice approach to equality and diversity may in fact require more than parity with the demographic characteristics of the local population, especially if the role of the public sector as a model employer is to be taken seriously. This remains an important conceptual question for representative bureaucracy theorists as much as an empirical concern for researchers and policy-makers.

At the same time, the evaluation of organizational influences on gender and minority ethnic representation suggests that large bureaucracies may struggle to be more representative. At both the central and local level, women are disproportionately occupying part-time posts. Further research is required to determine the extent to which this is attributable to organizational barriers, such as union resistance and casualization of certain jobs within the public sector, or enablers, such as active representation by senior bureaucrats, responsiveness to consumer demands, and sensitivity to the preference of female employees for more flexible working arrangements to meet childcare demands. The representation of minority ethnic groups follows a less consistent pattern across the settings. Subsequent quantitative and qualitative studies could examine the extent to which this is attributable to the barriers and enablers identified above, or whether it might be a product of the relationship between the respective organizations and their labor markets. Also important would be the role of elected officials in each governmental setting.

Despite the quality of the organizational level data used here, it nonetheless exhibits several limitations that constrain the possibilities for comprehensive research of all the issues surrounding representative bureaucracy. Crucially, it was not possible on this occasion to compare organizational influences on representation in senior management in central and local government due to data unavailability. Further research in this area would cast valuable light on whether the organizational influences on representation identified here hold true for the proportion of women and minorities in top management. Similarly, other aspects of representation are of considerable theoretical and practical interest. For example, age, disability, sexual orientation, and religious belief have all been a focus in the UK. Moreover, investigation of the class representativeness of senior public managers could build on Kingsley's classic (1944) study of the class base of the British civil service before World War II.

The advent of the Conservative–Liberal Democrat coalition government has led to a radical rethink of the relationship between government and society (Jordan, 2010). Although the provisions of the Equalities Act have come into force under the coalition government, it is highly conceivable that the practical experience, political goodwill, and managerial focus that became embedded in human resources practice in the UK public sector will face new challenges. For example, public service targets, which came to characterize the Labour government's approach to public services (Hood, 2006), have been discarded by the new government, thereby removing one source of pressure to progress the equality and diversity agenda in public organizations. It will be interesting to see if a voluntaristic approach to improving representativeness might yet prove more effective than the kind of top-down one that prevailed during the past decade.

In addition, over the coming years, the UK central government and local governments will all be subject to pressures to downsize, cutback, and make efficiency savings. In this cost-conscious context, it is quite possible that any progress made on the equality and diversity agenda will be subject to serious threat particularly given the hostility of some public organizations to the perceived burdens of the equalities agenda. For example, several local governments resisted the introduction of the Commission for Racial Equality Standard in 2001 on the 'grounds of cost' (Office of the Deputy Prime Minister, 2003, p. 16). At the same time, it is likely that these complex and possibly contradictory political and economic developments may yet result in changes in the rates of representation in public organizations. All of which is to say that the politics of representative bureaucracy in the UK is likely to continue to set the boundaries for organizational efforts to make their workforces more representative of the population.

PART III

Africa, Oceania, and Asia

12. Representative bureaucracy in South Africa

Robert Cameron and Chantal Milne

INTRODUCTION

Considerable attention has been paid to democratic consolidation in South Africa but substantively less has been written on public service transformation. There have only been a few comprehensive studies written on this topic (Picard, 2005; Cameron, 2009). Historically, white Afrikaner males held most middle and senior management positions in the country's public service. In 1990, 96.9 percent of employees in the total income categories of the South African public service were white (Commonwealth Secretariat, 1991, p. 53). Apartheid also discriminated against white women, and very few held senior management positions. In 1994 South Africa had its first democratic elections and one of the priorities of the new African National Congress (ANC) government was to create a more representative bureaucracy. Unlike countries such as the United States of America, which focused on minority representation, the discourse around representative bureaucracy in South Africa is centered on the representation of the majority in the public service. This makes it an exceptional and interesting case study.

This chapter looks at the extent to which the South African public service conforms to the concept of representative bureaucracy. It draws on previous work done by the authors on the topic of affirmative action in South Africa (Cameron and Milne, 2004, 2008; Milne, 2009). The data that is analysed in this chapter is on race and gender up to 2010, which was obtained from the South African Department of Public Service and Administration (DPSA) PERSAL (Personnel and Salaries Management System). The methodology used is that of a longitudinal study of this data across time periods, namely 1995, 2000, 2005, and 2010.

The research questions of the book were addressed in the following way: "What are the starting conditions and the setting of politico-administrative institutions in South Africa?"; as a stand-alone section. "What are the major push and pull factors as far as representative bureaucracy is concerned in South Africa?" and "How can the public/ political/intellectual debate about this issue and lines of conflict be described?" are combined under the headings "Affirmative action policy in South Africa" and "Representative Bureaucracy Actors and Debates". The research question around representation of people of different races in the public sector is included in the "Analysis of representative bureaucracy in the South African Public Service."

SOUTH AFRICAN POLITICO-ADMINISTRATIVE STRUCTURES AND TRADITIONS

Until 1994, apartheid policies had denied Africans citizenship rights. They were allowed into white areas for labor purposes only, and had to live in segregated residential areas. They were also not allowed to own land in white South Africa. The majority of South Africans were forced to live in poor rural areas called homelands (Welsh, 1982). Before 1994, apartheid had effectively divided South Africa into 11 separate quasi-states, each with its own government, legislation, and administrative system. The main South African public service consisted of the national government and four provinces. In the 1980s the government established separate ethnic administrations within the public service for whites, coloureds, and Asians. Ten ethnic administrations were created in the homelands reflecting different African ethnic groupings. Four of these homelands received nominal independence. In 1994 they were reintegrated into South Africa.

The Public Service in "white" South Africa largely provided services to its white constituents. Coloureds and Asians received second-class services. Africans received extremely limited services. The early 1990s saw major political changes in South Africa. Political organizations, most notably the African National Congress (ANC), were unbanned by the National Party (NP) government. Multi-party negotiations occurred in 1992 and 1993 during which a two-stage transformation was agreed upon. This was known as the Interim Constitution of 1993, which had transitional power-sharing mechanisms. The final Constitution was passed in 1996. A highly advanced Bill of Rights forms the cornerstone of the Constitution. Provision was made for a three-tier intergovernmental system, which comprises national, provincial and local governments. The public service consists of national and provincial government staff but not local government employees. The Constitution makes specific reference to public administration. Section 195 (1) states that public administration must be governed by the democratic values and principles. There are nine such principles. The Constitution also provides for an independent Public

Service Commission (PSC) whose powers include having to promote the Section 195 values and principles and to investigate, monitor, and evaluate the organization and personnel policies and practices of the public service.

Once in power, the ANC began to transform what had been an apartheid bureaucracy into a more democratic public service that put citizens first. Under President Thabo Mbeki (1999–2008) the notion of a development state became more prominent. The development state is intended to simultaneously promote economic growth and social objectives such as poverty alleviation, which facilitate state intervention in the market (Levin, 2007). Levin (2007, p. 6) stated that "the public service or the administration of a development state has to be strong, and capable of intervening, planning and channeling societal resources towards resolving national development strategies." The 1995 White Paper on the Transformation of the Public Service laid down the national policy framework for the transformation of the public service. The late 1990s saw further White Papers on public administration topics such as affirmative action, service delivery and training. The Presidential Review Commission (1998) was set up by the government to evaluate the public service. It made a number of wide-ranging recommendations, some of which were implemented. These reports laid the conceptual framework for public sector reform in South Africa. A number of reforms were influenced by global (NPM) reforms such as contract appointments, performance management, decentralized human resource management and rightsizing (Cameron, 2009) but affirmative action policies grew out of the internal imperative to transform apartheid.

AFFIRMATIVE ACTION POLICY IN SOUTH AFRICA

In 1994 the new predominantly black government was faced with a largely white senior public service. The jobs of existing public servants were guaranteed by a sunset clause in the Constitution so large scale retrenchment was not an option. Affirmative action understandably then became a major component of the new government's public reform program. The language of representative bureaucracy underpinned the government's affirmative action policies.

The interim Constitution (RSA, 1993) was the first document to make reference to the notion of a public service that is representative of the people of South Africa. Section 212(2)(b) on the Public Service states that the public service shall: "[p]romote an efficient public administration broadly representative of the South African community."

There are also a number of policies in the democratic South Africa, which look at or include affirmative action. The first document that discussed affirmative action in the policy context of democratic South Africa was the ANC's Reconstruction and Development Programme (RDP). This policy called for an affirmative action program specifically at senior management level, along the lines of race and gender (ANC, 1994). This document provided the foundation from which the government could change the face of the South African Public Service from one dominated by white males to one more representative of South African society as a whole. It was also specifically directed at the need to change the public service at the senior management level. The affirmative action policy of the White Paper on the Transformation of the Public Service (WPTPS) set out in 1995 the initial affirmative action targets for categories of people. All departments should, within four years, have 50 percent black[1] staff at management level. At least 30 percent of new recruits, within 4 years, at senior and management level should be women (DPSA, 1995). In addition to the targets, the WPTPS stated that each department needed to have detailed plans for affirmative action as part of the broader human resource development and capacity building, as it was viewed as part of the process of empowering disadvantaged people (DPSA, 1995). It was this document that expanded on how the public service would be changed to be more representative of society as the WPTPS outlined that the Public Service needed to have detailed plans on how affirmative action would be implemented and provided a timeframe within which to achieve the goals.

It is in the final Constitution (RSA, 1996) that the notion of a representative bureaucracy is codified through affirmative action and is enshrined in the Bill of Rights. Section 9(2) states that: "[e]quality includes the full and equal enjoyment of all rights and freedoms. To promote the achievement of equality, legislative and other measures designed to protect or advance persons or categories of persons, disadvantaged by unfair discrimination may be taken."

In the chapter on public administration in the Constitution, specific provision is made for affirmative action in the public sector. Section 195(1)(i) states that: "[p]ublic administration must be broadly representative of the South African people, with employment and personnel management practices based on ability, objectivity, fairness and the need to address the imbalances of the past to achieve broad representation."

It is clear from the above excerpts that the language that is used to underpin the rationale for affirmative action is that of achieving a representative bureaucracy in democratic South Africa. The White Paper on Human Resource Management also makes reference to affirmative action. The policy states that, in combination with affirmative action, improved human resource management can achieve a representative public service (DPSA, 1997). This marks a possible shift from narrow numbers to a representative bureaucracy that would aim to provide the public with a service that would be more responsive to their needs and therefore perform better. The White Paper on Affirmative Action in the Public Service was the policy document that directly addressed affirmative action and the theory of representative bureaucracy. This policy set out a framework for the creation of a representative public service stating that the public service should be representative of the population. This means that the targets set out in the WPTPS should be viewed as minimum guidelines only and are provisional steps to achieving full demographic representation. It was also stated in this affirmative action policy that the original targets would be reviewed and revised in 1999 and then at 3-yearly intervals (DPSA, 1998). The White Paper on Affirmative Action also provided additional rationale for the policy of affirmative action through a representative bureaucracy. It stated that, by having a public service that is more representative, the result would be a more responsive and effective public service and this would result in a better relationship between the bureaucracy and citizens. An example put forward by the policy is that "the increase of women in decision making levels will lead to greater sensitization of the workplace on gender issues and more responsive delivery to women" (DPSA, 1998).

The Employment Equity Act 55 of 1998 provides the implementation framework for the guidelines set out in the other affirmative action policies. All government departments had to have detailed employment equity plans. The act also explicitly includes a section on affirmative action where it details targets that are broader than those contained in the WPTPS. It states that there should be suitably qualified people from the target groups across all occupational categories and levels. This Act provides a restriction to affirmative action policy, indicating that it has moved far beyond being a mere symbolic change in what the public service looks like to become a human resource practice that is concerned with performance and the need to have qualified people in the positions specifically from target groups. It is also this affirmative action legislation that states explicitly that there must be representation across the whole public service and not just at management level; therefore, it aims to create a public service that is broadly representative of the population. Employers who do not comply with the Act will be referred to the Labor Court for possible disciplinary action.

The language of representative bureaucracy is evident in most of the policy documents that have been discussed above but they differ in the extent to which this principle is emphasized.

ANALYSIS OF REPRESENTATIVE BUREAUCRACY IN THE SOUTH AFRICAN PUBLIC SERVICE

The South African government makes use of four broad population groups within which to classify people; African, coloured, Indian or Asian, and white (Burger, 2010). However, in South Africa there is no official definition of these population groupings as when statistics are collected people are asked to classify themselves into the different groups. It is therefore a self-description and not any other method that is used for classification purposes (Statistics South Africa, 1998). Where the classification of African, Asian, and white is understood internationally the population grouping of coloured has different meanings; in the South African context it refers to a people who self-classify themselves as mixed-race (Van der Ross, 1997). For affirmative action targets the distinctions between African, coloured, and Asian were collapsed into one group and referred to as black, because all of these groupings were disadvantaged under apartheid (Statistics South Africa, 1998).

Table 12.1 below shows the four population groups as well for the combined population group of blacks for 2010 as for the whole South African population. It must be noted that although the affirmative action policy makes reference to the need for the public service to be representative of the population as a whole the government makes use of the Labour Force Surveys to assess whether the representation has been achieved. This is due to the survey providing the numbers of the population who would be able to be employed by the public service. The labor force consists of people who are classified as employed and unemployed (Statistics South Africa, 2010b).

Table 12.1   Mid-year population groups estimates, 2010

Population Group	Number	Number	Percent of total population
African	39 682 600		
Coloured	4 424 100		
Indian/Asian	1 299 900		
*Black		45 406 600	90.8
White		4 584 700	9.2
Total		49 991 300	100

Notes: *Black total includes, African, coloured, and Indian/Asian.

Source: Statistics South Africa (2010b)

Race

As pointed out, the original affirmative action target for race was that by 1999 all departments should have 50 percent blacks at management level. The national government cabinet reviews its affirmative action targets against the Labour Force surveys. Once the 50 percent threshold was met the national cabinet set a target of 75 percent for blacks in April 2005 (Public Service Commission, 2006).

The third quarter 2010 Labour Force survey revealed that the labor force consisted of 73.62 percent African, 12.08 percent white, 11.04 percent colored and 3.27 percent Asian. In terms of representative bureaucracy theory in the South African and the terminology used in the WPTPS the percentage of the labor force classified as black is 87.93 percent and white is 12.07 percent (Statistics South Africa, 2010a). These are the numbers or targets that need to be used as a basis for assessing the extent to which a representative public service has been achieved.

Gender

The target set by affirmative action policy for women was not disaggregated into different racial groups. As pointed out, the original target set for women was 30 percent at senior management level. This target was reached in March 2006, and in light of this being achieved, the cabinet revised the target to 50 percent by March 2009. The new target is applicable not only to senior management but across the whole of the public service (Public Service Commission (PSC), 2007). The revised target set by the cabinet is also roughly in line with a representative bureaucracy population level of 52 percent (Statistics South Africa, 2008). Females represent 44.81 percent of the labor force. In terms of targets, the legislation accordingly requires an overrepresentation of women in the public service.

ANALYSIS OF PERSONNEL AND SALARY INFORMATION SYSTEM DATA

Data was obtained from a detailed analysis of PERSAL (Personnel and Salaries Management System) which is a database of public service employees kept by the DPSA. The salary classifications on which the tables below are based are: senior management, management, highly skilled supervision, highly skilled production, skilled, and lower skilled. The level of management refers to the categories of management and senior management. Data for these two categories were separate until

Table 12.2   Total public service: race

	September 1995	December 2000	December 2005	December 2010
Whites in public service	312772	167272	126640	124683
Percent of total public service	24.67	16.02	12.24	9.71
Blacks in public service	954994	876685	908228	1158953
Percent of total public service	75.33	83.98	87.76	90.29
Total public service	1267766	1043957	1034868	1283636

Source: Statistics South Africa, 2011

December 2004. For the purpose of this chapter their numbers have been combined.

There has been a decline in the total public service employees from 1995 to 2000 (Table 12.2). This was part of the NPM reforms introduced by the government (Cameron, 2009).

From 2000 to 2005 there was a slight decrease in the number of public servants to 1034868 followed by a substantial increase to 1283636 in 2010 (Table 12.2). This increase could be accounted for by a move away from NPM ideas of a minimalist state towards strengthening the center of government in support of a stronger developmental state (Fraser-Moleketi, 2006). The plan is to develop a more professional public service, which entails growth in the higher echelons of the public service. There are now more people in the public service than there were in 2005.

The total number of blacks has increased from 75.33 percent of the public service in 1995 to 90.29 percent in December 2010, which is above the labor force total of 77.92 percent. Whites have fallen from 24.67 percent in 1995 to 9.71 percent in 2010, which is expected given the need to create a more representative bureaucracy.

In line with the rightsizing of the state in the late 1990s, the total number of women in the public service showed a decline from 618603 in 1995 to 533777 in 2000 (Table 12.3). However, in percentage terms this was a slight increase from 48.79 percent to 51.13 percent. There was then a slight increase in numbers in 2005 to 580122 followed by a substantial increase in 2010 to 723183, a total which is higher than the number of women in the total public service in 1995. This trend is also shown in the percentage representation of women in the public service as by 2010 women represent

Table 12.3   Total public service: gender

	September 1995	December 2000	December 2005	December 2010
Females in public service	618 603	533 777	580 122	723 183
Percent of total public service	48.79	51.13	56.06	56.34
Males in public service	649 163	510 180	454 746	560 453
Percent of total public service	51.21	48.87	43.94	43.66
Total public service	1 267 766	1 043 957	1 034 868	1 283 636

Source: Statistics South Africa, 2011

Table 12.4   Senior management level: race

	September 1995	December 2000	December 2005	December 2010
Whites in management	2161	2206	2024	3259
Percent of management	62.66	47.2	29.02	26.69
Blacks in management	1288	2468	4951	8950
Percent of management	37.34	52.8	70.98	73.31
Total management	3449	4674	6975	12 209

Source: Statistics South Africa, 2011

56.34 percent of the total public service. This increase is in line with affirmative action policies promoting an increase in the number of women in the public service.

In 2010, numbers of women exceeded the 50 percent target across public service. In comparison to the labor force total (44.81 percent), the percentage of women in the public service (56.34 percent) has exceeded the percentage representativeness in the public service.

There has been an increase in staff at the senior management level from 3449 in 1995 to 12 209 in 2010 (Table 12.4). This can be attributed to increasing the total number of people employed at management level in line with the need for more professional staff to run the development state.

At senior management level, the percentage of whites in 2010 has more than halved from the 1995 figures, but in terms of real numbers there has been an increase in the employment of whites in the management service

Table 12.5   Senior management level: gender

	September 1995	December 2000	December 2005	December 2010
Females in management	274	928	2045	4240
Percent of management	7.94	19.85	29.32	34.73
Total management	3449	4674	6975	12209

Source: Statistics South Africa, 2011

from 2161 in 1995 to 3259 in 2010. Comparatively, the number of blacks has risen from 1288 in 1995 to 8950. This shows substantive gains in terms of real numbers.

In terms of racial categories at the senior management level, the cabinet set the target for blacks at 75 percent in April 2005 (PSC, 2006). When the percentage of blacks is looked at in 2010 it is 73.31, which is just below the target. It is also lower than that of the overall percentages for the total public service (90.29 percent) and that of the labor force statistics. This shows that there still exists an overrepresentation of whites in the senior management service management level of the public service. This is to be expected given the longer experience and capacity of whites.

In terms of gender there has been a substantial gain in terms of representativeness, with the number of women at senior management level growing from a negligible level of 7.94 percent to over 34.73 percent from 1995 through to 2010 (Table 12.5). However, there have been a number of challenges encountered in attaining this and indeed the 50 percent target throughout the public service has not been reached at the management level. Geraldine Fraser-Moleketi (2008), the former Minister of DPSA stated that there has been a decline in the number of women at the level of directors-general. There are a greater number of women in the public service concentrated on traditional caring professions such as teaching and nursing (PSC, 2004; Ministry of Public Service and Administration, 2006). Despite vigorous recruiting, there appears to be a "glass ceiling" hindering the progress of women into the higher levels of bureaucracy. Women often have to balance child bearing, running households and a professional career.

Highly skilled supervision is the middle level of management. There has been a substantial increase in the total number of people employed in this category across all racial groups, in particular blacks, where the numbers have increased from 8572 in 1995 to 168679 in 2010 (Table 12.6). This increase is also reflected in the percentages where blacks represent 82.09 percent of this middle management level. There has been a substantial decrease in the percentage of whites in the highly skilled supervision ranks.

Table 12.6   Highly skilled supervision: race

	September 1995	December 2000	December 2005	December 2010
Whites in highly skilled supervision	12 577	16 510	24 464	36 810
Percent of highly skilled supervision	59.47	46.79	25.67	17.91
Blacks in highly skilled supervision	8572	18 772	70 837	168 679
Percent of highly skilled supervision	40.53	53.21	74.33	82.09
Total highly skilled supervision	21 149	35 282	95 301	205 489

Source: Statistics South Africa, 2011

Table 12.7   Highly skilled supervision: gender

	September 1995	December 2000	December 2005	December 2010
Females in highly skilled production	3901	9394	38 688	117 023
Percent of highly skilled production	18.45	26.63	40.6	56.95
Total highly skilled supervision	21 149	35 282	95 301	205 489

Source: Statistics South Africa, 2011

However, despite this 41.56 percent drop there has been a growth in real numbers of over 24 000 whites.

This increase is indicative of the efforts to increase the middle management level of the public service. The reasons for this include the need to increase the pool from which senior management comes from (Cameron and Milne, 2008).

The total number of women in this has also increased and in fact has exceeded the 50 percent target for women in 2010. In terms of gender composition, women now make up over 56.95 percent of the people employed at this level (Table 12.7). This shows an overrepresentation of women at middle management in relation to the labor force population statistic of 44.81 percent.

Table 12.8 Highly skilled production: race

	September 1995	December 2000	December 2005	December 2010
Whites in highly skilled production	184 006	120 761	82 331	60 312
Percent of highly skilled production	29.98	20.49	14.64	11.2
Blacks in highly skilled production	429 669	468 572	480 093	478 126
Percent of highly skilled production	70.02	79.51	85.36	88.8
Total highly skilled production	613 675	589 333	562 424	538 438

Source: Statistics South Africa, 2011

Table 12.9 Highly skilled production: gender

	September 1995	December 2000	December 2005	December 2010
Females in highly skilled production	324 866	324 866	339 115	328 576
Percent of highly skilled production	52.94	55.12	60.3	61.02
Total highly skilled production	613 675	589 333	562 424	538 438

Source: Statistics South Africa, 2011

Highly skilled production includes nurses, human resources, and financial clerks and administrative officers. There was a slight decrease in numbers in the category of highly skilled production from 1995 to 2010. Blacks are 88.8 percent of highly skilled production category and whites 11.2 percent. This is very close to the labor force totals of 77.92 percent and 12.08 percent, respectively.

The numbers and percentage of females has increased between 1995 and 2010. Females, as a percentage of this category are overrepresented in terms of the labor force, comprising 61.02 percent of the category.

The skilled category includes artisans, clerks, secretaries, drivers, and nursing assistants. There has been an increase in the number of skilled staff, from 249 919 in 1995 to 348 646 in 2010. However, in both number

Table 12.10   Skilled: race

	September 1995	December 2000	December 2005	December 2010
Whites in skilled	64 300	25 444	15 478	11 116
Percent of skilled	25.73	11.57	6.95	3.19
Blacks in skilled	185 619	194 531	207 072	337 530
Percent in skilled	74.27	88.43	93.05	96.81
Total skilled	249 919	219 975	222 550	348 646

Source: Statistics South Africa, 2011

Table 12.11   Skilled: gender

	September 1995	December 2000	December 2005	December 2010
Females in skilled	111 950	116 516	131 162	195 723
Percent of skilled	44.79	52.97	58.94	56.14
Total skilled	249 919	219 975	222 550	348 646

Source: Statistics South Africa, 2011

and percentage terms, whites have declined from 25.73 percent in 1995 to 3.19 percent in 2010 (Table 12.10). This shows a substantial under representation in terms of the labor force survey. This could be because a large number of blue-collar whites have left the public service (Cameron and Milne, 2008). In this category, Asians and coloureds come close to representing the population in 2008 with percentage representation at 1.47 percent and 9.91 percent, respectively. However, Africans are overrepresented in terms of the 2010 labor force at 85.43 percent.

The number of women has also increased at the skilled level of the public service, with women representing 56.14 percent of the total number of people employed (Table 12.11).

The lower skilled category includes cleaners, farmhands and laborers, messengers, road workers, and security guards. The total number in the lower skilled category has declined considerably from 379 574 to 112 442 in 2010. The percentage of whites in this category has declined from 13.1 percent in 1995 to 1.14 percent in 2010 (Table 12.12). In comparison the percentage of blacks has increased from 86.9 percent to 98.86 percent over the same period. However, the numbers across all the racial categories have decreased. This pattern can be explained by the increase of outsourcing at this level. A number of positions have also been reclassified to the

Table 12.12   Lower skilled: race

	September 1995	December 2000	December 2005	December 2010
Whites in lower skilled	49 728	2351	2284	1277
Percent of lower skilled	13.1	1.21	1.55	1.14
Blacks in lower skilled	329 846	192 342	145 187	111 165
Percent of lower skilled	86.9	98.79	98.45	98.86
Total lower skilled	379 574	194 693	147 471	112 442

Source: Statistics South Africa, 2011

Table 12.13   Lower skilled: gender

	September 1995	December 2000	December 2005	December 2010
Females in lower skilled	161 896	82 073	69 030	65 705
Percent of lower skilled	42.65	42.16	46.81	58.43
Total lower skilled	379 574	194 693	147 471	112 442

Source: Statistics South Africa, 2011

skilled category, which is a major reason for this decrease in numbers across this category (Cameron and Milne, 2008).

The numbers of both men and women have declined across the period under investigation. In percentage terms, however, the level of representation for women has grown by over 15 percent to 58.43 percent (Table 12.13).

REPRESENTATIVE BUREAUCRACY ACTORS AND DEBATES

While there is some debate within the ANC, the party is still firmly committed to the principle of affirmative action. For example, the ex-Minister of DPDA, Geraldine Fraser-Moleketi in response to a question whether affirmative action should be scrapped in the lower levels of the public sector given that the targets have been met, responded that affirmative action is not a numbers issue, but it is about creating economic opportunities.[2]

Jacob Zuma (2008) in his capacity as President of the ANC said that there is no sunset clause for affirmative action on the cards: "We have not reached a stage when we should say affirmative action is on the way out." The government has come under a great deal of pressure from black economic empowerment groupings to retain affirmative action. Jimmy Manyi, President of the Black Management Forum, has strongly opposed the abolition of affirmative action and argues that this policy should be strengthened. The official opposition in South Africa, the Democratic Alliance (DA) state that they are in favor of affirmative action, however, the way in which the policies have previously been implemented is viewed as conflicting with the spirit of the Constitution. "During Mr Mbeki's presidency, the real goal was control through the installation of cadres to operate the levers of power and through the imposition of demographic representativeness and cadre deployment" (Smuts, 2009). The DA maintains that the Constitutional provision that makes representativeness mandatory refers only to broad representation. They argue that gender and race composition should be broadly reflected upon, for employment appointments, and ability and fairness should carry as much weight as the need for redress. The opposition party views representativeness as being the ideal and not a mandatory head-counting measure: "It remains the primary consideration that appointees should be fit and proper" (Smuts, 2009).

The largest and oldest (white) trade union in South Africa, Solidarity, also has a critical view of the way in which affirmative action has been implemented. The perspective of Solidarity is that affirmative action is resulting in discrimination based on racial categories. This discrimination is said to lie with the rationale for the policies, where the success of the policies is measured primarily through attaining racial targets rather than substantial outcomes. The view of the trade union is that targets are not set equally across all levels of the public service. For example, there are no targets set for whites at the lower levels of the public service and this is a form of discrimination (Solidarity, 2010). Also, it is Solidarity's view that the category "black" is a masquerade, which allows for African people to be promoted at the expense of coloured and Asian people (Hermann, 2011).

There are divergent views within the ANC regarding the representation of the designated affirmative action groups. This is particularly noticeable in debates regarding the representation of coloured versus African representation. The (ANC-aligned) Congress of the South African Trade Unions (COSATU), the biggest trade union federation in the country has stated that coloured workers are generally underrepresented in terms of the implementation of affirmative action policies (Craven, 2011). In comparison an ANC's national spokesman has claimed that there is an "oversupply of coloureds" in the Western Cape province's people when regional percentages are looked at in relation to the national ones (Manyi, 2011). The former Minister of Finance, Trevor Manuel (a coloured) differs, arguing that coloured people are also black (Manuel, 2011). This debate stems from the differences in racial composition in South Africa's nine provinces and whether targets are assessed based on national as opposed to regional demographics.

Another debate within the ANC is whether gender policy should be amended. There is a view expressed most strongly by the Black Management Forum that white women have benefited disproportionately from affirmative action and should no longer be a beneficiary of the gender provisions of this policy.

CONCLUSION

The democratic aims of representative bureaucracy have largely been fulfilled in respect of race and gender with a few qualifications, namely that blacks are underrepresented at senior management level; whites are over-represented at senior management level; females are underrepresented at senior management level and whites are underrepresented at lower levels of public service. Representative bureaucracy also appears to have had positive spin-offs in that an increasing number of public servants are able to communicate in the variety of languages that citizens speak and have a greater understanding of the needs of communities who were neglected under apartheid. It has also had important symbolic value in that it indicates that the political system is open and democratic: a representative bureaucracy is understood to be one that consists of a workforce that reflects the composition of the citizens of the country.

A representative bureaucracy has also performed an important role in stabilizing South Africa's political situation. Census statistics have shown that the fastest growing income group is the black middle class. These increased Public Service affirmative action employees form a major component of this growing middle class. Without affirmative action, the racially based income differentials would have been starker than they are today. The disparity would have been a certain recipe for social unrest. One tenet of representative bureaucracy theory is that a representative public service will be more responsive to the population that it is representing. This is a difficult question to answer. There is general consensus that there are poor skills levels in the public service albeit co-existing with pockets of excellence. This has been acknowledged in government reports and by academics (see Butler, 2008; Cameron, 2009). However there has been no comprehensive empirical study, which examines the reasons for poor service delivery. While there is some evidence that representativeness is a cloak for patronage appointments (Cameron, 2009, 2011), the reasons for poor service delivery are multifaceted. Other reasons for poor service delivery include high management turnover, high vacancy rates, the brain drain to the private sector, and rapid vertical mobility in the public sector for officials who have not yet developed the necessary skills (Cameron, 2009). More systematic empirical research is needed to examine this relationship between representative bureaucracy and service improvement.

Finally, while the Constitution states, "Public Administration must be broadly representative of the South African people" it does not necessarily say that race must be the basis of that representativeness. Given the rise of the African middle class, is it not possible to consider a more class-based approach to affirmative action in the future?

NOTES

1. The term encompasses African, Coloured and Indian/Asian people.
2. Interview, November 28, 2008.

13. Politics of representative bureaucracy in India

Bas van Gool and Frank de Zwart

THREE POLITICS OF RESERVATIONS

The issue of group representation in public institutions has been at the heart of Indian politics since long before its independence in 1947. Given caste divisions and the ethnic, cultural, religious, and linguistic diversity of Indian society, this is hardly surprising. Politics of representation in India, however, do not primarily concern the question whether or not the state should build a representative bureaucracy. The need to do so is widely acknowledged and the Constitution of India supports staunch measures – such as reservations[1] in the form of job quotas – to help realize it. Governments in the center and the states use that opportunity – on an unrivalled scale – to promote employment of lower castes or classes in the public sector.

The Indian state is committed to enlarge representation in the bureaucracy of so-called "socially and educationally backward" groups. The latter is a constitutional category comprising an array of communities that make up about three-quarters of the population. From a comparative perspective, India's commitment to representative bureaucracy is remarkable. In most liberal democracies, preferential policies for ascribed groups generate fierce opposition because such policies violate equality before the law (Young, 1998). In India, however, this is not the main issue. The need for reservations as such is relatively uncontested because most people in India are acutely aware of the entrenched group inequalities that characterize their society, and of the problem that very large sections of the population are severely underrepresented in positions of power such as jobs in the bureaucracy (Galanter, 1984).

India's caste system is a textbook example of a rigid social stratification based on hereditary status. Ever since independence from British rule, India's modernizing elite has stressed that it aims to mitigate (if not eradicate) caste hierarchy, and reservation policy is a crucial instrument to realize this aim. Consensus over the need for reservations, however, does not mean that political issues are resolved. Reservations in India are still very controversial, but controversy and contention focus on the implementation rather than on the principle. For a good understanding of this controversy, elementary knowledge about India's caste system is required. Hence the first section below introduces the basic traits of caste in India.

We organize our account of the politics of representative bureaucracy in India around three controversial issues in the implementation of reservations: (1) Designating the beneficiaries – a contentious process that began in colonial times and continues today. (2) The so-called "creamy layer problem" – how to spread the benefits of reservations in a just way. (3) The question of active representation – whether group-identified bureaucrats use their administrative power to represent their groups' interests. Each of these issues generates a particular politics of reservations. We analyse these politics as they unfold for the two main categories of beneficiaries: the Untouchables and the "Backward Classes" (we shall explain that term below). Together these two categories constitute 80 percent of all beneficiaries, and about 60 percent of the population of India. India has been struggling with the politics of reservations for over 50 years. Our analysis suggests a few conclusions that may be instructive for other cases as well. First, the power of government to determine which "groups" will profit from a quota regime should not be overestimated. Second, in the context of electoral politics and a highly stratified society it is harder to curb the eligibility of "creamy layers" of beneficiaries than to expand reservations and allow proliferation of beneficiary categories. In effect, reservation regimes often become more complex and hard to administer and control over time. Third, quotas are no guarantee for the emergence of passively representative bureaucracies and there is no inevitable link between passive and active representation.

CASTE: DIVISION AND HIERARCHY

Division and hierarchy between communities characterize the caste system. The units of division are endogamous groups with a traditional occupation and a hereditary membership. The basic criterion for ranking these groups is ritual purity. Purity and pollution of castes follow from their traditional occupation and stick to castes as a whole. Most polluting are death and bodily emissions (Dumont, 1970 [1998]). Castes whose traditional occupation entails contact with them (for instance, washer men, leatherworkers, and barbers) rank low. Some traditional occupations (such as the skinning of animal carcasses, removal of human waste, and attendance at cremation grounds) bestow a massive and permanent impurity. The castes that specialize in them are considered untouchable by higher ranked castes and occupy the bottommost part of the caste hierarchy. All members of a caste – regardless of whether they follow its traditional occupation – share its rank in the hierarchy.[2] Caste hierarchy thus has a ritual basis and it is reflected in social and economic figures such as those concerning representation in government employment. The lower castes and the untouchables are strongly underrepresented in public sector employment, especially in the middle and higher levels (see below).

Caste identity follows the segmentary principle: the meaning of caste is relative to context. In the context of local events castes are small endogamous groups of people with the same name, spread over a few adjacent villages. On a regional level, castes are clusters of local castes, perceived by others as groups with similar status and subsumed under one name. In the context of a state or the nation, castes are clusters of regional clusters. In Indian languages these three segments are called jatis.[3]

Some authors specify the segmentary levels as caste, sub-caste, or sub-sub-caste. Others refer to castes of the first through the fourth order. Most, however, simply say "caste" and assume that the relevant level of segmentation is clear from context. The "castes" in government publications like the Census of India or the lists used for reservation policy are mostly regional or state-level caste clusters. But whereas outsiders, including the government, treat these clusters as groups with similar status they are still highly stratified for insiders. Many castes and sub castes are divided and ranked internally, and their units practice endogamy (just as castes do) or hypergamy (e.g. Mandelbaum, 1970, pp. 235–240). The same is true for the category "Untouchables," whose role in the politics of representation we discuss separately below. Untouchables are formally outside the caste system but in reality social structure among them follows the same principles: untouchable castes are made up of sub-castes with their own status ranking and marriage rules (Moffatt, 1979; Charsley, 1996; Deliège, 1999; Briggs, 1920 [1997]).

India's caste stratification has a sheer endless number of divisions, which makes the implementation of reservation policy very complicated and contentious. At present the central government recognizes well over 4000 castes as eligible for reservations, but that is not the end of it (we return to this below). Who exactly should a representative bureaucracy represent? Which group-boundaries are to be decisive for selecting the beneficiaries of reservation policy, and which criteria are used to establish that? These are a few of the hard questions in India's politics of representation.

POLITICS OF DESIGNATION

The politics of designating beneficiaries for reservations in India is path dependent. The foundation for the difficult issues today was laid by decisions made under British rule. The first part of this section discusses the colonial period; the second part concentrates on the period after 1947.

Reservations Under British Rule

In 1946, on the eve of independence from British rule, India's new political leadership set about the important task of drafting a new Constitution. This was done through a prolonged series of constituent assembly debates, spanning 3-years, in which over 300 prominent members of the nationalist movement participated. Most of the issues were pre-discussed in committees, one of which was the Sub-committee on Minorities. The major problem issue this deliberative body discussed was which "minority" groups, if any, were to be granted special protection by the new Constitution and what forms "special protection" should take. It was a pertinent issue because British colonial constitutions (1919 and 1935) contained special provisions for several officially recognized minorities. Muslims and the so-called "depressed classes" (an administrative euphemism for the Untouchables) were entitled to separate representation in the provincial legislatures and to reserved quotas in colonial public services.

These provisions under British rule were motivated by imperial self-interest. From the 1920s onwards, the British faced opposition and demands for self-rule from the Congress movement led by Mahatma Gandhi. The British were not willing to give up their rule but they did introduce limited forms of "native" political participation as a concession. In breaking up the unity of nationalist purpose, the British preferred strategy was to foster disagreements and rifts among native leaders and to facilitate the mobilization of minority groups that were willing to oppose the Congress movement and its claim to speak on behalf of the entire Indian nation. Groups that opposed the Congress movement – Muslims and Untouchables – received special benefits such as nominated seats in representative bodies, separate electorates, and reservations in the bureaucracy. The primary targets of this colonial divide and rule strategy were the Muslims (at the time around 23 percent of the population (Mondal, 2000)). The Untouchables (estimated at that time at 15 percent of the population) were added, however, because, as Secretary of State L.S. Amery put it, there were "politically very considerable advantages in having two substantial minorities to whom consideration has to be paid, and not to be put in the position of being merely labeled pro-Muslim and anti-Hindu" (cited in Shourie, 1997, pp. 85–86).

The promise of special benefits had an immediate effect. Until then, untouchable castes' attempts at social mobility had been primarily aimed at escaping untouchable ritual status, whether through the contestation of ascribed impurity, abandonment of stigmatizing activities, emulation of high caste religious, cultural and dietary practices (such as vegetarianism), or conversion to other religions (Christianity, Sikhism, Islam) (Deliège, 1999). The prospect of government jobs, however, turned untouchable status into an asset, especially so for educated untouchables. With an eye on improving their employment chances, untouchable caste organizations and associations all over India now started to cultivate their castes' lowliness and backwardness (see e.g. Bandyopadhyay, 1994; Deliège, 2002).

British efforts to mobilize a separate untouchable "community" divided the prominent Indian politicians of the time. Mahatma Gandhi considered the doctrine of untouchability a "horrible and terrible" stain on the Hindu faith, and an "insult to religion and humanity," but he still opposed special privileges for Untouchables. The latter, Gandhi argued, were an attack on Hinduism with its "divine," "harmonious," "organic," and "moral" order of castes. Gandhi wanted to purge Hinduism of the "sinful" belief in untouchability by means of religious reform, not through legislation or remedial state action (Bayly, 1999; Jaffrelot, 2003).

Other prominent political leaders, however, wanted to keep religion (and with it caste) out of all definitions of the nation. Jawaharlal Nehru (who would later become India's first Prime Minister) advocated a secular liberal democracy and rejected the idea that the state would define the Indian nation as built up from religious communities or castes. Nehru envisioned a nation of citizens, equal before the law, and wanted India's problem of group inequalities to be treated primarily as a class issue (De Zwart, 2000, pp. 53–54).

Gandhi's and later also Nehru's attempts to mobilize the Indian population under the Congress banner to oppose British rule were widely distrusted in South India. In the 1920s and 1930s, South India had a strong political movement – the non-Brahmin movement – that mobilized wide support on a caste-base. The non-Brahmins opposed Gandhi and the Congress movement. They did not share the ideal of independence from the British. Their stance was that Congress-rule would be Brahmin-rule, which would be worse than British rule. The non-Brahmins, by mouth of their political organization the Justice Party, thus repeatedly declared loyalty to the British (Irshick, 1969; Rajaraman, 1988).

Not surprisingly, the non-Brahmins played a role in the imperial strategy. In the 1920s and 1930s, the British started large-scale reservation programs – in the form of job quotas in the bureaucracy – to accommodate the non-Brahmin movement. The Justice Party mobilized wide political support among landholding castes (small, medium, and big landholders) in South India.

Their campaign focused on one clear grievance: the Brahmin monopoly on government jobs (Irshick, 1969).[4] The Justice Party demanded reserved job quotas for the non-Brahmin in order to break that monopoly. The British quickly conceded this demand and initiated a committee (the Miller Committee) to design reservation policies. This suited imperial strategy because the Brahmin monopoly on government jobs was a source of social unrest since Brahmin castes were accused of widespread nepotism and corruption (cf. Frykenberg, 1965; Irshick 1969). And, with the rise of democratic government in the provinces, the end of British rule impending, and the growing force of Mahatma Gandhi's Congress Movement, the British were in search of political support (see Brown, 1994).

In 1921 Mysore launched a program for "backward communities," defined by the Miller Committee as "all communities other than Brahmins who are not now adequately represented in the public service" (in Galanter, 1984, p. 156). Miller's scheme made 96 percent of the population eligible (Dushkin, 1979, p. 661). In 1925 Bombay introduced job quotas for all communities except Brahmins, Prahbus, Marwaris, Parsis, Banias, and Christians (Galanter, 1984, p. 156). The 1927 Communal Government Order in Madras reserved 5 of every 12 government jobs for non-Brahmin Hindus, 2 for Brahmins, 2 for Christians, 2 for Muslims, and 1 for "others" (Irshick, 1969, pp. 236–244; see also Radhakrishnan, 1996, pp. 113–114).

Caste-based reservations, then, were well established in several provinces from the 1920s. The Constituent Assembly that drafted the Constitution of independent India, we shall see below, struggled with this fact. Jawaharlal Nehru and B.R. Ambedkar (one of the principal drafters of the constitution) were liberal modernizers. They wanted to avoid recognition of castes in Constitutional articles, especially in articles that concerned the creation of a more representative bureaucracy (De Zwart, 2000).

B.R. Ambedkar was India's first Western-educated and professionally qualified untouchable.[5] In the decades preceding independence Gandhians and orthodox Hindu politicians found Ambedkar to be their key opponent on the issue of untouchability. Ambedkar considered the caste system inherently pernicious and oppressive. It had made "slaves" and "broken men" of the Untouchables and should, therefore, be "annihilated" altogether (Nehru shared that view). Throughout his life Ambedkar alternated between two different strategies to accomplish this goal – a pragmatic political strategy, aimed at obtaining specific representation for Untouchables in India's political institutions, and a more fundamental religious strategy, aimed at escaping "the poison of Brahminism" through conversion to another religion (Ambedkar, 1936 [1968]; Bayly, 1999; Jaffrelot, 2000).

A famous clash between Ambedkar and Gandhi occurred in 1932. In the consultations over the new Constitution, Ambedkar – like other minority leaders had done for their groups – demanded separate electorates for Untouchables (a claim that suited overall British strategy, as we saw). Gandhi, however, claimed to represent the "vast mass of untouchables" in his "own person," and he vowed to resist separate electorates for Untouchables with his life and started a fast "unto death" (Galanter, 1984; Gupta, 1985). In the end, Ambedkar saved Gandhi's life by dropping his demand for separate electorates in exchange for more reserved seats in the provincial assemblies. The deal between Gandhi and Ambedkar, known as the Poona Pact, was codified in the last colonial constitution – the Act of 1935. It triggered an intricate machinery of listing, or "scheduling" new special caste-based constituencies (Bayly, 1999). In 1936, these "scheduled caste" populations were also awarded 8.33 percent quota of jobs in the administration. At the time this was almost an "afterthought," because both the colonial authorities and Ambedkar reckoned that job quotas for Untouchables would not accomplish much since there were very few qualified candidates from among their ranks (Jaffrelot, 2000).

Reservations After Independence

After the British had left, in 1947, nothing would have prevented India's new leaders from abolishing the special provisions for colonially sponsored minorities. Indeed members of the constituent assembly, in line with the secular agenda now pursued by the political elite, led by Nehru, did decide to eliminate the special treatment of Muslims, Sikhs, Christians, Parsi, and other religious minorities (Rudolph and Rudolph, 1987). They felt "forced," however, to maintain (and even extend) the reservations for Untouchables, who were widely felt to be "unable to look after themselves." The Untouchables "needed" and "deserved" reservations in order to guarantee them a share in the administration and to make sure that their interests were represented in the bureaucracy; something which could not arguably be expected from the "machinery of the old pattern" operated by "officers belonging to Brahmin and allied castes" (Saksena, 1981; Chanchreek, 1991). The Constitution of independent India was to guarantee that entitlement.

The Constitutional provisions that give legal grounding to reservations in the bureaucracy are basically authorizations of special state-policies to assist deprived groups. They were written with an eye on existing quota policies, but they do not prescribe such policies explicitly. Article 46 (in the Directive Principles of State Policy), which prescribes that "the State shall promote with special care the educational and economic interests of the weaker sections of the people, and, in particular, of the Scheduled Castes and the Scheduled Tribes, and shall protect them from social injustice and all forms of exploitation," lays down the general commitment to preferential treatment of deprived groups. Articles 15(4) and 16(4) in the Fundamental Principles exempt preferential treatment of certain groups from the general ban on discrimination that articles 15 and 16 enact. Nothing in article 15 should prevent "any special provision for the advancement of any socially and educationally backward classes of citizens or for the Scheduled Castes and the Scheduled Tribes," amendment 15(4) reads, and amendment 16(4) says that nothing in article 16 can prevent "any provision for the reservation of appointments or posts in favor of any backward class of citizens which, in the opinion of the State, is not adequately represented in the services under the State." Both 15(4) and 16(4) were added to the Constitution in the first round of amendments in 1951.[6]

The terminology in these amendments is significant: Designated beneficiaries of preferential policies are named as "Scheduled Castes and Tribes," "weaker sections," and "Backward Classes" or "Socially and Educationally Backward Classes." But there is a crucial difference between these categories. The Constitution empowers the President of India to specify and list the Scheduled Castes (after consultation with authorities in the state) and once officially proclaimed, an Act of Parliament can only change this list. In 1950 the first President of independent India used this power and ordered a list of Scheduled Castes to be made. However, an authoritative list of Scheduled Castes did already exist at that time because this category was also mentioned in the 1936 Constitution (under British rule) and had been listed for policy purposes. In 1950 that older list was "basically re-enacted" (Galanter, 1984, p. 132). Afterwards it was adjusted periodically (mostly on the basis of new and better data from the Census) but not in any fundamental sense. "There have been no important policy departures . . . indeed there has been no further attempt to formulate any criterion for inclusion [in the Scheduled castes]" (Galanter, 1984, p. 132). Today India counts well over a thousand recognized Scheduled Castes.

For the Backward Classes a different situation evolved. The Constitution empowers the President of India to list the Backward Classes,[7] as it does for the Scheduled Castes, but in 1950 no such lists existed. The non-Brahmins, for whom job quotas existed in South India, were not exactly similar to the "weaker sections" or "backward classes" that the makers of the Constitution had in mind, and the backward class movement in North India was a loose coalition of numerous ill-defined groups. Indeed, when amendments 15(4) and 16(4) were defended and enacted in the Constituent Assembly in 1951 (for the explicit purpose of boosting representation in the bureaucracy of the backward classes), nobody knew exactly who these classes were (De Zwart, 2000).

This lack of clarity was more than just a matter of data shortage. Identifying the backward classes was (and still is) a very sensitive issue. Many in the constituent assembly expected the backward classes to be a list of low castes, but the political elite under leadership of Jawaharlal Nehru wanted to avoid official recognition of castes as a building block of Indian society. The constituent assembly was keenly aware that introducing reservations for castes would entrench and create vested interests in caste distinctions, which was exactly what the constitution aimed to avoid. Most policy-makers saw the caste system as the main cause of the group inequalities, which they wanted to combat with reservations. To reinvigorate caste distinctions by making them relevant for access to scarce goods such as government jobs and education, many thought, would make reservations self-defeating. Elsewhere De Zwart (2005) called this the "dilemma of recognition" and showed that using the category "backward classes" – exactly because it is vague – began as an attempt to resolve that dilemma.

But this attempt failed. To most people in India caste identities are concrete and of immediate relevance in daily life, whereas "Backward Classes" is an administrative abstraction. Moreover people commonly consider the fact that large sections of the population are underrepresented in public sector employment to be a consequence of caste-discrimination and therefore demand that remedial policies target castes. As Rajni Kothari, one of India's prominent political scientists aptly writes: "In dealing with the relationship between caste and politics . . . the doctrinaire moderniser suffers from a serious xenophobia . . . . Those in India who complain of 'casteism in politics' are really looking for a sort of politics which has no basis in society" (1970, p. 4).

Kothari made this point 40 years ago, long before the central government gave up its resistance to recognizing castes. Today, however, the authoritative list of Backward Classes – made by second national Backward Classes Commission – that is used to implement reservation policy is basically a list of castes: 3743 castes to be precise (Government of India, 1980). Together these castes comprise about 50 percent of the population of India.

This list of Backward Classes is not definitive, however. The composition of this list never ceased to be hotly debated ever since its making and it will certainly be changed again soon (we return to this below).

CREAMY LAYER POLITICS

One unintended and unwelcome consequence of preferential policies is that they create new inequalities among the beneficiaries. The reason is that the benefits of preferences are not distributed equally among the beneficiaries – relatively better-off and well-organized groups usually profit more. In India this is commonly referred to as the "creamy layer" problem. Reservation policy divides the beneficiary category in a creamy layer of people who profit or have profited from it, and a larger layer underneath of people who are formally eligible but have not yet profited. The creamy layer forms a painful problem for policy-makers because preferential treatment is meant to promote equality, not to create new inequalities. The creamy layer problem is not unique to India. It is more or less inherent to preferential policies – critiques of such policies have noted and documented is occurrence in cases around the world (e.g. Sowell, 1990, p. 157; Walzer, 1983). Given the large number of beneficiaries, however, and the fact that they are largely caste-based categories, the creamy layer problem in India is very complicated.

The creamy layer problem takes on specific characteristics in a caste system. It causes the larger categories that are targeted with job quotas – the backward classes and the Untouchables in this case – to fission into smaller segments (castes and sub-castes), claiming quotas of their own. The logic of this process follows from a few characteristics of reservation policy in India. First, there is discrepancy between the number of people who are eligible for quota and the number of jobs the government can share out. Second, the benefits reservations are unequally distributed among the people who fall into the eligible categories. Third, the rules that govern reservations recognize eligible collectivities, not individuals. In this situation, the best option for those who are eligible but have yet to profit from affirmative action is to define themselves as a collectivity apart from the rest and to demand separate quotas.

It is commonly believed that the benefits of reservations are cornered by certain castes or sub-castes and those who claim a fair share for their own in reaction to that also organize on the basis of caste. They can argue that the same problems – inequality or under-representation – that led the government to undertake reservations in the first place still exist, and they can appeal to existing rules and laws to demand their fair share. The courts have always found it hard to resist such pressure and consequently the lists of eligible castes have expanded over the years. Removing certain castes from the list of eligibles is much harder than adding new ones and assigning sub-quotas. India is a lively democracy and castes are vote blocks. Removing caste-privileges is risky for politicians.

Meanwhile the Supreme Court of India provides a less risky, and fairer, way to dam the number eligible for quota. In April 2008 the Court judged that the "creamy layer is to be excluded" from the backward classes. Identification of backward classes, the court says, is incomplete (and thus invalid) without exclusion of a creamy layer (Supreme Court of India, 2008). The government follows this ruling and defines the creamy layer on the basis of annual household income. The income ceiling it used at first was Rs 2.5 lakh.[8] With national and state elections nearing, however, this ceiling was raised to Rs 4.5 lakh. Politicians have an interest in keeping the creamy layer small, especially when elections are near.

Many politicians also have an interest in better information on the caste-identities of voters. A crucial step in the politics of designating beneficiaries of reservations is the recent decision to reintroduce caste-categories in the National Census, for the first time in 80 years (*Times of India*, 2010). This decision came after years of debate, pressure, and negotiation with caste representatives and caste-based political parties. It meant a final blow to the government's purposive policy, ever since independence, to refuse official recognition of "caste" as a relevant social category in representative bureaucracy.

The nature of India's caste system and immediate electoral interests promote the proliferation of beneficiary categories, not their restriction through the elimination of creamy layers. Proliferation is all the more attractive because it is cheap. As an involutionary strategy it spreads existing benefits ever more thinly over ever more categories and therefore does not require additional outlays of expenditure, nor the creation of government jobs.

POLITICS OF ACTIVE REPRESENTATION

Given the limited number of reserved jobs and the large numbers of candidates for these jobs, reservations, purely by design, can benefit only small segments of target populations. To illustrate, even if, by the late 1980s, the Untouchables had attained their statutory 15 percent of all government jobs (which they had not), there still would have been less than 2.6 million Untouchables in government jobs, or just over 2 percent of the total Untouchable population (Mendelsohn and Vicziany, 1998, p. 138). Even when counting bureaucrats' family members as beneficiaries, not more than around 10 percent of the Untouchables may ultimately profit from government employment made available under reservations (Isaacs, 1965; Galanter, 1984). The same holds true for the backward classes. Whereas the number of reserved jobs is counted in thousands, perhaps hundreds of thousands, the backward classes population runs into the hundreds of millions (De Zwart, 2000). At the time of their inception, Indian policymakers were no doubt aware of this inherent limitation of reservations but they nevertheless assumed that the compensatory effects of quotas might still be considerable. Their idea was that employees from backward categories would use their administrative power to safeguard and pursue the interests of their communities and, in so doing, remedy group-based inequalities.[9]

As students of representative bureaucracy know, such "active representation" of group interests on the part of in-group administrators does not occur as a matter of course. Active representation requires a fair number – a "critical mass" – of in-group administrators to provide "security in numbers" against the likely backlash of majority out-group representatives (Herbert, 1974; Meier, 1993). For the Untouchables such a critical mass has by and large been realized over the past six decades. Although initially awarded for a limited period of 10 years in 1950, reservations for Untouchables have since then been routinely extended, until this day. The credit for these routine extensions goes in large part to elected untouchable politicians who, largely dependent themselves on reserved constituencies for their election to state and federal assemblies, have developed a vested interest in the continuation of reservations (Galanter, 1984; Jaffrelot, 2003).[10] The filling up of reserved positions had a slow start in the first decades after independence because of a lack of qualified untouchable candidates (an old problem), patchy regulation, and internal bureaucratic obstruction. Though it is seldom openly expressed, upper caste resentment of reservations for Untouchables was – and still is – widespread. But under the cumulative pressure of politicians, bureaucratic oversight bodies, and untouchable public employees unions, quotas have increasingly been fulfilled ever since the 1970s (Mendelsohn and Vicziany, 1998).

Limiting ourselves to the central services (see Table 13.1), the increase of Untouchable representation has been most notable in the three highest classes covering senior administrative (Class I), other administrative (Class II), and clerical (Class III) positions. In these service classes, Untouchables' shares increased roughly 25-fold, 10-fold, and 4-fold, respectively, in the first 50 years after independence. These proportional increases entail dramatically large increases in absolute numbers. The inconspicuously small minority of 20 Untouchable officials who worked in the highest echelons of New Delhi's federal bureaucracy in 1953, for example, had by 1995 been replaced by an over 6000-strong army of senior untouchable administrators.[11]

As for the backward classes, the 27 percent job quota reserved for them in the central services (introduced in 1990) has not yet proven effective in boosting their representation. There were 2.6 percent (Class I),

Table 13.1   Representation of Untouchables in central services, 1953–95

Year	Class I		Class II		Class III		Class IV		Pop.
	N	%	N	%	N	%	N	%	%
1953	20	0.4	113	1.3	24819	4.5	161958	20.5	
1960		1.2		2.5		7.2		17.2	14.7
1963	250	1.8	707	3.0	84714	9.3	151176	17.2	
1965		1.6		2.8		8.9		17.8	
1970		2.3		3.8		9.9		18.1	14.8
1974	1094	3.2	2401	4.6	161775	10.3	230864	18.6	
1975		3.4		5.0		10.7		18.6	
1980		5.0		8.5		13.4		19.5	
1984		6.9		10.4		14.0		20.2	15.6
1987	4746	8.2	7847	10.5	307980	14.5	234614	20.1	
1995	6637	10.2	13797	12.7	378172	16.2	221380	21.3	

Source: Galanter, 1984, pp. 88–89; Kumar, 1994; Mendelsohn and Vicziany, 1998, p. 135; NCSCST, 1998, p. 176; Radhakrishnan, 1991, p. 1920

4.0 percent (Class II), and 8.4 percent (Class III and IV) backward class bureaucrats in the central government in 1980 (Government of India, 1980). Today, 30 years later, and 20 years after the enactment of quota laws, they still occupy only 7 percent of central government jobs (*Times of India*, 2008). This figure stands in sharp contrast with the situation in some of the south Indian states, however, where reservations for Other Backward Classes (OBCs) have been in force for much longer and where, in some cases, OBCs are effectively overrepresented in government service (Radhakrishnan, 1990, 1993).

In a society where jobs in the organized sector are extremely scarce[12] while government employment is widely regarded as the best deal for educated youth (cf. Taub, 1969, p. 79), or the only clear goal in the life of a middle-class boy (van Gool, 2008, p. 213), securing such employment is almost a national obsession (Mendelsohn and Vicziany, 1998, p. 133). The benefits for backward individuals of landing government jobs through reservations are real and substantial. Public employment not only allows them to avoid, or escape from, poverty; it also automatically confers elite status to those in the higher echelons.

The benefits of reservations for those represented by these "new elites" of backward administrators are less self-evident, however. A recent study by van Gool (2008) shows that, in India, more representative bureaucracies do not necessarily produce the kind of compensatory, redistributive effects that policy-makers envisaged. Though official rules delegate wide-ranging powers to bureaucrats in the implementation of public policy, bureaucrats' actual powers in this regard are more limited. Politicians often capture the public benefits under the nominal control of administrative agencies in order to use them as patronage for electoral purposes. (Most politicians in India act on the assumption that votes can only be successfully won by channeling concrete material benefits to their constituencies.) Since politicians can easily punish "uncooperative" officials – particularly by way of transfers to undesirable postings – there is usually little that bureaucrats can do against politicians' appropriation of de jure administrative discretion. Left without discretion, Indian bureaucrats often simply lack the opportunity to act as the active representatives of in-group interests in their jurisdictions.

Opportunities apart, bureaucrats may also lack the desire to assume representative roles. Many Untouchable bureaucrats, for instance, continue to experience their untouchability as a stigma, as something deeply discrediting that disqualifies them from full social acceptance by their colleagues and neighbors. Hence, they typically try to minimize the unwelcome effects of stigma by downplaying or concealing their caste identities to outsiders. Since their stigma is an invisible one (Untouchables are physically indistinguishable from "pure" caste Hindus) they often succeed. That is, they simply disappear in the "white-shirted mass" of other white-collar workers in the cities and towns where most of them live (cf. Isaacs, 1965; see also Roy and Singh, 1987; Ram, 1988; Saavala, 2000). For these officials, the choice between downplaying their identities or "staying with our people" through active representation is easily made. Downplaying caste identity has likely rewards such as a relatively successful career, secure income, and the possibility to bring one's family ahead, whereas acting as a representative has likely costs such as stalled careers, frequent transfers, suspensions, and unsteady incomes.

CONCLUSION

India's extended experience with representative bureaucracy is fascinating and instructive. Some of the intense politics over this issue can only be properly understood within the context of Indian history, culture, and social and political structure. However, some of the mechanisms we have analysed may be relevant to other cases as well. Governments that start preferential policies often overestimate their powers to determine the beneficiaries of these policies (cf. Sowell, 1990). Moreover, it is difficult to curb the eligibility of "creamy layers" of beneficiaries, especially in a democratic context. As a consequence the administration of preferential programs tends to become increasingly complex over time. And finally, India's experience with reservations shows that quotas are no guarantee for the emergence of passively representative bureaucracies, and that the incentive structures of electoral patronage politics and hierarchical caste society may draw group-identified bureaucrats away from the active representation of in-group interests. In short, studying India's struggle with the creation of a representative bureaucracy draws our attention to mechanisms that other countries can anticipate.

NOTES

1. In India "reservations" is the common term used for affirmative action in the form of reserved quota in government jobs, elective seats in representative political institutions, and in institutes of higher education.
2. This does not mean that the present occupation of caste members is completely irrelevant to status. Castes are not immobile. Given time, means, organization, and a favorable political climate, castes (not individuals) can rise in the status hierarchy (Kothari and Maru, 1965; Rudolph and Rudolph, 1967; Mandelbaum, 1970, pp. 23–24).
3. "Caste" also refers to the four categories into which the Hindu scriptures divide society at large: Brahmins (priests and scholars), Kshatryas (rulers and soldiers), Vaishyas (traders and merchants), and Shudras (agriculturalists). These latter categories –varnas in Indian languages – are not actual groups. They form an ideological scheme that people use to quickly classify others (Mandelbaum, 1970, p. 13). In this scheme there is no place for the untouchables. They are considered avarna – without varna – and therefore outside the caste system (hence "outcasts", a term also used to describe them).
4. Traditionally, Brahmins held a religiously sanctioned monopoly on education. Consequently, under British rule "Western educated Brahmins entered the professions and services in large numbers. Those who entered Government and other services used the ties of kinship and affinity to recruit more Brahmins . . . . [I]n the first quarter of the [twentieth] century their representation in professional, administrative, and managerial positions . . . was extremely high" (Kothari, 1970, pp. 268–269).
5. Ambedkar graduated from Columbia University. He also studied at Grays Inn, where he got his Law degree in 1916, and at the London School of Economics (Jaffrelot, 2000).
6. The amendments were intended to save extant and future reservation schemes from the Supreme Court Ruling that had declared the "communal allotment scheme" in Madras (see above) unconstitutional because it violated articles 15 and 16.
7. More precisely, the President can appoint Backward Class Commissions for that purpose.
8. A lakh equals 100 000 rupees.
9. As Constituent Assembly member Professor Yashwant Rai phrased this expectation for the Untouchables: "I cannot believe that the Federal Public Service Commission or other Commissions will not be injustice (sic) in the case of Harijans [Untouchables] . . . there should be some representatives of the Harijans on the Federal Public Service Commission and the Commission which are formed in the States and provinces so that they may watch over the interests of the candidates who apply for different posts and who may prevent any injustice being done to Harijans" (cited in Saksena, 1981, p. 431).
10. Very few untouchable politicians have successfully competed in non-reserved, or "general" constituencies.

11. Considerable variety in Untouchable representation remains, however. It is typically better at the national level than in the states; in the highest and lowest echelons than in the upper-middle ones (Class I and II); and in the regular civil service than in the public banks and public sector undertakings. Besides, in most states untouchable bureaucrats are disproportionally drawn from large (and hence electorally important) castes with an early history of caste organization under colonial rule.

12. In India, the organized sector provides only roughly 10 percent of employment opportunities. The large majority of Indians earn their living in the unorganized, informal, "mud-floored" economy (cf. Panini, 1996; Harriss-White, 2003).

14. Bureaucratic representation in Israel

Moshe Maor

INTRODUCTION

Gender and minority equity in the Israeli civil service provide a unique case study. This is because Israel is the most ideological of all contemporary democracies (i.e. Zionism is the dominant ideology); social architecture is widely accepted as a government task (e.g. immigration absorption, dispersion of population, and so on); government is in charge of making critical choices as it faces direct threats to the survival of the state and society, and there is a scarcity of strategic thinking. As well, Israel has a highly fragmented political system, no professional civil service elite compensating for the weakness of the political system, and political structures, processes, and cultures that inhibit administrative reforms (Dror, 2002, pp. vii–x). Indeed, no comprehensive reform of the Israeli administrative system has been undertaken since the establishment of the State of Israel in 1948.[1] A few committees were established and reports published – the Kubersky Commission Report (The Kubersky Commission, 1989) being the most wide-ranging – but aside from a very few islands of excellence and professionalism, the civil service system as a whole remains fragmented, politicized, and devoid of a sense of identity, cohesiveness and esprit de corps.

Against this background, this chapter examines the representation of women, Israelis of Ethiopian Descent, Arab Citizens of Israel, Druze and Circassians in the Israeli governmental ministries and subsidiary units. It discusses the factors affecting the representation of these groups during the last decade, and identifies actors and practices that facilitate or prevent minority access to senior positions. Attention is focused on actual achievements and failures rather than the governments' promises and commitments. The argument advanced here is that although the issues of gender and minority equality have been firmly on the political agenda, certain groups have remained underrepresented in the Israeli civil service. Specifically, despite some principles of formal equality, the higher the grade, the fewer women and Arabs. These groups are the two most underrepresented groups in the Israeli civil service. Legislation, which was supposed to cater for these groups, was by-passed and diffused by a combination of organizational obstacles and personal barriers. There is therefore an urgent need for women and minority groups to be placed into positions for which they are qualified, rather than to satisfy political demands for a diverse workforce.

THE ORGANIZATIONAL FRAMEWORK

Public sector organizations in Israel are divided into three categories: the governmental sector (civil service), the non-governmental sector (e.g. Office of the President, State Comptroller, Knesset Administration and the Bank of Israel), and local authorities. The governmental sector is divided into three categories, namely, governmental ministries and subsidiary units, statutory authorities, and government corporations. Governmental ministries are in charge of policy formation, funding, implementation, and evaluation. Each ministry is headed by a minister who is accountable to the Knesset. Due to their distinct policy areas, responsibilities, tasks, and in many cases also culture, the ministries are quite distinguishable from one another. Furthermore, because hiring and promotion for senior posts are largely undertaken within each ministry, a narrower policy view in each ministry is common and loyalty of senior employees rests with the ministry rather than with the civil service system as a whole. It is therefore hardly surprising that the Israeli civil service system resembles a loose federation of ministries. This system can be traced back to the federative structure of the government ministries in 1948 (Kfir, 2002). As of 2011, there are 28 government ministries whose numbers and boundaries are frequently changing due to coalitional considerations. A few of them employ less than 15 civil servants.

These government ministries house 29 subsidiary units, not including the 22 government hospitals. Subsidiary units include, for example, the central Bureau of Statistics in the Office of the Prime Minister, the Meteorological Service in the Transportation Ministry, and Veterinary Services and Animal Health at the Ministry of Agriculture. There is no clear definition of the status or function of a subsidiary unit. The Civil Service Commissioner has the authority, upon a request from a ministry's director general, to design a unit within a government ministry as a subsidiary unit. Such a designation implies that the unit will be semi-independent in matters of budget, human resources, accounting, legal matters, etc., and its head will usually report directly to the minister.

Governmental hospitals are special subsidiary units within the Ministry of Health and enjoy even greater administrative autonomy. The Civil Service Commissioner can extend or restrict the authorities of a subsidiary unit at any time on the recommendation of the ministry's director general or with his or her approval, or terminate its status as a subsidiary unit upon the request of a ministry's director general or with his or her approval.

By the end of December 2009, there were 56 993 employees in the government ministries and subsidiary units, up from 53 503 in 2004 (Civil Service Commission, 2005; Shachar-Rosenfeld and Berger, 2010; Central Bureau of Statistics, 2010).[2] Focusing on the three highest grades of government ministries and subsidiary units, there were 350 employees in the highest grade, 649 in the second highest grade, and 1340 in the third highest grade (Shachar-Rosenfeld and Berger, 2010, p. 25). This is also the place to note that the screening and examination of candidates for senior positions, for which the Civil Service Commission is responsible, are vulnerable to external (read: political) pressures (State Comptroller, 2004, 2006, 2007). The fact that the civil service is not mentioned in Israel's Basic Laws, and that laws relevant to the civil service are not strictly enforced, extends politicians' room for maneuverability in this regard.

THE LEGAL FRAMEWORK

Theoretically, the trickling down of political norms of behavior into public management is supposed to be limited by a series of legal barriers. Article 32 of Basic Law: The Government (2001) determines that the government must act solely and exclusively within the framework of the powers set by law. The Administrative Procedures Amendment (Decision and Reasoning) (1958) also determines that any governmental organization must act in accordance with its powers as defined by law. All decisions by the government and its bureaucracy are therefore subject to judicial review, meaning that the court can force any government agency to comply with the law if it exceeds its powers without due cause. Hiring and promotion of civil service employees on the basis of a merit system, public tenders and impartial examinations are regulated by the Civil Service (Appointment) Law (1959). The requirement imposed on civil servants to resign if they wish to enter the political arena and compete in an election is specified in the Civil Service (Curtailment of Partisan Activity and Fundraising) Law (1959) and disciplinary procedures and sanctions are laid down in the Civil Service (Discipline) Law (1963). Entitlement to state pension and its regulation is set in the Civil Service (Pension) Law (1970). Regulations and directives regarding the rights and obligations of civil servants, collective agreements about wage and other employment conditions are laid down in the Civil Service Regulations (Personal Code). The Civil Service Commission, which is in charge of enforcing the aforementioned laws, is an autonomous subsidiary unit in the Prime Minister Office. Its head, the Civil Service Commissioner, is appointed by the Prime Minister with the approval of the government, and has independent powers guaranteed by law over appointments, discipline, pensions and so on. Overall, these "laws do not reflect a clear and consistent concept about the nature and desirable patterns of public management. Instead, they present the broad range of problems that have arisen over the years for which *ad hoc* legislation has sought solutions" (Galnoor, 2011, p. 41, italics in original).

PATTERNS OF BEHAVIOR AND ADMINISTRATIVE CULTURE

According to Galnoor (2011, pp. 45–48), there are four patterns of behavior of the Israeli civil service. These patterns include: (1) centralization in the relationships between central government and citizens, central government and local authorities, and "strong" ministries (e.g. Defense, Finance, and Justice) and the other ministries; (2) pragmatism, which devalues any notion of planning because of a fatalist presumption that the unexpected will most likely occur, and its derived by-product of improvisation, meaning "an extemporaneous action undertaken to cope with a problem or seize an opportunity" (Sharkansky and Zalmanovitch, 2000, p. 321); (3) organizational territoriality; and (4) secrecy, or more specifically, "compartmentalization of secrets between government ministries and sometimes between units within the same ministry" (Galnoor, 2011, p. 47). Not surprisingly, turf battles and interorganizational rivalries are common and policy coordination for crosscutting issues is rare. Regarding administrative culture, political appointments are prevalent (Galnoor, 2011), corruption by high-level civil servants is rare (although in recent years there have been some highly visible cases such as, for example, at the Tax Authority and the Ministry of Interior), a bond between the wealthy and senior civil servants has been recorded in numerous instances, and a relaxed public attitude towards corruption is common.

THE CHANGING ROLE OF THE STATE

The changing role of the state is evident in Israel by the decreasing proportion of the public sector in the GDP: from 70.5 percent in 1980 to 54.8

percent in 1990, 46.9 percent in 2000, and 42.7 percent in 2009 (Bank of Israel, 2010). The most significant, comprehensive, and consistent change in Israeli public management is rooted in the process of privatization that has been carried out in practice since the 1980s. The process includes both transparent privatization decisions, and secret administrative decisions regarding budget cuts and reducing the supply of public services and goods (Paz-Fuchs and Kohavi, 2011). Additionally, it spans all government offices and policy areas, and takes place regardless of political changes or the identity of the Prime Minister and the minister in charge. Parallel to the process of privatization, outsourcing is taking place, encompassing two phenomena: First, entire fields are transferred from the state to subcontractors (for example, cleaning, computing, security). Second, manpower contractors supply workers and government units employ their services only as long as they are required (Paz-Fuchs and Kohavi, 2011; Meron, 2011). This process occurs without thorough public debate with regard to its consequences for a young democracy still striving to build its foundations in various domains, and without an orderly procedure to examine the profitability of privatization in each individual area (Paz-Fuchs and Kohavi, 2011). The privatization touches upon matters of internal and external security, among others, while the outsourcing relates to areas of welfare and social security, among others. A central feature of these processes is weakness in supervision, both in terms of resources and expertise, and a lack of commitment by policymakers to deal with this weakness (Paz-Fuchs and Kohavi, 2011).

Bureaucratic Representation

A convenient starting point is a 1995 amendment to Article 15A of the Civil Service (Appointment) Law (1959), which laid down the principle of affirmative action in the civil service. This principle reads as follows: "Among employees of the civil service, expression shall be given, taking the circumstances into consideration, to the appropriate representation of members of both genders." In subsequent amendments, Article 15A was expanded as follows: "Among employees of the Civil Service at all grades and professions, in every ministry and subsidiary unit, expression shall be given, taking the circumstances into consideration, to the appropriate representation of members of both genders, people with disabilities, Arab members of the population, including Druz, Circassians, and anyone who was, or whose parents were, born in Ethiopia" (quoted from Galnoor, 2011, pp. 79, 169). In 1996, the Unit for the Advancement and Integration of Women in the Civil Service Commission was formed by the Civil Service Commissioner (Shaked, 2004). An in depth analysis of its structure and operation can be found elsewhere (Maor, 2001; Shaked, 2004).

Gender Equity

Since the 1980s, there have been more women than men in the civil service – 62 percent during 1997–98, 63 percent during 1999–2000, 64 percent during 2001–03, and 65 percent during 2004–09 (Shachar-Rosenfeld and Berger, 2010, p. 26; figures do not include employees at the Ministry of Defense). Although some improvement is noticeable in recent years, Table 14.1 clearly indicates that the higher the rank, the fewer the women. Perhaps most important is that in 2002, women filled 38 percent of the positions in the civil service in the highest rank – defined as grade 46 in the humanities and social sciences professional ranking and its equivalent ranks in the remaining 17 specialized fields. This figure has increased to 60 percent in 2006 and remained stable until 2009. A similar, albeit less dramatic trend has been recorded in the second highest grade, with 44 percent of women filling positions at this grade in 2002, rising to 49 percent in 2005 and 2007, and reaching 50 percent in 2009. The question that has arisen is whether women are being appointed to token positions to fulfill affirmative action goals (Dolan, 2004). Table 14.2 presents the number of women whose working conditions are stipulated in personal contracts – commonly known as Senior Contracts. At face value, an increase in the number of women is recorded, from 27 percent in 2002 to 30 percent in 2009. However, if one excludes registrars who have no influence over policy, the share of women ranges between 23 percent in 2002 and 28 percent in 2009. Putting these figures in perspective, in 2009 women constituted 17.5 percent of members of the 18th Knesset (21 of 120 members), 28.5 percent of the Supreme Court (4 of 14 judges; 2011 figures), 65 percent of the civil service at large, 60 percent of the highest rank of the civil service, and only 28 percent in positions that afford opportunities to influence governmental decision-making. Women at large, and executive-level women in particular, have undoubtedly benefited from the equal employment opportunity provisions of the 1995 amendment to Article 15A of the Civil Service (Appointment) Law (1959) and its subsequent modifications. However, more needs to be done to ensure that female advancement into positions of power and influence takes place.

Arab Citizens of Israel, Druze and Circassians

Arabs, Druze and Circassians (hereafter referred to simply as Arabs), comprise about 20.5 percent of the Israeli population,[3] and yet, in 2010, less than 8 percent of civil servant positions were filled by this sector of society (Table 14.3). In 2010, 4717 Arabs were employed in the Israeli governmental offices and subsidiary units, 2941 men and 1776 women.

Representative bureaucracy in action

Table 14.1   *The representation of women in the civil service according to rank, 2002–09**

Rank	2002		2003		2004		2005	
	Total**	Women	Total	Women	Total	Women	Total	Women
1	555	38%	556	40%	571	41%	307	57%
2	586	44%	566	47%	558	48%	606	49%
3	950	35%	970	36%	977	37%	1239	33%
4	2754	44%	2776	43%	2823	44%	3015	45%
5	4113	47%	4251	47%	4317	47%	4444	48%
6	4692	52%	4648	53%	4584	54%	4661	55%
7	5905	62%	6026	63%	6144	64%	6267	66%
8 and below	29954	72%	30589	73%	31242	72%	30835	73%
Total	49509	31550 (64%)	50382	32443 (64%)	51216	33051 (65%)	51374	33466 (65%)

Rank	2006		2007		2008		2009	
	Total	Women	Total	Women	Total	Women	Total	Women
1	311	60%	331	60%	344	60%	350	60%
2	558	48%	600	49%	625	48%	649	50%
3	1160	35%	1163	35%	1264	37%	1340	38%
4	2907	47%	2950	47%	3082	48%	3228	49%
5	4373	48%	4461	48%	4615	49%	4840	49%
6	4969	56%	5641	59%	5615	60%	5973	61%
7	6546	65%	6577	66%	7287	67%	8206	68%
8 and below	31147	72%	30252	72%	30237	72%	30238	71%
Total	51971	33797 (65%)	51975	33980 (65%)	53069	17995 (65%)	54824	35755 (65%)

Notes:
*   The data displayed above is according to grades across different rankings that do not necessarily reflect seniority and organizational hierarchy. Only government offices with over 50 employees were included in the data presented here. Employees at the Ministry of Defense are excluded.
**   "Total" refers to men and women.

Source: Shachar-Rosenfeld and Berger (2007, 2008, 2009, 2010); Civil Service Commission (2005)

Table 14.2   Women employed under senior contracts, divided by types of contracts, 2002–09

Type of contract	2002		2003		2004		2005	
	Total	Women	Total	Women	Total	Women	Total	Women
Registrars	78	41 (53%)	82	41 (50%)	79	42 (53%)	80	45 (56%)
Senior Contracts	146	25 (17%)	135	22 (16%)	124	21 (17%)	478	121 (26%)
Deputy Minister	3	0	5	0	2	0	2	0
Legal Advisers	32	15 (47%)	34	15 (44%)	34	16 (47%)	37	20 (54%)
Senior Contract (New)	301	78 (26%)	320	78 (24%)	334	89 (28%)	–	–
CEOs (New)	35	2 (6%)	38	5 (13%)	37	5 (15%)	44	7 (16%)
Total	595	161 (27%)	614	161 (26%)	610	176 (29%)	641	193 (30%)

Type of contract	2006		2007		2008		2009	
	Total	Women	Total	Women	Total	Women	Total	Women
Registrars	87	52 (60%)	80	46 (58%)	85	48 (56%)	92	53 (58%)
Senior Contracts	481	119 (25%)	482	125 (26%)	495	130 (26%)	541	151 (28%)
Deputy Ministers	1	0	1	0	1	0	1	0
Legal Advisers	39	19 (49%)	40	20 (50%)	39	16 (41%)	40	16 (40%)
Senior Contracts (New)	–	–	–	–	–	–	–	–
CEOs (New)	44	7 (16%)	43	7 (16%)	47	8 (17%)	47	6 (13%)
Total	652	197 (30%)	646	198 (31%)	667	202 (30%)	721	226 (30%)

Source: Berger and Shaked (2004); Civil Service Commission (2005, 2006); Shachar-Rosenfeld and Berger (2010)

Table 14.3   Arab citizens employed in the Israeli Civil Service Commission

Year	Men	Women	Total Arab employees	Percentage of civil servants
1992	n.a.	n.a.	1117	2.1
1993	n.a.	n.a.	1369	2.5
1994	n.a.	n.a.	1679	3.0
1995	n.a.	n.a.	1997	3.5
1996	n.a.	n.a.	2231	4.0
1997	n.a.	n.a.	2340	4.1
1998	n.a.	n.a.	2537	4.4
1999	n.a.	n.a.	n.a	n.a.
2000	n.a.	n.a.	n.a.	n.a.
2001	n.a.	n.a.	3176	5.7
2002	n.a.	n.a.	3440	6.1
2003	n.a.	n.a.	2798	5.6
2004	n.a.	n.a.	3154	5.5
2005	2123	1128	3251	5.7
2006	2215	1174	3389	5.9
2007	2312	1265	3577	6.2
2008	2452	1431	3883	6.7
2009	2650	1595	4245	7.0
2010	2914	1776	4717	7.5

Source: Haidar (2005); Civil Service Commission (2010)

To enter the civil service, Arabs can compete in tenders open solely to the Arab population or in general tenders open to all segments of Israeli society. The share of tenders open solely for the Arab population out of all tenders available rose from 4.5 percent (36 of a total of 805) in 2005 to 15.4 percent (182 of 1366) in 2008, and then dropped back down to 9.4 percent (145 of 1546) in 2010 (Civil Service Commission, 2010).

The very few Arabs employed in the Israeli civil service enter at the lowest levels, and are distributed across the following professional rankings: 1518 (32 percent) in the specialized field of nursing, 849 (18 percent) in the administrative rankings, which include low level technical employees and clerks, 518 (11 percent) in the ranking of doctors, 302 (6.4 percent) as Imams (i.e. worship leaders of mosques), 231 (4.8 percent) in the professional ranking of social sciences and humanities, 172 (3.6 percent) employed as social workers, and the rest in other rankings (Civil Service Commission, 2010, p. 25). Another finding that comes out of the data is that Arab civil servants are employed in positions that require knowledge of Arabic. The defining characteristics of these positions are that they are geographically centered in the north of Israel and that they are positions

Table 14.4   Distribution of civil servants of Ethiopian descent

Year	Civil servants of Ethiopian descent			Total number of civil servants	Percentage of civil servants
	Men	Women	Total		
2007	292	337	629	57 946	1.09
2008	330	386	716	59 505	1.2
2009	372	410	782	61 338*	1.27
2010	388	453	841	64 062**	1.31

Notes:
*   Data is correct for June 15, 2010.
**   Data is correct for February 11, 2011.

Source: Civil Service Commission (2011)

that cater almost exclusively to Arab society. According to the 2010 data, 1628 (34.5 percent) are employed in the Northern District, 1195 (25.3 percent) in the Haifa District, 416 (8.8 percent) in the Jerusalem District, and the rest in other regions (Civil Service Commission, 2010, p. 15). Regarding the upper ranks, only 38 Arabs were at the highest senior grade of the civil service (i.e. professional as well as administrative rankings) in 2010 (Civil Service Commission, 2010, p. 27).

The fact that many of the positions held by Arab civil servants are in the administrative ranking, and therefore do not require academic knowledge, does not mean that these employees do not possess academic knowledge. In fact, 52.5 percent of all Arab civil servants have an academic degree, an increase of 3 percent since 2008 (Civil Service Commission, 2008, 2010, p. 10).

Israelis of Ethiopian Descent

In 2010, the community of Israelis of Ethiopian descent constituted just under 2 percent of the general population (Central Bureau of Statistics, 2010). The number of Israelis of Ethiopian descent employed by the civil service stood at 1.09 percent in 2007, and showed a slight increase to 1.2 percent in 2008 and 1.31 percent in 2010 (Table 14.4; Civil Service Commission, 2011). Regarding their distribution according to rankings, of the 841 citizens of Ethiopian descent employed by the civil service in 2010, 518 are at the administrative rankings, 146 at the nurses' professional ranking, 49 as academics in the humanities and social sciences, and the remaining at all other rankings. Most of these civil servants work at the Ministry of Welfare and Social Services, the Immigration and Border

Control Authority, and the Tax Authority. Of those employed in the civil service in 2010, over 13 percent have elementary education, over 35 percent have secondary education and 19 percent have academic education (Civil Service Commission, 2011).

ORGANIZATIONAL OBSTACLES AND PERSONAL BARRIERS

At first glance, Israel is seemingly one of the most progressive societies in regards to minority rights and representation. Women have always had the right to vote in Israel, women serve beside men in the military, and early legislation was already protecting women's rights in the workplace. When one begins to scratch the surface, however, a more complicated picture appears. The military, for example, while it accepts women, does not recruit Arabs and exempts any female who declares herself religious. Furthermore, within the army, the rank of combat soldier was closed to females until a few years ago. Family law is under the sole jurisdiction of the Rabbinical Courts, and religious political parties, which hold enormous power as pivotal parties in Israeli coalition governments, refuse to loosen the grip of those Rabbinical Courts, making civil marriage and divorce unattainable in Israel, and leaving women vulnerable to their husbands and the rulings of all-male courts (Golan, 2011).

Despite a plethora of legislation and high court rulings on matters of gender, ethnic, and national equality, Israel still encounters problems with underrepresented minorities in the workforce and discriminatory hiring and general workplace practices. With regard to the Arab citizens of Israel, the Orr Commission investigation (2003), which followed the killing of 13 Arab citizens by Israeli police during the political riots in 2000, has determined that that there is discrimination against this group. The data clearly indicates that this is still the case. According to Galnoor (2011, p. 81), "The Discrimination is collective – Arabs work in the civil service in small numbers because they are Arab, not because they lack qualifications (thousands of Arab university graduates are employed), or because they pose a security risk [. . .]." On top of that, the representation of all minority groups in the civil service is undermined by decision makers' flaunting and bypassing of the laws. Let me elaborate on this point.

According to the Civil Service (Appointments) Law (1959), tenders are to be used to fill positions and, when confronted with two qualified individuals, the one from an under-represented minority is to be chosen for the job. However, there is a list of positions that are exempt from tender. The "Exemption List" includes, for example, directors general, senior positions in the Prime Minister Office and the Finance Ministry, the Cabinet Secretary, and others. Since 2002, contenders for other positions that are exempted from tenders must appear before a Candidate Search Committee. As for the remaining senior positions, the law is circumvented all too often by appointing a civil servant to the job in an acting capacity (e.g. acting director, acting manager), or as a temporary appointment or replacement. Once a tender is undertaken in order to make a permanent appointment, the acting, temporary, or replacement civil servant has, of course, an advantage over all other candidates as he or she has already been trained for the position in question and will need no further transition period (Maor, 2001; Tirosh, 2009). In fact, out of all of the tenders issued between 2002 and 2004, 55 percent of those positions were filled by people who had worked at that job or a similar job for an average of 21 months before the tender. In the Ministry of Justice the percentage was 66 percent, and in the Treasury Department it rose as high as 88 percent (Tirosh, 2009, p. 715). Another way in which hiring tactics are skewed is by issuing tenders that are specifically biased towards a preferred candidate (Maor, 2001; Tirosh, 2009).

According to Tirosh (2009), when positions are filled through an appointment process, as opposed to a public tender, there are two adverse results. First, the immediate position is far more likely to be filled by someone of the hegemony, which directly harms underrepresented minorities despite their qualifications. This is because people tend to hire those most similar to them and those they are familiar with. Underrepresented minorities are less likely to be within the network of people who come in contact with the person hiring, thus unable to make themselves familiar and prove their qualifications. Second, since many of the tenders are internal and interdepartmental tenders, based on the wrong assumption that the original hiring process was fair and representative, underrepresented minorities are again harmed by not being eligible to apply for those tenders (Tirosh, 2009). Moreover, these tenders often only have one applicant, and office norms dictate that it is "rude" to apply for a position that was not tailored for you (Tirosh, 2009, p. 717).

Furthermore, the tenders that are issued do not always follow the guidelines of proper tenders. The reviewers are not anonymous, which means that they can be swayed by friends and co-workers to accept someone familiar and from within the office (Tirosh, 2009). Often, no written test is administered to the candidates, thereby making it difficult to properly assess two candidates in comparison with each other. In many cases, there is no written protocol for the reviewers' decision-making process, nor is there any explanation for the final decision (Tirosh, 2009). In addition, an important aspect of the Civil Service (Appointments) Law (1959) is the text reading "as much as possible under the circumstances." This short addition effectively renders any law impotent of real meaning. It provides a clear loophole for anyone not wishing to comply with the law (Maor, 2001; Shaked, 2004). Consequently, the current hiring practices in the Civil Service Commission effectively shut out underrepresented minorities from many professional and senior level positions (Tirosh, 2009).

CONCLUDING REMARKS

This analysis yields several conclusions. First, bureaucratic representation varies across gender and other minority groups, with significant advances made with regard to women. However, there is still a need to recruit and promote Israelis of Ethiopian descent to medium and senior positions, and to undertake a persistent and targeted effort to bring into the civil service highly qualified Israeli Arabs and ensure their equal representation at all rankings and grades. Women and minority groups must be placed into positions for which they are qualified, rather than to satisfy political demands for a diverse workforce. Second, policy-makers must ensure that executive-level women continue to benefit from equal-opportunity provisions, and that gains will be noticeable within the upper ranks, especially where they can influence policy in ways that bestow rewards upon their social groups.

ACKNOWLEDGMENTS

The author would like to thank Hayah Eichler for her research assistance.

NOTES

1. Other countries, however, have experienced wide-ranging reforms insofar as recruitment and training of senior civil servants are concerned. See, for example, Maor (1997, 1999a, b, c), Maor and Stevens (1997), and Maor and Jones (1998).
2. These numbers were calculated as follows: overall number of employees (not included the Ministry of Defense) – drawn from the Civil Service Commission reports (2004, 2009) – combined with the number of employees at the Ministry of Defense – drawn from the Central Bureau of Statistics (2010). These figures do not include temporary and special contract employees as well as subcontracted employees.
3. As of December 2010, the Israeli population is comprised of 1 587 000 (20.5 percent) Arab citizens out of a total of 7 746 000 (Central Bureau of Statistics, 2011).

15. Representative bureaucracy in Australia: a post-colonial, multicultural society

Rodney Smith

INTRODUCTION

Given its status as a former British colony, it is not surprising that Australia has developed a public sector that belongs within the anglophone or Westminster family. Over the past 40 years, Australia's bureaucratic structures and traditions have undergone reform in response to changing political, economic, and ideological imperatives. Over the same period, governments have responded to Australia's increasing social diversity by deliberately attempting to create socially representative public sector agencies. These efforts are analysed in this chapter, with particular attention given to the representation of minority immigrant ethnic groups and Aboriginal and Torres Strait Islander people (the latter group will also be referred to as Indigenous Australians in this chapter). The argument in the chapter is that while the Australian public sector has made great strides toward representing social diversity within its ranks, the deeper implications of Australia's status as a multicultural, post-colonial society for bureaucracy have not been fully recognized or acted upon.

AUSTRALIAN POLITICO-ADMINISTRATIVE STRUCTURES AND TRADITIONS

The Australian public sector falls within an 'anglophone' family that includes the United Kingdom, Canada, and New Zealand (Halligan, 2010). Its core structure and practices reflect the traditions associated with Westminster systems. The influential Northcott Trevelyan Report of 1853 on the organization of the British civil service just preceded the beginnings of responsible self-government in the Australian colonies. The Westminster bureaucratic norms of permanency, professionalism, expertise, and neutrality in the service of the government of the day were not imprinted on the colonial bureaucracies from the outset; however, by the federation of the colonies in 1901, these norms had a reasonable hold (see Golder, 2005).

The basic relationship between the elected executive and the public service has persisted since 1901. Cabinets are comprised of ministers typically drawn in their entirety either from the center-left Labor Party or from a coalition of the center-right Liberal and National parties. Ministers are drawn from the Parliament and are answerable to it both for their policy decisions and for the performance of the public sector agencies within their portfolio areas. Public servants are expected to serve Labor or Liberal–National ministries neutrally, offering "frank and fearless" advice on policy and administrative matters to ministers. They must also carry out the ministers' directions to the best of their abilities, regardless of their own views about these directions.

The permanence and professional expertise of the public service have meant that senior public servants usually possess a knowledge advantage over the ministers to whom they present policy alternatives. Until the 1970s, most public servants worked in a single department for their whole careers. Against this expertise, ministers may have no real knowledge of their portfolio areas and may therefore rely heavily on the public service to determine the best policy direction (Thynne, 1983). Public servants, in turn, may have been formally or informally socialized to shared closed views of the world, which cause them to reject or overlook some policy options (Pusey, 1991). These points suggest one effect of bureaucratic representation on policy formulation: the wider interests and lived perspectives contained in a more representative bureaucracy should make it less prone to the unconscious exclusion of some policy alternatives.

The 1970s saw the start of several long waves of public sector change from the classical Westminster model. Ministers in Gough Whitlam's Labor Government (1972–75) were convinced that conservative senior public servants were not acting neutrally but were undermining Labor's policies. These ministers employed advisers to counter the public service monopoly on policy knowledge. More significantly, the Government set up the Royal Commission on Australian Government Administration in 1974, headed by the widely respected economist and public servant H.C. Coombs. Among other things, the Coombs Commission recommended formalizing arrangements for employing the newly emerging class of ministerial advisers, opening up public service employment to allow public servants to move between agencies and to allow movement between the public and private sectors, strengthening the merit principle over seniority in appointments and promotions, and establishing performance-based senior executive positions that lacked the tenure protection typical of public service posts (Hazlehurst and Nethercote, 1977).

Consistent with these steps toward a more open public sector, the Coombs Commission promoted the benefits of greater social diversity within the public service and proposed equal employment opportunity measures to achieve that goal. Its recommendations for a more representative public sector dovetailed with two contemporaneous developments. First, in 1973, Labor Minister for Immigration Al Grassby rejected the previous Liberal–National Government's policy of integrating immigrants into a "monoculture." Grassby promoted the idea of a multicultural Australia, which would "appreciate, embrace and preserve all those diverse elements which find a place in the nation today" (1973, p. 15). Second, the late 1960s and early 1970s saw an increase in organized campaigns for social, economic, and civic equality by groups such as women and Aboriginal and Torres Strait Islander people (Horne, 1980).

Although Labor lost office before Coombs reported in 1976, most of his key recommendations received bipartisan support and were acted on by Malcolm Fraser's Liberal–National Government (1975–83) and the Labor governments of Bob Hawke and Paul Keating (1983–96). Equal Employment Opportunity (EEO) programs were established in 1981. By the 1990s, the elected executive had established greater control over the public sector. The abolition of the Public Service Board gave ministers and agency heads power over the staffing of public sector agencies. The conditions of Senior Executive Service contracts meant that agency heads and other senior public sector staff could be easily removed by their ministers (Weller, 2001). Public servants' influence over ministers was reduced by ministerial advisers, who often kept public servants at arm's length from their ministers (Tiernan, 2007).

These developments were mirrored at the sub-national level, with state and territory governments implementing equal opportunity programs and establishing managerialist norms and structures throughout their public sector agencies (Halligan and Power, 1992; Alaba, 1994; Laffin, 1995). National and sub-national bureaucracies began to shrink from the late 1980s, as governments outsourced, commercialized and privatized a range of their activities. The Australian Public Service, for example, fell from about 169 000 staff in 1988 to 114 000 in 2000. Since 2000, the number of public servants has gradually returned to 1980s' levels, as governments have paid greater attention to monitoring and coordinating services that are now delivered by a mix of organizations across the public, private, and community sectors (Halligan, 2010; Simon-Davies, 2010).

This Australian evolution of the traditional anglophone model might be expected to have had mixed effects on bureaucratic representation. On the one hand, the opening up of public service positions, combined with EEO measures, should have produced a better alignment between the composition of Australian bureaucracies and that of the wider society. In its policy development role, the public service is likely to be more representative of the range of social identities and interests found in the community. On the other hand, the fact that governments increasingly use contracted private businesses and community groups in partnership with public sector agencies to provide frontline services might make the representativeness of those public sector agencies on their own less relevant to the way that policies are actually implemented.

WHO IS TO BE REPRESENTED IN AUSTRALIAN BUREAUCRACIES?

Australian public sector bodies regularly advertise their dedication to diversity and inclusion. They do so largely in terms of individual equity and access to public sector employment. Thus their primary focus is on drawing people from a range of backgrounds into the public sector, rather than on the effects that the resulting diversity might have on the performance of the public sector for Australian society and its various parts.

The Australian Public Service Commission's 2009–10 State of the Service Report is typical in this regard. It devotes a chapter to diversity, which begins:

> The Australian Public Service (APS) is committed to progressing equity and diversity to ensure the public service workforce is representative of the broader Australian community. To support this commitment, agencies are required to improve workforce representation across the diversity groups through a number of whole-of-government initiatives. (2010, p. 147)

The report notes that diversity is legally mandated by the Public Service Act 1999. The report states briefly that "[d]iversity is important if the APS is to draw on the full range of skills and experience to build its capability" (2010, p. 148). It later indicates that diversity helps the APS to deal sensitively with particular groups (2010, p. 150). Beyond this, the report says little about the objectives that might be served by a commitment to representative bureaucracy.

Which groups ought to be properly represented in Australian bureaucracies to achieve these goals? As the Australian Public Service Commission itself notes, diversity could potentially encompass a wide range of criteria:

> Diversity has a broad connotation and includes many facets of differences in gender, age, language, ethnicity, cultural background, religious belief and family responsibilities. In the context of the workplace, diversity encompasses all of these characteristics, as well as differences between individuals in educational level, life experience, work experience, socio-economic background and personality. (2010, p. 172)

Out of such broad considerations, contemporary Australian governments consistently emphasize four criteria when measuring and addressing public sector representativeness: indigenous status, ethno-linguistic status, gender, and physical and intellectual disability.

For many years, Australian governments had no expectation that bureaucracy would be representative of broader society on such measures. Indeed, some groups were overtly or covertly excluded. Between 1902 and 1966, for example, married women were explicitly barred from permanent employment in the Australian Public Service. They could only apply for low paid temporary jobs that involved no supervision of other public servants. Understandably, most women resigned on becoming married (Briggs, 2006). More covertly, sectarian tensions led to accusations that certain public service departments were bastions either of Catholics or Protestants (especially Protestants who belonged to Orange Lodges), to the exclusion or serious disadvantage of members of the other religion (Hogan, 1987).

From the 1970s, state and national anti-discrimination legislation and EEO measures formalized the new expectation that the staff of bureaucracies would look increasingly like the wider society. What would this mean for representation of Aboriginal and Torres Strait Islander peoples and of minority immigrant communities, the two broad categories of people most relevant to the concerns of this volume? In neither case has establishing a good measure of representation been easy.

ABORIGINAL AND TORRES STRAIT ISLANDERS

The definition of aboriginality has been deeply contested in Australia. Until the 1970s, Australian authorities decided who counted as Aboriginal in terms of purity of descent, or "blood." Officials habitually reserved the status of Aboriginal for what they termed "full bloods" or "Aboriginal natives," separating them from "half castes" and others with a mix of Aboriginal and non-Aboriginal forebears. Indigenous people's own identifications with their aboriginality were considered irrelevant. Moreover, Aboriginal people were not counted in the official Australian Census until 1971, following a referendum in 1967 (Chesterman and Galligan, 1997).

More recently, official definitions of aboriginality have shifted to include anyone of part or full Aboriginal or Torres Strait Islander descent who identifies themselves as Indigenous. For some purposes, acceptance by an Indigenous community is also required. This newer definition allows individuals and communities, rather than governments, to set the observable boundaries of aboriginality. Contention about who has a genuine claim to aboriginality has not disappeared, with rival Indigenous families and clans sometimes disputing each other's claims. In addition to this problem, the broad "Aboriginal and Torres Strait Islander" category might not be seen as a satisfactory basis for bureaucratic representation, since the category is an amalgam of many distinct clan groups across Australia, each of whom have their own traditional lands, language and authority structures (Jordan, 1985; McCorquodale, 1997).

MINORITY ETHNO-LINGUISTIC COMMUNITIES

The definition of minority ethnic communities is difficult for similar reasons. Australia has experienced several waves of post-war immigration that have reshaped its ethnic composition. These waves are indicated in Table 15.1, which shows the major birthplaces of Australians at three points roughly 25 years apart.

Several trends are evident. First, the proportion of native-born Australians has fallen consistently over the post-war period. The Australian Anglo-Celtic majority is in decline. Second, immigrants from Europe (especially Greeks and Italians) increased in the first period but then declined in relative and absolute terms between 1981 and 2008. Third, the newer growth has come from Asia, with the numbers of people born in China, India, Vietnam, the Philippines and Malaysia all over 120 000 by 2008. Fourth, as a result of these shifts, the picture is one of greater diversity in 2008, with a larger number of countries contributing more even proportions of the immigrant total than in the past.

The result is a social mosaic; however, its precise implications for bureaucratic representation are not entirely obvious. For one thing, immigrants' places of birth alone will often provide an incomplete and potentially misleading guide to their traditions, interests and identities. This is true, for example, of the immigrants born in Australia's neighbor New Zealand, who may well come from either the indigenous Maori community or the European "Pakeha" community. In addition, by 2008, the "Australian-born" category included large numbers of people whose parents were immigrants from outside the United Kingdom and other anglophone states. Many of these children will have grown up

Table 15.1   Main countries of birth, Australian population (000s and %)

Birthplace*	Year					
	1954		1981		2008	
	000s	%	000s	%	000s	%
Australia	7700	85.7	11389	79.4	15946	74.4
United Kingdom	664	7.4	1076	7.5	1167	5.4
New Zealand	43	0.5	161	1.1	495	2.3
China**	12	0.1	41	0.3	401	1.9
India	12	0.1	41	0.3	239	1.1
Italy	120	1.3	275	1.9	222	1.0
Vietnam	–	–	41	0.3	193	0.9
Philippines	–	–	15	0.1	155	0.7
South Africa	6	–	27	0.2	136	0.6
Greece	26	0.3	146	1.1	131	0.6
Germany	65	0.7	109	0.8	127	0.6
Malaysia	2	–	31	0.2	120	0.6
Others Combined	336	3.7	988	5.7	2099	9.8
Total Overseas	1286	14.3	2951	20.6	5486	25.6
Total	8987	100.0	14340	100.0	21432	100.0

Notes:
*   Countries contributing more than 120000 immigrants in 2008 shown individually.
**   Includes Hong Kong.

Source: Australian Bureau of Statistics.

in households where English was rarely spoken and where traditions brought by parents from overseas were still followed. Others will have assimilated into the dominant Anglo-Celtic culture (see Smith, 2001). The varied identities and interests of these "second generation immigrants," as much as those of their first generation immigrant parents, will be relevant considerations for representative bureaucracy.

Australian governments have responded to these identity conundrums in different ways. The Australian Public Service has focused attention on people who have migrated to Australia and whose first language is not English. In official Australian documents, these people are categorized "Non-English Speaking Background 1" or "NESB1," with the "1" referring to their first generation immigrant status. The New South Wales, Queensland, and Tasmanian official categories include anyone whose first language is not English, regardless of where they were born, thus drawing in a wider "Non-English Speaking Background" or "NESB" group. South Australia and Western Australia include anyone who migrated from a country where English is not the main language, regardless of their individual language backgrounds. Victoria includes people who currently speak a language other than English in their homes (see Table 15.2 below).

These categories all focus on a presumed difference that separates the experiences and identities of immigrant groups from those of mainstream Anglo-Celtic Australian culture; however, none of them entirely captures these ethno-linguistic differences. Moreover, the differences in categories make it difficult to compare bureaucratic representation across Australian jurisdictions. Finally, as with aboriginality, the issue of generality arises. It is difficult to argue, for example, that a public servant who grew up speaking Mandarin has a particular ability to represent the interests of a Turkish-speaking citizen, simply because both are "NESB."

MINORITY GROUPS AND AUSTRALIAN REPRESENTATIVE BUREAUCRACY

Bearing in mind the points made above, how well do Australian bureaucracies represent minority ethnic groups? The simplest answer is moderately well. Table 15.2 presents data, drawn from the most recent official government publications, on the proportions of Aboriginal and Torres Strait Islanders and members of cultural minorities working in the Commonwealth and state public sectors, as well as their proportions in the wider community. Data on women are presented for comparative purposes. As noted earlier, the data are far from perfect. Most of the figures rely on individual self-reporting, which may vary in accuracy over time and between agencies. Information on membership of specific minority ethnic groups is generally not collected and/or presented comprehensively in official documents (for these problems, see Australian Public Service Commission, 2010, Chapter 8). The rounding of small percentages in the Victorian and Tasmanian cases makes comparisons less precise than they might be.

Table 15.2 suggests that Australian public sector agencies have been far more successful at the inclusion of women than they have in recruiting Aboriginal and Torres Strait Islanders or members of cultural minorities. Women make up half the population but three-fifths to two-thirds of public sector workers. By contrast to this over-representation, Indigenous Australians are underrepresented. Setting aside the rounded percentage from Victoria, the only jurisdiction in which Indigenous public sector workers appear to be (slightly) overrepresented is in New South Wales. The three states with the highest proportion of Aboriginal and Torres Strait Islanders in their populations – Western Australia, Queensland, and

Table 15.2   Representation of diversity in Australian Commonwealth and State public sectors

	People from minority cultural backgrounds		Aboriginal and Torres Strait Islanders		Women	
	In public sector (%)*	In population (%)**	In public sector (%)	In population (%)	In public sector (%)	In population (%)
Commonwealth***	6.3	15.8	2.2	2.5	57.4	50.2
New South Wales****	15.2	20.1	2.3	2.2	60.2	50.4
Victoria**	16	20.4	1.0	0.6	67	50.4
Queensland***	9.5	7.8	2.1	3.6	63.8	50.0
Western Australia***	11.9	11.6	2.4	3.8	67.5	49.3
South Australia*****	3.6	12.2	1.5	1.7	65.2	50.6
Tasmania***	4	3.5	2	3.4	69	50.6

Notes:
*	Figures for the Commonwealth are for the non-English Speaking Background 1 or 'NESB1' group; that is, people who have migrated to Australia and whose first language is not English. Figures for NSW, Queensland, and Tasmania are for non-English Speaking Background or 'NESB'; that is, anyone whose first language is not English. SA and WA migrated to Australia from a country where English is not the main language. Victoria, language other than English spoken at home.
**	Language other than English spoken at home.
***	2010 for public sector, 2006 for population.
****	2009 for public sector, 2006 for population.
*****	2007 for public sector, 2006 for population.

Sources: Australian Public Service Commission, 2010; Commissioner for Public Employment, 2007; Director of Equal Opportunity in Public Employment, 2010; Equal Opportunity in Public Employment, 2009; Office of the State Service Commissioner, 2010; Public Service Commission, 2010; State Services Authority, 2009.

Tasmania – are the states with the largest apparent underrepresentation of Indigenous public sector workers. Why this should be so is unclear, although historically the cultures of these states have tended to be less supportive of Indigenous aspirations than have states with smaller and less visible Indigenous populations (Smith, 2001, pp. 147–148).

The pattern for minority ethnic groups is blurred by the different measures used in official sources from different jurisdictions (see above). The second column of Table 15.2 presents the proportions of the population who speak a language other than English at home, so as to indicate the relative levels of minority ethnic public sector representation that should be expected in the different Australian jurisdictions. By this measure, the highest levels should occur in New South Wales and Victoria and the lowest levels in Tasmania. This appears to be the case. The three states that use an identical measure for ethnic minorities in the public sector – New South Wales, Queensland, and Tasmania – appear in the order that the population data would predict. Victoria is the only jurisdiction in Table 15.2 for which it is possible to compare the public sector and population using the same measure of minority ethnic representation (language spoken at home). The results (20 percent versus 16 percent) show that minority ethnic groups are somewhat underrepresented in the Victorian public sector (see also State Services Authority, 2009). The same may well be true in other jurisdictions, and particularly in South Australia (see Commissioner for Public Employment, 2007).

The official government reports on which Table 15.2 is based reveal two further details to add to this broad picture of Indigenous and ethnic minority underrepresentation. The first is that the underrepresentation of Aboriginal and Torres Strait Islanders (and women) tends to increase at the higher levels of the public sector and particularly at Senior Executive Service level. Members of minority ethnic groups, by contrast, tend to be overrepresented at more senior levels (see, for example, Director of Equal Opportunity in Public Employment, 2010; Equal Opportunity in Public Employment, 2009). Second, Indigenous public sector workers tend to be concentrated in a narrow range of public sector agencies. In the Australian Public Service, for example, 60 percent of Indigenous employees were concentrated in just four agencies (Australian Public Service Commission, 2010). Australian bureaucratic representation is thus extremely uneven both vertically and horizontally.

Unsurprisingly, given Australian government commitments to achieving more diverse bureaucracies, agency reports emphasize successes in improving Indigenous and minority ethnic staffing, while playing down any decreases as statistical aberrations or short-term reversals. All jurisdictions have programs to improve diversity and some national coordination of employment targets has begun. In 2009, the body that coordinates policies across the Australian federation, the Council on Australian Government, agreed to a National Partnership Agreement on Indigenous Economic Participation. This agreement committed the Commonwealth and all states to increase their public sector Indigenous employee levels to 2.7 percent by 2015. Beneath such high profile umbrella agreements, individual agency diversity programs are patchier in character. In 2010, for example, just 68 percent of Australian Public Service agencies had a diversity program, a drop of 9 percent from 2 years earlier. As the Australian Public Service Commission has noted, this decline is "a concerning trend, given that it is mandatory for all agencies to have one" (2010, p. 148).

UNRESOLVED ISSUES: MULTICULTURALISM AND POST-COLONIALISM

From one perspective, the increased diversity across Australian public sector agencies is a triumph for the policies of multiculturalism, anti-discrimination, and equal opportunity begun in the 1970s. Although public sector agencies may not be perfectly representative, they are far more representative than they were until the 1970s. Immigrants' pre-1970s experiences of bureaucracy were overwhelmingly alienating and confusing (Martin, 1978). Two or three decades later, Australians from minority ethnic groups had the same expectations of fair treatment by bureaucracy as the rest of the community (Smith, 2001).

From another perspective, public sector diversity disguises the failure of multicultural policies and programs to ask fundamental questions about the best way to represent different ethnic communities and deliver programs to them. When a range of conservative critics began to assert that immigration and multiculturalism were undermining Australian national identity in the 1980s and 1990s, the government's response was to define national identity around shared commitments to citizenship and democracy (National Multicultural Advisory Council, 1999). If citizenship rather than ethnicity was going to be the glue that held Australia together, little room was allowed for experimenting with bureaucratic structures and programs that would address the particular needs and expectations of specific ethnic communities. Individuals from those communities could join the public sector, and be served by it, but only if they conformed to the uniform model of policy delivery established by the dominant Anglo-Celtic community (see Hage, 1998).

This unresolved issue of the potential (or threat) of minority ethnic representation to reshape bureaucratic institutions and services is more sharply revealed in the participation of Aboriginal and Torres Strait Islander people in bureaucratic institutions. The starting point here is Australia's status as a post-colonial society, one deeply marked by ongoing tensions and conflicts between the values of the dominant white (Anglo-Celtic) settler society and those of the first Australians (see Ivison et al., 2000).

These conflicts have been repeatedly played out through public sector bureaucracies in three forms. The first has been white settler efforts to impose "normal" living conditions on indigenous Australians, often by imposing special bureaucratic rules, controls and procedures not applied to the non-indigenous community. Examples include the systematic separation of Indigenous children from their parents between 1910 and 1970 and the extraordinary power over many Indigenous Australians exercised by white Chief Protectors during much of the same period (National Inquiry into the Separation of Aboriginal and Torres Strait Islander Children from Their Families, 1997; Chesterman and Galligan, 1998). The current example of this is the Northern Territory Emergency Response, which commenced in 2007 and has seen massive bureaucratic efforts to normalize conditions in the remote Aboriginal communities of northern Australia. The imposition of a range of social and economic controls on remote Aboriginal people that were not also imposed on white communities required the suspension of the Commonwealth Racial Discrimination Act 1975 (Pounder, 2008).

The second form has been resistance by Indigenous Australians, both from outside and within the public sector, to bureaucratic policies and norms imposed by white settler society. Resistance by Indigenous Australians to the policy of removing their children, for example, was common (National Inquiry into the Separation of Aboriginal and Torres Strait Islander Children from Their Families, 1997). Prominent Aboriginal officials such as Charles Perkins, who served as Secretary of the Commonwealth Department of Aboriginal Affairs in the 1980s, have refused to abandon strategies of public advocacy, campaigning, and protest, despite the norms attached to their bureaucratic positions (Read, 2001).

The third manifestation of Australia's post-colonial social relations has been the creation of hybrid bureaucratic forms that reflect the representation of values drawn from both the white settler and Indigenous communities. The most ambitious experiment with this hybrid representation was the Aboriginal and Torres Strait Islander Commission (ATSIC), established by Bob Hawke's Labor Government in 1990. ATSIC's structure combined elected and bureaucratic representation for Indigenous Australians. Indigenous people voted for ATSIC Commissioners, who in turn oversaw policy delivery to Indigenous communities. While ATSIC involved a significant move toward policy self-determination by Indigenous Australians, its structures of elections and accountability were drawn from the dominant Anglo-Celtic models. Ultimately, ATSIC satisfied neither Indigenous nor non-Indigenous standards of governance. John Howard's Liberal–National Government abolished the organization in 2005, returning the administration of Indigenous affairs to mainstream bureaucratic structures, supplemented by an Indigenous advisory committee. Although ATSIC was widely seen as a failure, its abolition has not resolved the problem of designing a representative bureaucratic structure that incorporates Indigenous people's aspirations for policy self-determination (Anthony, 2010; Muir, 2010).

CONCLUSION

As the previous section indicates, Australian government moves toward representative bureaucracy since the 1970s can be viewed in two ways. The project of replacing a male, Anglo-Celtic bureaucracy with one that accurately represents the diversity of Australian society is unfinished; however, it has transformed the face of the Australian public sector. In 2011, Australians interacting with public sector agencies, as well as government ministers drawing on those agencies for policy advice are likely to deal with people who have a range of social characteristics. This project of diversity has been implemented without any challenge to the dominant anglophone patterns of bureaucratic behavior or structure.

For critics, this lack of challenge reflects the failure of a representative project that focuses on the insertion of diverse individuals into a common bureaucratic system established by the dominant culture. They look for evidence that the representation of ethnic minorities and Indigenous Australians has diversified Australian bureaucracy, rather than Australian bureaucrats, and fail to find it. While most Australians might be satisfied that public sector agencies are more socially representative than they once were, for the critics, the transformative promise of Australian multicultural and Indigenous bureaucratic representation is yet to be achieved.

ACKNOWLEDGMENTS

The author wishes to acknowledge the research assistance of Patrick Hurley.

Bibliography

Abed, G. and Gupta, S. (2002). The economics of corruption. In G. Abed and S. Gupta (eds), *Governance, Corruption, and Economic Performance.* Washington, D.C.: International Monetary Fund.

Aberbach, J.D. and Rockman, B.A. (1998). Mandates or Mandarins? Control and discretion in the modern administrative states. *Public Administration Review,* **48**, 606–612.

Aberbach, J.D., Putnam, R.D., and Rockman, B.A. (1981). *Bureaucrats and Politicians in Western Democracies.* Cambridge, MA: Harvard University Press.

Abu-Laban, Y., and Gabriel, C. (2002). *Selling Diversity: Immigration, Multiculturalism, Employment Equity, and Globalization.* Peterborough, UK: Broadview Press.

Adams, I. (2010). *Beyond National Models. Immigrant Integration Policies of the Belgian Regions (1980–2006).* Brussels: Vrije Universiteit.

African National Congress (ANC) (1994). *The Reconstruction and Development Programme.* Cape Town, South Africa: African National Congress.

Alaba, R. (1994). *Inside Bureaucratic Power.* Sydney, Australia: Hale and Iremonger.

Algemene Directie voor Statistiek en Economische Informatie (2008). *Bevols per Nationaliteit, Geslacht en Leeftijd op 1/1/2008,* accessed March 1, 2011 at http://statbel.fgov.be/nl/modules/publications/statis-tiques/bevolking/Bevolking_nat_geslacht_leeftijdsgroepen.jsp.

Algemene Directie voor Statistiek en Economische Informatie (2010). Wettelijke Bevolking per Gemeente op 1 Januari, accessed March 3, 2011 at http://statbel.fgov.be/nl/modules/publications/statistiques/bev olking/cijfers_bevolking_1_1_2009.jsp.

Altermatt, B. (2005). Die institutionelle Zweisprachigkeit der Stadt Fribourg–Freiburg: Geschichte, Zustand und Entwicklungstendenzen. *Bulletin Suisse de Linguistique Appliquée,* **82**, 63–82.

Ambedkar, B.R. (1936 [1968]). *Annihilation of Caste.* Jullundur, India: Bheem Patrika Publications.

Andrews, R., Boyne, G.A., Meier, K.J., O'Toole, J., and Walker, R.M. (2005). Representative bureaucracy, organizational strategy, and public service performance: an empirical analysis of English local government. *Journal of Public Administration, Research and Theory*, **15**(4), 489–504.

Andrews, R., Boyne, G.A., and Walker, R. (2006). Workforce diversity in the public sector: an evaluation of the performance of English local authorities. *Policy and Politics*, **34**, 287–306.

Anthony, T. (2010). A new indigenous representative body . . . again. *Indigenous Law Bulletin*, **7**, 5–9.

Arena, M. (2003). *De Wereld is in Beweging. Samen Gaan we de Uitdaging van het Nieuwe Federaal Openbaar Ambt aan. Beleidsnota Ambtenarenzaken*. Brussels: Federale Overheid.

Audit Commission (2007). *Best Value Performance Indicators*. London: Audit Commission.

Audit Commission (2008). *Best Value Performance Indicators*. London: Audit Commission.

Australian Public Service Commission (2010). *State of the Service Report 2009–2010*. Canberra, Australia: Commonwealth of Australia.

Bakan, A. and Kobayashi, A. (2000). *Employment Equity Policy in Canada: An Interprovincial Comparison*. Ottawa, Canada: Status of Women Canada.

Ball, W. (1987). Local authority policy-making on equal opportunities: corporate provision, co–option and consultation. *Policy and Politics*, **15**, 101–110.

Bandyopadhyay, S. (1994). Caste, class and politics in colonial Bengal: a case study of the Namasudra Movement of 1872–1937. In K.L. Sharma (ed.), *Caste and Class in India*. Jaipur and New Delhi, India: Rawat Publications, pp. 19–52.

Bank of Israel (2010). *Bank of Israel Report for 2009*. Jerusalem: Bank of Israel.

Barnard, C.I. (1968). *The Functions of the Executive*. Cambridge, MA: Harvard University Press.

Bauböck, R. (1996). Social and cultural integration in a civil society. In R. Bauböck, A. Heller, and A. Zolberg (eds), *The Challenge of Diversity: Integration and Pluralism in Societies of Immigration*. Aldershot, UK: Avebury, pp. 67–132.

Bauböck, R. (2004). Multiculturalism. In A. Harrington, B. Marshall, and H.-P. Müller (eds), *Routledge Encyclopedia of Social Theory*. Abingdon, UK: Routledge.

Bayly, S. (1999). *Caste, Society and Politics in India from the Eighteenth Century to the Modern Age*. Cambridge: Cambridge University Press.

Bekke, H.A.G.M., Perry, J.L., and Toonen, T.A.J. (1996). Introduction: conceptualizing civil service systems. In H.A.G.M. Bekke, J.L. Perry, and T.A.J. Toonen (eds), *Civil Service Systems in Comparative Perspective.* Bloomington, IN: Indiana University Press, pp. 1–13.

Berger, Y. and Shaked, R. (2004). *Activity Report. Division for the Advancement and Integration of Women.* Jerusalem: Civil Service Commission.

BQN Berlin (2007). Newsletter Ausbildung im Öffentlichen Dienst, Berlin.

Bovens, M.A.P. (1998). *The Quest for Responsibility: Accountability and Citizenship in Complex Organizations.* Cambridge: Cambridge University Press.

Bradbury, M.D. and Kellough, J.E. (2008). Representative bureaucracy: exploring the potential for active representation in local government. *Journal of Public Administration Research and Theory*, **18**(4), 697–714.

Briggs, L. (2006). *Celebration of the 40th Anniversary of the Lifting of the Marriage Bar.* Canberra, accessed at http://www.apsc.gov.au/media/briggs201106.htm.

Briggs, W. (1920 [1997]). *The Chamars.* Delhi: Low Price Publications.

Brimelow, E. (1981). Women in the civil service. *Public Administration*, **59**, 313–335.

Brown, J.M. (1994). *Modern India: The Origins of an Asian Democracy.* Oxford: Oxford University Press.

Bulgaria: National Statistical Institute (2010). http://www.nsi.bg, accessed October 3, 2012.

Bundesamt für Statistik (2004). *Religionslandschaft in der Schweiz.* Neuenburg, Germany: Bundesamt für Statistik.

Bundesamt für Statistik (2005). *Eidgenössische Volkszählung 2000: Sprachenlandschaft der Schweiz.* Neuenburg, Germany: Bundesamt für Statistik.

Burger, D. (ed.) (2010). *Pocket Guide to South Africa 2010/11.* Pretoria, South Africa: Government Communication and Information System.

Butler, A. (2008). Consolidation first: institutional reform priorities in the creation of a developmental state in South Africa. In B. Turok (ed.), *Wealth Does Not Trickle Down. The Case for a Developmental State in South Africa.* Cape Town: New Agenda, pp. 183–201.

Cameron, R. and Milne, C. (2004). Affirmative action in the South African Public Service, unpublished paper, Cape Town.

Cameron, R. and Milne, C. (2008). Consociational bureaucracy in the South African Public Service, unpublished paper, Cape Town.

Cameron, R.G. (2009). New public management reforms in the South African Public Service: 1999–2009, *Journal of Public Administration*, **44**(4.1), 910–942.

Cameron, R.G. (2011). New Public Management and Patronage within the South African State, Paper presented at 15th IRSPM Conference April 10–13, 2011, Dublin.

Campbell, J.L. (2004). *Institutional Change and Globalization*. Princeton, NJ: Princeton University Press.

Capano, G. (2006). L'evoluzione storica della pubblica amministrazione. In G. Capano and E. Gualmini (eds), *La Pubblica Amministrazione in Italia*. Bologna, Italy: Il Mulino, pp. 27–55.

Capano, G. and Vassallo, S. (eds) (2003). *La Dirigenza Pubblica. Il Mercato e le Competenze Dei Ruoli Manageriali*. Soveria Mannelli, Italy: Rubbettino.

Carboni, N. (2008). *Il Circolo Virtuoso del Controllo Politico: Concetti, Variabili e Modelli della Relazione tra Politica e Amministrazione in Italia e in Prospettiva Comparata*. Soveria Mannelli, Italy: Rubbettino.

Carboni, N. (2010a). Professional autonomy vs. political control: how to deal with the dilemma. Some evidence from the Italian Core Executive. *Public Policy and Administration*, **25**(4), 1–22.

Carboni, N. (2010b). The changing relationship between politicians and bureaucrats in contemporary democracies: an empirical analysis of the Italian case. *International Public Management Review*, **11**(1), 90–109.

Cassese S. (1980). *Esiste un governo in Italia?* Rome: Officina.

Cassese, S. (1984). *Il Sistema Amministrativo Italiano*. Bologna, Italy: Il Mulino.

Cassese, S. (1999). Italy's senior civil service: an ossified world. In E.C. Page and V. Wright (eds), *Bureaucratic Elites in Western European States*. Oxford: Oxford University Press, pp. 55–64.

Central Bureau of Statistics (2010). *Statistical Abstract of Israel*. Jerusalem: Central Bureau of Statistics, Section 10.12.

Central Bureau of Statistics (2011). Press Release 08/05/2011. Jerusalem: Central Bureau of Statistics.

Cerase, F. (1994). *I Dipendenti Pubblici. Profilo Socio–Statistico Dei Dipendenti delle Pubbliche Amministrazioni in Italia*. Bologna, Italy: Il Mulino.

Chanchreek, K.L. (ed.) (1991). *Dr. B.R. Ambedkar: Patriot, Philosopher and Statesman: Fight for the Rights of the Depressed Classes*. Delhi: H.K. Publishers and Distributors.

Charsley, S. (1996). Untouchable: what is in a name? *Journal of the Royal Anthropological Institute* (N.S.), **2**, 1–23.

Chesterman, J. and Galligan, B. (1997). *Citizens Without Rights: Aborigines and Australian Citizenship*. Cambridge: Cambridge University Press.

CIA (2011). *World Fact Book*. Washington DC: CIA, accessed October 3, 2012 at https://www.cia.gov/library/publications/download/download–2011/index.html.

Civil Service (2008). *Promoting Equality, Valuing Diversity. A Strategy for the Civil Service*. London: Cabinet Office.

Civil Service Commission (2005). Appropriate Representation and the State of Women Advancement in the Civil Service, report submitted to the Knesset's Constitution, Law and Justice Committee. Jerusalem: Civil Service Commission.

Civil Service Commission, the Unit for the Advancement and Integration of Women (2004). *Annual Report for the Year 2003*. Jerusalem: Civil Service Commission, Hebrew, accessed at http://www.civil–service.gov.il/Civil–Service/TopNavHe/Units/Woman/Reports/.

Civil Service Commission, the Unit for the Advancement and Integration of Women (2009). *Annual Report for the Year 2008*. Jerusalem: Civil Service Commission, Hebrew, accessed at http://www.civil–service.gov.il/Civil–Service/TopNavHe/Units/Woman/Reports/.

Civil Service Commission, the Unit for the Advancement and Integration of Women (2010). *Annual Report for the Year 2009*. Jerusalem: Civil Service Commission, Hebrew, accessed at http://www.civil–service.gov.il/Civil–Service/TopNavHe/Units/Woman/Reports/.

Civil Service Commission, the Unit for the Advancement and Integration of Women (2011). *Annual Report for the Year 2010*. Jerusalem: Civil Service Commission, Hebrew, accessed at http://www.civil–service.gov.il/Civil–Service/TopNavHe/Units/Woman/Reports/.

Coleman Seldon, S. (1997). *The Promise of Representative Bureaucracy: Diversity and Responsiveness in Government Agencies*. New York: M.E. Sharpe.

Comisión Nacional para el Desarrollo de los Pueblos Indígenas (CDI) (2006). *Informe Sobre Desarrollo Humano de los Pueblos Indígenas de México 2006*. México City: CDI–PNUD.

Comisión Nacional para el Desarrollo de los Pueblos Indígenas (CDI) (2010). *Acciones de Gobierno Para el Desarrollo de los Pueblos Indígenas. Informe 2009*. México City: CDI.

Commissioner of Official Languages (2003). *Annual Report 2002–2003*. Ottawa: Ministry of Public Works and Government Services Canada.

Commissioner of Official Languages (2005). *Annual Report, Special Edition, 35th Anniversary, 1969–2004*. Ottawa: Ministry of Public Works and Government Services Canada.

Commissioner of Official Languages (2007). *Annual Report 2006–2007*. Ottawa: Ministry of Public Works and Government Services Canada.

Commissioner for Public Employment (2007). *The South Australian Public Sector Workforce Information: June 2007 Summary Report*. Adelaide, Australia: Department of Premier and Cabinet, Government of South Australia.

Commonwealth Secretariat (1991). *Report of a Commonwealth Expert Group, Human Resources in a New South Africa.* London: James Currey.

Craven, P. (2011). Coloured job–loss claim dismissed. *Business Day*, February 22, 2011.

D'Auria, G. and Bellucci, P. (eds) (1995). *Politici e burocrati al governo dell'amministrazione.* Bologna, Italy: Il Mulino.

Dawson, A.S. (1998). From models for the nation to model citizens: indigenismo and the "revindication" of the Mexican Indian, 1920–1940. *Journal of Latin American Studies*, **30**, 279–308.

De Zwart, F. (2000). The logic of affirmative action: caste, class and quotas. *Acta Sociologica*, **43**, 235–249.

De Zwart, F. (2005). The dilemma of recognition: administrative categories and cultural diversity. *Theory and Society*, **34**, 137–169.

Decat, A. and Scheepers, S. (2005). Genderanalyse van de Copernicushervorming. In A. Hondeghem and R. Depré (eds), *De Copernicushervorming in Perspectief. Veranderingsmanagement in de Federale Overhead.* Brugge: Vandenbroele, pp. 293–323.

Deliège, R. (1999). *The Untouchables of India.* Oxford and New York: Berg.

Deliège, R. (2002). Is there still untouchability in India? Heidelberg Papers in South Asian and Comparative Politics, Working Paper No. 5, June 2002.

Dente, B. (2001). Riforme e (Controriforme) Amministrative. *Il Mulino*, **6**, 1050–1059.

Department of Public Service and Administration (DPSA) (1995). *White Paper on the Transformation of the Public Service.* Pretoria: Government Printer.

Department of Public Service and Administration (DPSA) (1997). *White Paper on Human Resource Management in the Public Service.* Pretoria: Government Printer.

Department of Public Service and Administration (DPSA) (1998). *White Paper on Affirmative Action in the Public Service.* Pretoria: Government Printer.

Department of Public Service and Administration (2011). *Public Service Employment Statistics.* Pretoria: DPSA.

Derlien, H.–U. and Peters, B.G. (2008). *The State at Work*, 2nd edn. Cheltenham, UK and Northampton, MA: Edward Elgar.

Deschouwer, K. (2004). *Ethnic Structure, Inequality and Governance of the Public Sector in Belgium.* Geneva: United Nations Research Institute for Social Development.

Dieckhoff, A. (2000). *La Nation Dans tous ses États. Les Identités Nationales en Mouvement.* Paris: Flammarion.

Dienst Emancipatiezaken (2010). Algemeen, accessed at http://emancipa tiezaken.vlaanderen.be/nlapps/docs/default.asp?fid=36.

DiMaggio, P.J. and Powell, W.W. (1991). The iron cage revisited: institutional isomorphism and collective rationality in organizational fields. In P.J. Di Maggio and W.W. Powell (eds). *The New Institutionalism in Organizational Analysis.* Chicago, IL: University of Chicago Press, pp. 63–82.

Dion, L. (1973). Quebec and the future of Canada. In D.C. Thomson (ed.), *Quebec Politics and Society: Views from the Inside.* Toronto, Canada: McClelland and Stewart, pp. 251–262.

Director of Equal Opportunity in Public Employment (2010). *Annual Report.* Perth, Australia: Office of Equal Employment Opportunity.

Dolan, J. (2004). Gender equity: illusion or reality for women in the federal executive service? *Public Administration Review*, **64**(3), 299–308.

Dolan, J. and Rosenbloom, D.H. (2003). Preface. In *Representative Bureaucracy: Classic Readings and Continuing Controversies.* New York: M.E. Sharpe, pp. xi–xiii.

Dror, Y. (2002). Foreword. In M. Maor (ed.), *Developments in Israeli Public Administration.* London: Fran Cass, pp. vii.

Drumaux, A. (2009). How to compare public reforms in strategic management? A way to identify pathologies. Paper presented at EGPA Conference 2009.

DT and RGS (The State General Accounting Department) (2010). *Public Administration Personnel: The Annual Count Survey*, accessed at http:// www.rgs.mef.gov.it.

Dudek, S. M. (2009). *Diversity in Uniform? Geschlecht und Migrationshintergrund in der Berliner Schutzpolizei.* Wiesbaden, Germany: VS Verlag.

Dumont, L. (1970 [1998]). *Homo Hierarchicus: The Caste System and its Implications.* Oxford: Oxford University Press.

Durr, M., and Logan, J.R. (1997). Racial submarkets in government employment: African–American managers in New York State, *Sociological Forum*, **12**, 353–370.

Dushkin, L. (1979). Backward class benefits and social class in India, 1920–1970. *Economic and Political Weekly*, July 14, 661–667.

Easton, D. (1965). *A Systems Analysis of Political Life.* New York: Wiley.

Easton, D. (1975). A re–assessment of the concept of political support. *British Journal of Political Science*, **5**(4), 435–457.

Easton, M., Ponsaers, P., Demarée, C., Vandevoorde, N., Enhusm, E., Elffers, H., Moor, L.G. (2009). *Multiple Community Policing: Hoezo? Reeks Samenleving and Toekomst.* Ghent, Belgium: Academia Press.

Eidgenössische Ausländerkommission. (2005). *Öffnung der Institutionen.*

Empfehlungen der Eidgenössischen Ausländerkommission. Bern, Switzerland: EKA.

Equal Opportunity in Public Employment (2009). *Equal Opportunity Employment Report 2008–2009.* Sydney: NSW Government.

Escalante, F. (2006). México, Fin de Siglo. In H.A. Camín (ed.). *Pensar en México.* México City: FCE, pp. 19–36.

Escalante, F. (2009). *Ciudadanos Imaginarios: Memorial de los Afanas y Desventuras de la Virtud y Apología del Vicio Triunfante en la República Mexicana. Tratado de Moral Pública.* México City: El Colegio de México.

Esman, M. (1999). Public administration and conflict management in plural societies: the case for representative bureaucracy. *Public Administration and Development,* **19**, 353–366.

European Commission (2008). *Report from the Commission to the European Parliament and the Council on Progress in Romania under the Co–operation and Verification Mechanism.* Brussels: European Commission.

European Commission (2010a). *Report from the Commission to the European Parliament and the Council on Progress in Bulgaria under the Co–operation and Verification Mechanism.* Brussels: European Commission.

European Commission (2010b). *Report from the Commission to the European Parliament and the Council on Progress in Romania under the Co–operation and Verification Mechanism.* Brussels: European Commission.

Eurostat database (2010). http://www.epp.eurostat.ec.europa.eu, accessed October 3, 2012.

Evans, P. (1974). Defining representative bureaucracy. *Public Administration Review,* **34**(6), 628–631.

Facon, P., Hondeghem, A., and Nelen, S. (2004). *Gelijkekansenbeleid onderweg: een international vergelijkend onderzoek.* Bruge, Belgium: Die Keure.

Federal Government of Germany (2007). *Answer to Interpellation No. 16/4480, German Federal Parliament no. 16/4703.* Berlin: Federal Government of Germany.

Federale Overheidsdienst Personeel en Organisatie (2005). *Actieplan 2005–2007 voor het Bevorderen van de diversiteit.* Brussels: FOD Personeel en Organisatie.

Federale Overheidsdienst Personeel en Organisatie (2006). *Handvest Diversiteit [van de Federale Overheid].* Brussels: FOD Personeel en Organisatie.

Federale Overheidsdienst Personeel en Organisatie (2010a). *Gelijke kansen en diversiteit,* accessed at http://www.fedweb.belgium.be/nl/

over_de_organisatie/over_de_federale_overheid/missie_visie_waarden/
gelijke_kansen_en_diversiteit/index.jsp.

Federale Overheidsdienst Personeel en Organisatie (2010b). *Een Diversiteitsbeleid Uitwerken. Methodologische Handleiding.* Brussels: FOD Personeel en Organisatie.

Federale Overheidsdienst Werkgelegenheid, Arbeid en Sociaal Overleg (2011). *Non–Discriminatie en Diversiteit,* accessed at http://www.werk.belgie.be/defaultTab.aspx?id=444.

Fire and Rescue Service (2009). *Equality and Diversity Report 2009.* London: FRS.

Fox, J. (1994). The difficult transition from clientelism to citizenship: lessons from Mexico. *World Politics,* **46**, 151–184.

Fraser-Moleketi, G. (2006). Notes for Incoming President at President's CAPAM 2006 Biennial Conference, October 10, 2006, Sydney, Australia.

Fraser-Moleketi, G. (2008). Raps gender bias in top state jobs. *Cape Argus,* July 2, 2008.

Frykenberg, R. E. (1965). *Guntur District 1788–1848: A History of Local Influence and Central Authority in South India.* Oxford: Clarendon Press.

Gagnon, A.-G., Turgeon, L., and de Champlain, O. (2006). La Bureaucratie Représentative au sein des Etats Multinationaux. *Revue française d'administration publique,* **118**, 291–306.

Galanter, M. (1984). *Competing Equalities: Law and the Backward Classes in India.* Berkeley and Los Angeles: University of California Press.

Galnoor, I. (2011). *Public Management in Israel: Development, Structure, Functions and Reforms.* London: Routledge.

Germann, R. E. (1996). *Administration Publique en Suisse. L'Appareil Ètatique et le Gouvernement.* Bern, Switzerland: Haupt.

Golan, G. (2011). Women and Political Reform in Israel. In F. Sadiqi and M. Ennaji (eds), *Women in the Middle East and North Africa: Agents of Change.* London: Routledge.

Golder, H. (2005). *Politics, Patronage and Public Works: The Administration of New South Wales 1842–1900.* Sydney, Australia: UNSW Press.

Gool, S.M. van (2008). Untouchable bureaucracy: unrepresentative bureaucracy in a North Indian State. PhD Thesis. Leiden, the Netherlands: Leiden University.

Government of India (1980). *Report of the Backward Classes Commission 1980.* New Delhi: Government of India Press.

Grabosky, P.N. and Rosenbloom, D.H. (1975). Racial and ethnic integration in the federal service. *Social Science Quarterly,* **56**, 71–84.

Grassby, A. (1973). *A Multi-Cultural Society for the Future.* Canberra, Australia: Australian Government Publishing Service.

Greer, S., and Jarman, H. (2010). What Whitehall? Definitions, demographics and the changing home civil services. *Public Policy and Administration*, **25**, 251–270.

Grin, F. (1997). Language policy developments in Switzerland: Needs, opportunities and priorities for the next few years. *Swiss Political Science Review*, 3(4), 108–113.

Groeneveld, S., and Van de Walle, S. (2010). A contingency approach to representative bureaucracy: power, equal opportunities and diversity. *International Review of Administrative Sciences*, **76**(2), 239–258.

Groeneveld, S. and Verbeek, S. (2010). Diversity policies in public and private sector organizations: an empirical comparison of incidence and effectiveness. Paper presented at the EGPA Conference 08–10/09/2010, Toulouse, France.

Gualmini, E. (2007). Restructuring Weberian bureaucracy: comparing managerial reforms in Europe and the United States. *Public Administration*, **86**, 75–94.

Guarnieri, C. (1988). Burocrazie Pubbliche e Consolidamento Democratico: Il Caso Italiano. *Rivista Italiana di Scienza Politica*, **1**, 73–103.

Gupta, S.K. (1985). *The Scheduled Castes in Modern Indian Politics: Their Emergence as a Political Power*. New Delhi: Munshiram Manoharlal Publishers.

Hage, G. (1998). *White Nation: Fantasies of White Supremacy in a Multicultural Society*. Sydney, Australia: Pluto Press.

Haidar, A. (2005). The representation of Arab citizens in the civil service, government corporations and local government. The Sikkuy Report 2004–2005, accessed at www.sikkuy.org.il/english/2005/ali_haidar05.pdf.

Halford, S. (1988). Women's initiatives in local government: where do they come from and where are they going? *Policy and Politics*, **16**, 251–259.

Hall, P.A. and Taylor, R.C.R. (1996). Political science and the three new institutionalisms. *Political Studies*, **XLIV**(4), 936–957.

Halligan, J. (2010). The fate of administrative tradition in anglophone countries during the reform era. In M. Painter and B.G. Peters (eds). *Tradition and Public Administration*. Houndmills, UK: Palgrave Macmillan, pp. 129–142.

Halligan, J., and Power, J. (1992). *Public Management in the 1990s*. Melbourne, Australia: Oxford University Press.

Hamburg–Personalamt (2009). *Pressemitteilung: Ausbildung ist Zukunft – 380 Nachwuchskräfte für Verwaltung und Justiz*, accessed March 22, 2012 at http://www.hamburg.de/pressearchiv–fhh/1817324/2009–10–01–pr–verwaltungsauszubildende.html.

Harriss–White, B. (2003). *India Working: Essays on Society and Economy.* Cambridge: Cambridge University Press.

Hazlehurst, C., and Nethercote, J.R. (1977). *Reforming Australian Government: The Coombs Report and Beyond.* Canberra, Australia: Royal Institute of Public Administration (A.C.T.) in association with Australian National University Press.

Heisler, M.O. (1977). Managing ethnic conflict in Belgium. *The Annals of the American Academy of Political and Social Science,* **433**, 32–46.

Hendricks, R. (2008). *Social Democrats (SPD) Parliamentary Group, Parliament of North–Rhine Westfalia, February 21st, Interpellation No. 14/6242.* Düsseldorf: NRW Government.

Herbert, A. W. (1974). The minority administrator: problems, prospects, and challenges. *Public Administration Review,* **34**(6), 556–563.

Hermann, D. (2011). Solidarity vows to fight affirmative action in concourt. Business Report 18/03/2011.

Hessischer Landtag (2007). Antwort des Ministers des Innern und Sport auf die Kleine Anfrage des Abg. Frömmrich (Bündnis 90/Die Grünen) vom 17.09.2007, Drucksache 16/7816, 18.12.2007.

HM Treasury (2009). *Public Expenditure: Statistical Analyses 2009.* London: HM Treasury.

Hoffman, A.J. (2001). *From Heresy to Dogma: An Institutional History of Corporate Environmentalism.* Stanford, CA: Stanford University Press.

Hogan, M. (1987). *The Sectarian Strand.* Ringwood, UK: Penguin.

Hondeghem, A. (1999). The National Civil Service in Belgium. In H.A.G.M. Bekke and F.M. van der Meer (eds). *Civil Service Systems in Western Europe.* Cheltenham, UK and Northampton, MA, USA: Edward Elgar Publishing Limited. pp. 121–146

Hood, C. (2000). *The Art of the State: Culture, Rhetoric, and Public Management.* Oxford: Oxford University Press.

Hood, C. (2006). Gaming in Targetworld: the targets approach to managing British public services. *Public Administration Review,* **66**, 515–521.

Horne, D. (1980). *Time of Hope: Australia 1966–72.* Sydney, Australia: Angus and Robertson.

Hudon, M.-È. (2009). *Official Languages in the Public Service: from 1973 to the Present.* Ottawa, Canada: Parliamentary Information and Research Service.

Hupe, P. (2007). *Overheids beleid als politiek, Over de grondslagen van beleid.* Assen, the Netherlands: Van Gorcum.

IJsselmuiden, P.G. van (1988). *Binnenlandse Zaken en the Ontstaan van de Moderne Overheidsbureaucratie in Nederland 1813–1940.* Kampen, the Netherlands: Kok.

Ilieva, M. (2010). Why Go Back? Return Migration of Skilled Labor:

Case Study of Bulgaria 2001–2009. B.A. Thesis, American University in Bulgaria.

Immergut, E.M. (1998). The theoretical core of the new institutionalism. *Politics and Society*, **26**(1), 5–34.

Institut für Arbeitsmarkt– und Berufsforschung (IAB). (2011). *IAB–Kurzbericht: Ostdeutsche Frauen häufiger in Führungspositionen.* No. 3, February, accessed at www.iab.de.

Institute Cattaneo data (2002). http://www.cattaneo.org/index. asp?l1=archivi&l2=adele, accessed October 3, 2012.

Instituut voor de Gelijkheid van Mannen en Vrouwen (2009). *Actiedomeinen. Besluitvorming.* accessed at http://igvm–iefh.belgium.be/nl/actiedomeinen/besluitvorming/Politiek/.

Irshick, E.F. (1969). *Politics and Social Conflict in South India: The Non–Brahman Movement and Tamil Separatism, 1916–1929.* Berkeley and Los Angeles, CA: University of California Press.

Isaacs, H. R. (1965). *India's Ex–Untouchables.* Bombay, India: Asia Publishing House.

Italian National Institute of Statistics (ISTAT) (2001). *General Census*, accessed at http://www.istat.it.

Ivison, D., Patton, P., and Sanders, W. (eds) (2000). *Political Theory and the Rights of Indigenous Peoples.* Cambridge: Cambridge University Press.

Jacobs, D. and Rea, A. (2005). Construction et Importation des Classements Ethniques. Allochtones et immigrés aux Pays–Bas et en Belgique. *Revue Européenne des Migrations Internationalles,* **21**(2), 35–59.

Jaffrelot, C. (2000). *Dr. Ambedkar and Untouchability: Analysing and Fighting Caste.* London: Hurst and Company.

Jaffrelot, C. (2003). *India's Silent Revolution: The Rise of the Lower Castes in North India.* London: Hurst and Company.

Janvier, R., Hendrickx, E., Segers, J., and Valkene, R. (2011). Meer Discriminatie door meer Diversiteit: Een Paradox voor het Belgisch Publiek Management? *Burger, Bestuur en Beleid*, **7**(1), 3–20.

Jenkins, B., and Sofos, S.A. (2006). *Nation and Identity in Contemporary Europe.* London: Routledge.

Jordan, B. (2010). *Why the Third Way Failed: Economics, Morality and the Origins of the "Big Society".* Bristol, UK: Policy Press.

Jordan, D. (1985). Census categories: enumeration of aboriginal people, or construction of identity? *Australian Aboriginal Studies*, **1**, 28–36.

Katznelson, I. and Weingast, B.R. (2005). *Preferences and Situations: Points of Intersection Between Historical and Rational Choice Institutionalism.* New York: Russel Sage Foundation Publications.

Kearns, A. and Forrest, R. (2000). Social cohesion and multilevel urban governance. *Urban Studies*, **37**, 995–1017.

Keiser, L.R., Wilkins, V.M., Meier, K.J., and Holland, C. (2002). Lipstick or logarithms: gender, identity, institutions and representative bureaucracy. *American Political Science Review*, **96**(35), 553–564.

Kellough, J.E. (1990). Integration in the public workplace: determinants of minority and female employment in federal agencies. *Public Administration Review*, **50**, 557–566.

Kfir, A. (2002). The development of the Israeli government offices. In M. Maor (ed.), *Developments in Israeli Public Administration*. London: Frank Cass, pp. 2–24.

Kingsley, J.D. (1944). *Representative Bureaucracy. An Interpretation of the British Civil Service*. Yellow Springs, OH: The Antioch Press.

Kingsley, J.D. (2003). Representative bureaucracy. In J. Dolan and D.H. Rosenbloom (eds), *Representative Bureaucracy: Classic Readings and Continuing Controversies*. Armonk, NY: M.E. Sharpe, pp. 12–19.

Kirton, G., and Greene, A. (2010). *The Dynamics of Managing Diversity. A Critical Approach*. Oxford: Elsevier.

Kothari, R. (1970). *Politics in India*. Boston, MA: Little, Brown and Company.

Kothari, R. and Maru, R. (1965). Caste secularism in India: case study of a caste federation. *The Journal of Asian Studies*, **25**, 33–50.

Kriesi, H. (ed.). (1996). *Le Clivage Linguistique: Problèmes de Compréhension entre les Communautés Linguistiques en Suisse*. Berne, Switzerland: Office Fédéral de la Statistique.

Kriesi, H., Lachat, R., Selb, P., Bornschier, S., and Helbling, M. (eds) (2005). *Der Aufstieg der SVP. Acht Kantone im Vergleich*. Zürich, Switzerland: NZZ Verlag.

Krislov, S. (1967). *The Negro in Federal Employment: The Quest for Equal Opportunity*. St. Paul, MN: North Central Publishing Company.

Krislov, S. (1974). *Representative Bureaucracy*. Englewood Cliffs, NY: Prentice-Hall, Inc.

Krueger, A.O. (1974). The political economy of the rent–seeking society. *American Economic Review*, **64**(3), 291.

The Kubersky Commission (1989). *Report of the Professional Public Committee for Comprehensive Examination of the Civil Service and Entities Supported by the State Budget*, Jerusalem: The Kubersky Commission.

Kübler, D. (2009). La Langue Originale des Actes Législatifs. In Fichier français de Berne (ed.), *Côtoyer: Cohabiter: 50e Anniversaire du Fichier Français de Berne*. Neuchâtel, Switzerland: H. Messeiller, pp. 29–36.

Kübler, D., and Piñeiro, E. (2011). *Migration und Verwaltung: politische*

Strategie und Transkulturelle Praxis. Basel, Switzerland: Institut Sozialplanung und Stadtentwicklung.

Kübler, D., Papadopoulos, Y., Mazzoleni, O., Andrey, S., and Kobelt, E. (2009). *Le Plurilinguisme de la Confédération: Représentation et Pratique Linguistiques dans l'Administration Fédérale. Résumé du rapport final.* Basel, Switzerland: Institut Sozialplanung und Stadtentwicklung, FHNW.

Kübler, D., Andrey, S., and Kobelt, E. (2011). Vers une Bureaucratie Représentative. La promotion de la Représentation et de la Diversité Linguistiques dans l'Administration Fédérale en Suisse et au Canada. *Revue canadienne de science politique/Canadian Journal of Political Science*, **44**, 1–25.

Kumar, V. (1994). Nature and crisis of Dalit leadership in India: a macro sociological analysis. Unpublished M. Phil dissertation, Jawaharlal Nehru University, New Delhi.

Kymlicka, W. (2009). *Multicultural Odysseys: Navigating the New International Politics of Diversity.* Oxford: Oxford University Press.

Kymlicka, W. (2010). The rise and fall of multiculturalism? New debates on inclusion and accommodation in diverse societies. In S. Vertovec and S. Wessendorf (eds), *The Multiculturalism Backlash. European Discourses, Policies and Practices.* London and New York: Routledge, pp. 32–49.

Laffin, M. (1995). The public service. In M. Laffin and M. Painter (eds), *Reform and Reversal.* Melbourne, Australia: Macmillan.

Leacy, F.H., Urquhart, M.C., and Buckley, K.A.H. (1983). *Historical Statistics of Canada.* Ottawa, Canada: Supply and Service Canada.

Levin, R. (2007). Building a capable development state in South Africa. Paper presented at the 7th Africa Governance Forum October 24–26, 2007, Ouagadougou, Burkina Faso.

Lewanski, R. (1997). Italian Civil Service: A Pre–Modern Bureaucracy in Transition? Paper prepared for the Conference on "Civil service Systems in Comparative Perspective," April 5–8, 1997. Bloomington, IN: University of Indiana.

Lewanski, R. and Vassallo, S. (2002), I nuovi dirigenti comunali. Esterni o interni: fa differenza? *Rivista Italiana di Politiche Pubbliche*, **1**, 99–135.

Liebig, T. and Widmaier, S., 2009. *Children of Migrants in the Labour Market of EU and OECD Countries: An Overview.* Paris: OECD.

Lijphart, A, (1975) *The Politics of Accommodation: Pluralism and Democracy in the Netherlands.* Berkeley, CA: University of California Press.

Lijphart, A. (1999). *Patterns of Democracy.* New Haven, CT: Yale University Press.

Lim, H.–H. (2006). Representative bureaucracy: rethinking substantive effects and active representation. *Public Administration Review*, **66**, 193–204.

Lindblom, C. E. (2002). *The Market System: What It Is, How It Works, and What to Make of It*, new edition. London: Yale University Press.

Linder, W. (2010). *Swiss Democracy. Possible Solutions to Conflict in Multi–cultural Societies*, 3rd edn. New York: St. Martin's Press.

Linder, W., and Steffen, I. (2006). Ethnic structure, inequality and governance in the public sector in Switzerland. In Y. Bungura (ed.), *Ethnic Inequalities and Public Sector Governance*. Houndmills and New York: Palgrave Macmillan, pp. 221–238.

Lippi, A. (1998). Esercizi di Controllo di Gestione: l'Implementazione dei Decreti Legislativi 29/93 e 77/95 nei Governi Locali. *Il nuovo governo locale*, **2**, 85–116.

Lipsky, M. (1980). *Street–Level Bureaucracy: Dilemmas of the Individual in Public Services*. New York: Russell Sage Foundation.

Local Government Association (2010). *Quarterly Public Sector Employment Survey*. London: LGA.

Lomnitz, C. (1996). *La Insoportable Levedad*. Fractal. Retrieved from http://www.fractal.com.mx/.

Lomnitz, C. (2000). La construcción de la Ciudadanía en México. *Metapolítica*, **15**, 128–149.

Ludwig, M., and Vogel S. (2006). Expertise "Vorbereitung auf Einstellungstests", *Berliner Beiträge zur Integration und Migration*, Berlin.

Lum, J.M. (1995). The Federal Employment Equity Act: goals vs. implementation. *Canadian Public Administration*, **38**, 45–76.

Maertens, K. (2002). De Rechten van Etnische, Culturele en Religieuze Minderheden. *Jura Falconis,* **39**(1), 129–160.

Mallory, J.R. (1971). *The Structure of Canadian Government*. Toronto, Canada: Gage Publishing.

Mandelbaum, D. G. (1970). *Society in India* (two volumes). Berkeley and Los Angeles, CA: University of California Press.

Manuel, T., (2011). Manyi you are a racist. *Cape Times*, March 2, 2011.

Manyi, J. (2011). Manyi's remarks on coloured people seen as "crude racism". *Cape Times*, February 25, 2011.

Maor, M. (1997). The impact of European integration and NPM on recruitment and training of senior public officials: a methodology. *Current Politics and Economics of Europe*, **7**(1), 59–81.

Maor, M. (1999a). The paradox of managerialism. *Public Administration Review,* **59**(1), 5–18.

Maor, M. (1999b). Recruitment and training of senior civil servants in

Denmark and Norway, 1970–1995: the impact of new public management and European integration. *Current Politics and Economics of Europe*, **8**(4), 321–340.

Maor, M. (1999c). Recruitment and training of senior civil servants in Germany and the UK, 1970–1995: the impact of new public management and European integration. *Current Politics and Economics of Europe,* **8**(4), 341–355.

Maor, M. (2001). The advancement of women in the Israeli Civil Service: the gender equity policy approach. *Social Security*, **61**, 127–153.

Maor, M., and Jones, G.W. (1998). Varieties of administrative convergence. *International Journal of Public Sector Management*, **12**(1), 49–62.

Maor, M., and Stevens, H. (1997). The impact of new public management and European integration on recruitment and training in the UK civil service, 1970–1995. *Public Administration*, **75**(3), 531–551.

March, J.G., and Olsen, J.P. (1989). *Rediscovering Institutions: The Organizational Basis of Politics*, Vol. 1. New York: The Free Press.

Margetts, H. (1996). Public management change and sex equality within the state. *Parliamentary Affairs*, **49**, 130–142.

Martin, J. (1978). *The Migrant Presence: Australian Responses 1947–1977*. Sydney, Australia: George Allen and Unwin.

Mason, D. (2003). Changing patterns of ethnic disadvantage in employment. In D. Mason (ed.), *Explaining Ethnic Differences: Changing Patterns of Disadvantage in Britain*. Bristol, UK: Policy Press.

Massey, D.S., Arango, J., Hugo, G., Kouaouci, A., Pellegrino, A., Taylor, J.E. (1993). Theories of international migration: a review and appraisal. *Population and Development Review,* **19**(3), 431–466.

Mattar, S. (2002). *A Senior Public Service that Reflects Canada's Linguistic Duality*. Ottawa, Canada: Office of the Commissioners of Official Languages.

McCorquodale, J. (1997). Aboriginal identity: legislative, judicial and administrative definitions. *Australian Aboriginal Studies*, **2**, 24–35.

McLaughlin, E. (2007). From negative to positive equality duties: the development and constitutionalisation of equality provisions in the UK. *Social Policy and Society,* **6**, 111–121.

McRae, K.D. (2007). Towards language equality: four democracies compared. *International Journal of the Sociology of Language*, **187/188**, 13–34.

Medina Peña, L. (2010). *Hacia el nuevo Estado. México, 1920–2000*. México: Fondo de Cultura Económica.

Meer, F.M. van der and Roborgh, L.J. (1993), *Ambtenaren in Nederland. Omvang, bureaucratisering en representativiteit van het ambtelijk apparaat.* Alphen aan den Rijn, the Netherlands: Samsom H.D. Tjeenk Willink.

Meer, F.M. van der and Roborgh, L.J. (1996a). Representatieve Bureaucratie: de Ambtenaar Tussen Mens en ambt. In A.H. Berg et. al (eds). *Strategie en Beleid in de Publieke Sector.* Alphen aan den Rijn, the Netherlands: Samsom Tjeenk Willink.

Meer, F.M. van der and Roborgh, R. (1996b). Civil Servants and Representativeness. In A.J.G.M. Bekke, J.L. Perry, and Th. A.J. Toonen (eds). *Civil Service Systems in Comparative Perspective.* Bloomington/ Indiana: Indiana University Press, pp. 119–137.

Meier, K.J. (1975). Representative bureaucracy: an empirical analysis. *American Political Science Review*, **69**, 526–542.

Meier, K.J. (1993). Latinos and representative bureaucracy: testing the Thompson and Henderson hypothesis. *Journal of Public Administration Research and Theory*, **3**(4), 393–414.

Meier K.J. (1997). Bureaucracy and democracy: the case for more bureaucracy and less democracy. *Public Administration Review*, **57**(3), 193–199.

Meier, K.J. and O'Toole, L.J. (2002). Political control versus bureaucratic values: reframing the debate. *Public Administation Review*, **66**(2), 177–192.

Meier, K.J. and Stewart, J.J. (1992). The impact of representative bureaucracies: educational systems and public policies. *American Review of Public Administration*, **22**(3), 157–171.

Meier, K.J., and Hawes, D.P. (2008). Ethnic conflict in France: a case for representative bureaucracy? *The American Review of Public Administration*, **39**(3), 269–285.

Meier, K.J., Wrinkle, R.D., and Polinard, J.L. (1999). Representative bureaucracy and distributional equity: addressing the hard question. *Journal of Politics*, **61**(4), 1025–1039.

Melis, G. (1996). *La Burocrazia.* Bologna, Italy: Il Mulino.

Mendelsohn, O. and Vicziany, M. (1998). *The Untouchables: Subordination, Poverty and the State in India.* Cambridge: Cambridge University Press.

Merit System Protection Board (2006). *The Federal Government: A Model Employer or a Work in Progress?* Washington DC: Merit System Protection Board.

Meron, A. (2011). *Privatization Processes and Trends in the Israeli Social Services.* Jerusalem: The Van Leer Jerusalem Institute.

Meyers, M.K. and Vorsanger, S. (2004). Street-level bureaucracy and the implementation of public policy. In B.G. Peters and J. Pierre (eds), *Handbook of Public Administration.* London: Sage, pp. 245–256.

Michalak, K. (2008). *Civil Service Reform and the Quality of Governance in Romania.* Columbus, OH: Ohio State University.

Miller, K. (2009). Public policy dilemma: gender equality mainstreaming in UK policy formulation. *Public Money and Management,* **29,** 43–50.

Milne, C. (2009). Affirmative action in South Africa. from targets to empowerment. *Journal of Public Administration,* **44**(4.1), 969–990.

Ministry of the Interior (2007). Het Personeels- en Mobiliteitsonderzoek over 2006. The Hague: BZK.

Ministry of the Interior (2008–09). Groeiboek diversiteit Rijk I,II,III, The Hague: BZK.

Ministerie van Binnenlandse Zaken (1976). *Kerngegevens Bezoldiging Overheidspersoneel.* The Hague, the Netherlands: Ministerie van Binnenlandse Zaken.

Ministerie van Binnenlandse Zaken en Koninkrijkrelaties (2008a). *Kwalitatieve Rapportage: Diversiteit Maakt Overheid sterker.* The Hague, the Netherlands:: Ministerie van Binnenlandse Zaken.

Ministerie van Binnenlandse Zaken en Koninkrijkrelaties (2008b). *Traag Maar Gestaag? Beleidsdoorlichting Diversiteitbeleid Rijk.* The Hague, the Netherlands:: Ministerie van Binnenlandse Zaken.

Ministerie van Binnenlandse Zaken en Koninkrijkrelaties (2010). *Trendnota Arbeidszaken Overheid.* The Hague, the Netherlands: Ministerie van Binnenlandse Zaken.

Ministry of Public Service and Administration (2006). *Budget Vote.* Cape Town: Ministry of Public Service and Administration.

Mintchev, V., and Boshnakov, V. (2007). Stay or leave again? New evidence for Bulgarian return migration. *Economic Thought,* **7,** 107–126.

Mladenka, K.R. (1989). Blacks and Hispanics in urban politics. *American Political Science Review,* **83,** 165–191.

Moffatt, M. (1979). *An Untouchable Community in South India: Structure and Consensus. Princeton.* Princeton, NJ: Princeton University Press.

Mondal, S.R. (2000). Muslim population of India: some demographic and socio–economic features. *International Journal of Anthropology,* **15**(1–2), 91–107.

Mosher, F (1968). *Democracy in the Public Service.* Oxford: Oxford University Press.

Muir, S. (2010). The new representative body for Aboriginal and Torres Strait Islander people: just one step. *Australian Indigenous Law Review,* **14,** 86–97.

National Commission for Scheduled Castes and Scheduled Tribes (NCSCST) (1998). *Special Report.* New Delhi: National Commission for Scheduled Castes and Scheduled Tribes.

National Inquiry into the Separation of Aboriginal and Torres Strait

Islander Children from Their Families (1997). *Bringing Them Home.* Canberra, Australia: Commonwealth of Australia.

National Multicultural Advisory Council (1999). *Australian Multiculturalism for a New Century: Towards Inclusiveness.* Canberra, Australia: Australian Government Publishing Service.

Newman, J. (2002). Changing governance, changing equality: New Labour, modernization and public services. *Public Money and Management,* **22,** 7–14.

Newman, J. and Ashworth, R.E. (2008). Changing equalities: politics, policies and practice. In T. Bovaird and E. Loeffler (eds), *Public Management and Governance.* London: Routledge.

Niskanen, W. (1971). *Bureaucracy and Representative Government.* Chicago, IL: Aldine–Atherton Press.

Nunberg, B. (1999). *The State After Communism. Administrative Transitions in Central and Eastern Europe.* Washington DC: World Bank.

O'Neill, M. (2000). Belgium: language, ethnicity and nationality. *Parliamentary Affairs: A Journal of Representative Politics,* **53**(1), 114–134.

OECD (2009). *SOPEMI Country Notes 2009: Bulgaria.* Paris: OECD.

Office Fédéral du Personnel (2009). *Promotion du Plurilinguisme dans l'Administration Fédérale de 2004 à 2008. Rapport d'Èvaluation au Conseil Fédéral.* Berne, Switzerland: Département Fédéral des Finances.

Office for National Statistics (2008). *Civil Service Statistics.* London: ONS.

Office for National Statistics (2009a). *Civil Service Statistics.* London: ONS.

Office for National Statistics (2010). *Civil Service Statistics.* London: ONS.

Office for National Statistics (2009b). *Labour Force Survey.* London: ONS.

Office of the Deputy Prime Minister (2003). *Equality and Diversity in Local Government in England: a Literature Review.* London: HMSO.

Office of the State Service Commissioner (2010). *Tasmanian State Service Employee Survey 2010.* Hobart, Australia: Office of the State Service Commissioner.

Ossipow, W. (1994). Le Système Politique Suisse ou l'Art de la Compensation. In Y. Papadopoulos (ed.), *Elites Politiques et Peuple en Suisse. Analyse des Votations Fédérales 1970–1987.* Lausanne, Switzerland: Réalités Sociales. pp. 9–55.

Painter, M., and Peters, B.G. (2010). Administrative traditions in comparative perspective: families, groups and hybrids. In M. Painter and

B.G. Peters (eds), *Tradition and Public Administration*. Basingstoke: Palgrave MacMillan, pp. 19–30.

Panini, M.N. (1996). The political economy of caste. In M.N. Srinivas (ed.), *Caste: Its Twentieth Century Avatar*. New Delhi: Viking Penguin India, pp. 28–68.

Papaux, A. (1997). Droit des Langues en Suisse: Ètat des Lieux. *Revue Suisse de Science Politique*, 3(2), 3–6.

Parekh, B. (2006). *Rethinking Multiculturalism*, 2nd edn. London: Palgrave Macmillan.

Paz–Fuchs, A. and Kohavi, Z. (2011). *On the Seam between the Public and the Private: Privatization and Nationalization in Israel Annual Report 2010*. Jerusalem: The Van Leer Jerusalem Institute.

Perrott, S. (2002). Gender, professions and management in the public sector. *Public Money and Management*, **22**, 21–4.

Peters, B.G. (2001). *The Politics of Bureaucracy*, 5th edn. London: Routledge.

Peters, B.G. (2011). *Institutional Theory in Political Science: The "New Institutionalism"*, 2nd edn. London: Continuum.

Picard, L.A. (2005). *The State of the State: Institutional Transformation, Capacity and Political Change in South Africa*. Johannesburg: Wits University Press.

Pipan, T. (1992). La Gestione del Personale nel Pubblico Impiego. *Rivista Trimestrale di Scienza dell'Amministrazione*, **2**, 121–142.

Piracha, M. and Vickerman, R. (2002). *Immigration, Labour Mobility and EU Enlargement. Studies in Economics*. Canterbury, UK: University of Kent, Department of Economics.

Pitkin, H. (1967). *The Concept of Representation*. Berkeley, CA: University of California Press.

Pitts, D.W., Hicklin, A.K., Hawes, D.P., and Melton, E. (2010). What drives the implementation of diversity management programs? Evidence from public organizations. *The Journal of Public Administration Research and Theory*, **20**(4), 867–886.

PNUD (2010). *Informe Sobre el Desarrollo Humanos de los Pueblos Indíenas de México*. México City: Programa de las Naciones Unidas para el Desarrollo, Organización de las Naciones Unidas y CDI.

Pounder, L. (2008). Never mind human rights, let's save the children: the Australian government's emergency intervention in the Northern Territory. *Australian Indigenous Law Review*, **12**, 2–21.

Presidenza del Consiglio dei Ministri (2003). *La Presenza femminile nella P.A.: il contesto italiano, il quadro normativo e la promozione delle pari opportunità*, accessed at http://www.sspa.it/wp–content/uploads/2010/04/Donne_nella_PA.pdf.

Prodolliet, S. (2005). Öffnung der Institutionen: Mit Vielfalt Gewinnen. *Terra Cognita*, **7**(05), 4–5.

Public Service Commission (PSC) (2004). *State of the Public Service Report*. Pretoria, South Africa: Public Service Commission.

Public Service Commission (PSC) (2006). *An Audit of Affirmative Action in the Public Service*. Pretoria, South Africa: Public Service Commission.

Public Service Commission (PSC) (2007). *State of the Public Service Report*. Pretoria, South Africa: Public Service Commission.

Public Service Commission (PSC) (2010). *State of the Public Service Report 2010. Integration, Coordination and Effective Service Delivery.* Pretoria, South Africa: Public Service Commission.

Public Service Commission of Canada (2010). Annual Report 2009–2010, accessed at http://www.psc–cfp.gc.ca/arp–rpa/2010/rpt–eng.pdf.

Pusey, M. (1991). *Economic Rationalism in Canberra: A Nation–Building State Changes its Mind.* Cambridge: Cambridge University Press.

Putnam, R. D. (2000). *Bowling Alone: The Collapse and Revival of the American Community.* New York: Simon and Schuster.

Raadschelders, J.C.N., Meer, F.M. van der, Roborgh L.J., and Toonen, Th.A.J. (1991). Representativeness in the Netherlands. In V. Wright (ed.), *La Représentativité de l'Administration Publique.* Brussels: IIAS.

Radhakrishnan, P. (1990). Backward classes in Tamil Nadu: 1872–1988. *Economic and Political Weekly*, March 10, 1990, 509–520.

Radhakrishnan, P. (1991). Ambedkar's legacy to Dalits: has the nation reneged on its promises? *Economic and Political Weekly*, August 17, 1991, 1911–1922.

Radhakrishnan, P. (1993). Communal representation in Tamil Nadu, 1850–1916. *Economic and Political Weekly*, July 31, 1993, 1585–1597.

Radhakrishnan, P. (1996). Backward class movements in Tamil Nadu. In M.N. Srinivas (ed.), *Caste: Its Twentieth Century Avatar.* New Delhi: Viking, pp. 110–134.

Ragioneria Generale dello Stato (RGS) (2009). *Conto Annuale dei dipendenti delle pubbliche amministrazioni*, Rome: RGS.

Rajan, A., Martin, B., and Latham, J. (2003). *Harnessing Workforce Diversity to Raise the Bottom Line.* London: Centre for Research in Employment and Technology in Europe.

Rajaraman, P. (1988). *The Justice Party. A Historical Perspective, 1916–37.* Madras, India: Poompzhil Publishers.

Ram, N. (1988). *The Mobile Scheduled Castes: Rise of a New Middle Class.* Delhi: Hindustan Publishing Corporation.

Read, P. (2001). *Charles Perkins: A Biography.* Ringwood, UK: Penguin.

Regierungsrat des Kantons Basel–Stadt (1999). *Leitbild und Hand-lungskonzept des Regierungsrates zur Integrationspolitik des Kantons*

Basel–Stadt, Basel, Switzerland: Regierungsrat des Kantons Basel–Stadt.

Région Wallonne (2007). Charte de la Diversité dans l'Enterprise, accessed at http://emploi.wallonie.be/THEMES/EMPLOI/Documents/Charte%20de%20la%20Diversit%C3%A9.doc.

Republic of South Africa (RSA) (1993). *Constitution of the Republic of South Africa, Act No. 200 of 1993.* Pretoria, South Africa: Government Printer.

Republic of South Africa (RSA) (1996). *The Constitution of the Republic of South Africa, Act No. 108 of 1996.* Cape Town, South Africa: Government Printer.

Ricucci, N. (1990). *Women, Minorities, and Unions in the Public Sector.* New York: Greenwood Press.

Riggs, F. W. (2002). Globalization, ethnic diversity, and nationalism: the challenge for democracies. *Annals of the American Academy of Political and Social Science*, **581**(1), 35–47.

Rose, R. (1984). *Understanding Big Government: The Programme Approach.* London: Sage.

Rose, R. (ed.). (1985). *Public Employment in Western Nations.* Cambridge: Cambridge University Press.

Roy, R. and Singh, V.B. (1987). *Between Two Worlds: A Study of Harijan Elites.* Delhi: Discovery Publishing House.

Royal Commission on Bilingualism and Biculturalism (1969). *Report, Part 2: The Federal Administration.* Ottawa, Canada: Queen's Printer.

Rudolph, L.I. and Rudolph, S.H. (1967). *The Modernity of Tradition: Political Development in India.* Chicago, IL and London: The University of Chicago Press.

Rudolph, L.I. and Rudolph, S.H. (1987). *In Pursuit of Lakshmi: The Political Economy of the Indian State.* New Delhi: Orient Longman.

Saavala, M. (2000). Erasing untouchability in the city: about religious strategies for gaining middle-class status. Paper prepared for the 16th European Conference on Modern South Asian Studies 05–09/09/2000, Edinburgh.

Saksena, H.S. (1981). *Safeguards for Scheduled Castes and Tribes: Founding Fathers' Views. An Exploration of the Constituent Assembly Debates.* New Delhi: Uppal Publishing House.

Scheepers, S. (2007). Meanings of equality and diversity in the Belgian public sector. Paper presented at the EGPA Conference 17–22/09/2007, Madrid.

Schönwälder, K. (2010). Germany: integration policy and pluralism in a self–conscious country of immigration. In S. Vertovec and S. Wessendorf (eds), *The Multiculturalism Backlash. European Discourses, Policies and Practices.* London and New York: Routledge, pp. 152–169.

Scott, W. R. (1994). Institutions and organizations: toward a theoretical synthesis. In W. R. Scott and J. W. Meyer (eds.), *Institutional Environments and Organizations.* Thousand Oaks, CA: Sage, pp. 55–80.

Scott, W. R. (2001). *Institutions and Organizations.* Thousand Oaks, CA: Sage.

Selden, S. C. (1997), *The Promise of Representative Bureaucracy: Diversity and Responsiveness in a Government Agency.* New York: M.E. Sharpe.

Selden, S. C. and Selden, F. (2001). Rethinking diversity in public organizations for the 21st century. *Administration and Society*, **33**(3), 303–329.

Self, P. (1993). *Government by the Market? The Politics of Public Choice.* Boulder, CO: Westview Press.

Self, P. (2000). *Rolling Back the Market: Economic Dogma and Political Choice.* London: Palgrave Macmillan.

Selor (2011). Werken bij de Overheid? Gelijke kansen, accessed at http://www.selor.be/selordiversity.aspx.

Selznick, P. (1948). Foundations of the Theory of Organization. *American Sociological Review*, **13**(1), 25–35.

Selznick, P. (1957). *Leadership in Administration.* Berkeley, CA: University of California Press.

Selznick, P. (1996). Institutionalism "Old" and "New." *Administrative Science Quarterly*, **41**, 270–277.

Sen, A. (2009). *The Idea of Justice.* Cambridge, MA: Harvard University Press.

Sepe, S. (1995). *Amministrazione e Storia. Problemi della Evoluzione degli Apparati Statali dall'Unità ai Nostri Giorni.* Rimini, Italy: Maggioli Editore.

Shachar-Rosenfeld, T. and Berger Y. (Various Years). *Activity Report.* Jerusalem: Civil Service Commission, Division for the Advancement and Integration of Women.

Shaked, R. (2004). The application of affirmative action law in the civil service commission. In A. Maor (ed.), *Affirmative Action and Equal Representation in Israel.* Tel Aviv: Ramot Press, pp.174–194.

Sharkansky, I. and Zalmanovitch, Y. (2000). Improvisation in public administration and policy making in Israel. *Public Administration Review*, **60**, 321–329.

Shourie, A. (1997). *Worshipping False Gods: Ambedkar, and the Facts which have been Erased.* New Delhi: ASA Publications.

Sieben, L. (1987). De Talentellingen: Een Korte Historische Echets. In E. Witte, H. Van Velthoven, L. Sieben, B. Martin and S. Parmentier (eds),

Taalgebruik, Talentellingen en Identiteitskaarten in Brussel–Hoofdstad. Brussels: VUB – Onderzoekscentrum voor Interdisciplinair Onderzoek naar de Brusselse Taaltoestanden en Vlaams Onderwijscentrum Brussel, pp. 42–54.

Simon-Davies, J. (2010). *How Many are Employed in the Commonwealth Public Sector?* Sydney, Australia: Parliament of Australia, Parliamentary Library Background Note, accessed at Http://www.aph.gov.au/library/pubs/bn/stats/PublicSector.htm#_Toc278533055.

Simon, R. and Sikich, K.W. (2007). Public attitudes toward immigrants and immigration policies across seven nations. *International Immigration Review*, **41**, 956–962.

Sirianni, C. and Negrey, C. (2000). Working time as gendered time. *Feminist Economics*, **6**, 59–76.

Smith, R. (2001). *Australian Political Culture.* Sydney, Australia: Longman.

Smith, S.R. (2004). Street-level bureaucracy and public policy. In B.G. Peters, and J. Pierre (eds), *Handbook of Public Administration.* London: Sage, pp. 245–256.

Smuts, D. (2009). *Time for an Equality Check.* Pretoria, South Africa: Minister of Justice and Constitutional Development, accessed at http://www.da.org.za/newsroom.htm?action=view–news–itemandid=6760.

Solidarity (2010). Frequently asked questions, accessed at http://www.solidaritysa.co.za.

Sowa, J.E., and Selden, S.C. (2003). Administrative discretion and active representation. an expansion of the theory of representative bureaucracy. *Public Administration Review*, **63**(6), 700–710.

Sowell, T. (1990). *Preferential Policies: An International Perspective.* New York: William Morrow and Company, Inc.

Spehar, A. (2008). Gender equality policy development in Post-Communist Central- and Eastern Europe. Good or bad for women? *Inblick Osteuropa* 1/2008.

Stadler, M. (2007). *German Liberal Democrats (FDP) Parliamentary Group, German Parliament, 28 February, interpellation no. 16/4480.*

Standing Senate Committee on Human Rights (2007). *Employment Equity in the Federal Public Service.* Ottawa, Canada: The Standing Senate Committee on Human Rights, accessed at http://www.parl.gc.ca/Content/SEN/Committee/391/huma/rep/rep07feb07–e.pdf.

State Comptroller (2004). *Report on Political Appointments and Inappropriate Appointments at the Ministry of Environment.* Jerusalem: State Comptroller.

State Comptroller (2006). *Report on the Small and Medium Businesses Authority: Political Appointments.* Jerusalem: State Comptroller.

State Comptroller (2007). *Annual Report*, Jerusalem: State Comptroller.

State Services Authority (2009). *The State of the Public Sector in Victoria 2008–09*. Melbourne, Australia: State Services Authority.

Statistics Canada (2006). Ethnocultural portrait of Canada highlight tables, 2006 Census, accessed June 7, 2011 at http://www12.statcan.ca/census–recensement/2006/dp–pd/hlt/97–562/sel_geo.cfm?Lang=F&Geo=PR&Table=2.

Statistics Canada (2007). *The Evolving Linguistic Portrait, 2006 Census*. Ottawa, Canada: Statistics Canada Catalogue 97-555-XIE.

Statistics Canada (2008a). *Canada's Ethnocultural Mosaic, 2006 Census*. Ottawa, Canada: Statistics Canada Catalogue 97-562-X.

Statistics Canada (2008b). *Aboriginal Peoples in Canada in 2006: Inuit, Métis and First Nations, 2006 Census*. Ottawa, Canada: Statistics Canada Catalogue 97-558-XIE.

Statistics South Africa (1998). *Definitions*. Pretoria, South Africa: Statistics South Africa

Statistics South Africa (2008). *Mid-year Population Estimates*. Pretoria, South Africa: Statistics South Africa.

Statistics South Africa (2010a). *Quarterly Labour Force Survey*. Pretoria, South Africa: Statistics South Africa.

Statistics South Africa (2010b). *Mid-year Population Estimates*. Pretoria, South Africa: Statistics South Africa.

Statistisches Bundesamt. (2007). Beschäftigte der öffentlichen Arbeitgeber am 30. Juni 2006. *Wirtschaft und Statistik,* Nr. 11, Wiesbaden.

Statistisches Bundesamt (2011). Entwicklung der Beschäftigten im öffentlichen Dienst. *Wirtschaft und Statistik*, November. Wiesbaden.

StemVrouw (2007). *Homepage*, accessed at http://www.stemvrouw.be/nl/index.aspx?Id=Home.

Stinchcombe, A.L. (1997). On the virtues of the old institutionalism. *Annual Review of Sociology*, **23**, 1–18.

Stojanovic, N. (2006). Direct democracy: a risk or an opportunity for multicultural societies? The experience of the four multilingual cantons. *International Journal on Multicultural Societies*, **8**(2), 183–202.

Subramaniam, V. (1967). Representative bureaucracy: a reassessment. *The American Political Science Review*, **61**(4), 1010–1019.

Subramaniam, V., Dolan, J., and Rosenbloom, D.H. (2003). Preface. In J. Dolan and D.H. Rosenbloom (eds). *Representative Bureaucracy: Classic Readings and Continuing Controversies*. New York: M.E. Sharpe, p. xi–xiii.

Supreme Court of India (2008). *Judgement: 2008(4) SCRI, 2008(6) SCCI, 2008 (5) SCALEI, 2008(5) JTI*. New Delhi: Supreme Court of India.

Taub, R. P. (1969). *Bureaucrats under Stress: Administrators and Administration in an Indian State.* Berkeley and Los Angeles, CA: University of California Press.

Taylor, C. and Gutman, A. (eds) (1994). *Multiculturalism: Examining the Politics of Recognition.* Princeton, NJ: Princeton University Press.

Thomas, D.A. and Ely, R.J. (1996). Making differences matter: a new paradigm for diversity management. *Harvard Business Review*, **74**(5), 79–90.

Thynne, I. (1983). Accountability, responsiveness and public service officials. In A. Kouzmin (ed.), *Public Sector Administration: New Perspectives.* Melbourne, Australia: Longman Cheshire.

Tiernan, A. (2007). *Power Without Responsibility? Ministerial Staffers in Australian Governments from Whitlam to Howard.* Sydney, Australia: UNSW Press.

Times of India (2010). Cabinet nod for first caste census in 80 years. *Times of India*, September 10, 2010.

Tirosh, Y. (2009). Fair representation in Israeli Law: a realistic summary. In A. Barak, Y. Zamir, and Y. Marzel (eds), *Mishael Cheshin Book.* Mishpatim, pp. 699–741.

Treasury Board of Canada Secretariat (2010a). Annual report on official languages, 2008–2009, accessed at http://www.tbs–sct.gc.ca/reports–rapports/ol–lo/08–09/arol–ralo/arol–ralo–eng.pdf.

Treasury Board of Canada Secretariat (2010b). Employment equity in the public service of Canada. Annual report to Parliament, 2008–09, accessed at http://www.tbs–sct.gc.ca/reports–rapports/ee/2008–2009/ee–eng.pdf.

Valgaeren, E., Hendrickx, K., De Biolley, I., Reymenants, G., and Van Hove, H. (2008). *Vrouwen aan de Top.* Brussels: Instituut voor de Gelijkheid van Vrouwen en Mannen.

Van der Ross, R.E. (1997) Foreword. In J.M. Spencer (ed.), *The New Colored People: The Mixed–Race Movement in America.* New York: New York University Press.

Van Riper, P. (1958). *History of the United States Civil Service.* Evanston, IL: Row, Peterson and Company.

Varone, F. (2007). The Federal Administration. In U. Klöti, P. Knoepfel, H. Kriesi, W. Linder, Y. Papadopoulos and P. Sciarini (eds), *Handbook of Swiss Politics*, 2nd edn. Zurich: NZZ Publishing, pp. 281–308.

Vervotte, I. (2009). *Algemene Beleidsnota Ambtenarenzaken.* Brussels: Federale Overheid.

Villoro, L. (2005). *Los Grandes Momentos del Indigenismo en México.* México City: Fondo de Cultura Económica.

Vladimirova, K. (2010). *Management of the Different: New Challenges for Public and Corporate Policies. Sustainable Development and Diversity in Bulgaria.* Sofia, Bulgaria: Institute of Economics at BAS.

Walsh, J. (2007). Equality and diversity in British Workplaces: The 2004 Workplace Employment Relations Survey. *Industrial Relations Journal*, **38**, 303–319.

Walzer, M. (1983). *Spheres of Justice: A Defence of Pluralism and Equality*. Oxford: Blackwell.

Weil, S. (1995). Présentation de la Situation Plurilingue dans l'Administration Fédérale: Un Exemple de Communication en Entreprise. *Bulletin Suisse de Linguistique Appliquée*, **62**, 35–55.

Weller, P. (2001). *Australia's Mandarins: The Frank and the Fearless?* Sydney, Australia: Allen and Unwin.

Welsh, D. (1982). The politics of control: blacks in the common areas. In R. Schrire (ed.), *South Africa: Public Policy Perspectives*. Cape Town: Juta, pp. 87–111.

White, L. D. (1954). *The Jacksonians: A Study in Administrative History*. New York: Macmillan.

Widmer, J. (1987). Statut des Langues dans une Administration Plurilingue. In B. Py and R. Jeanneret (eds), *Mobilisation Linguistique et Interaction: Actes du Symposium*, Vol. 41. Neuchâtel, Switzerland: Université de Neuchâtel, pp. 115–121.

Wilson, V.S., and Mullins, W.A. (1978). Representative bureaucracy: linguistic/ethnic aspects in Canadian public policy. *Canadian Public Administration*, **21**, 513–38.

Wimmer, A. (1997). Who owns the State? Understanding ethnic conflict in post–colonial societies. *Nations and Nationalism*, **3**(4), 631–665.

Wise, L.R. (2003). Representative bureaucracy. In B.G. Peters, and J. Pierre (eds), *Handbook of Public Administration*. London: SAGE, pp. 343–353.

World Bank (2010). www.worldbank.org/en/country/bulgaria, accessed October 3, 2012.

World Values Survey Association (2000). *World Values Survey. Official Data File*. Madrid, Spain: ASEP /JDS, accessed at www.worldvalues-survey.org.

Young, C. (ed.) (1998). *Ethnic Diversity and Public Policy: A Comparative Inquiry*. New York: St. Martin's Press, Inc.

Young, K. (1997). Beyond Policy and Politics: Contingencies of Employment Equity. *Policy and Politics*, **25**, 361–374.

Zamaro, N., D'Autilia, M., and Ruffini, R. (eds) (2009). *Il Lavoro Pubblico tra Cambiamento e Inerzie Organizzative*. Milan, Italy: Mondadori.

Zuma, J. (2008). Affirmative action stays. *Cape Argus*, September 9, 2008.

Index